PHILOSOPHICAL EXPLORATIONS
A Series Edited by George Kimball Plochmann

On Manly Courage:
A Study of Plato's *Laches*

WALTER T. SCHMID

Foreword by
GEORGE KIMBALL PLOCHMANN

SOUTHERN ILLINOIS UNIVERSITY PRESS

CARBONDALE AND EDWARDSVILLE

For my father and L. S.
Vivere Militaire!

Copyright © 1992 by the Board of Trustees,
   Southern Illinois University
All rights reserved
Printed in the United States of America
Edited by Mara Lou Hawse
Designed by Bookworks, Inc.
Production supervised by Natalia Nadraga

95 94 93 92   4 3 2 1

Library of Congress Cataloging-in-Publication Data

Schmid, Walter T.
   On manly courage: a study of Plato's *Laches* / Walter T. Schmid;
foreword by George Kimball Plochmann.
      p.   cm.—(Philosophical explorations)
   Includes bibliographical references and index.
   1. Plato. *Laches*.   2. Courage.   3. Socrates.   4. Virtue.
I. Plato. *Laches*. English. 1992.   II. Title.   III. Series.
B373.S36   1992
170—dc20   91-30776
ISBN 0-8093-1745-1   CIP

Contents

Foreword

George Kimball Plochmann

SYSTEMATIC SCHOLARLY WRITING ON Plato began in the United States not much further back than Paul Shorey's editing of an august journal of Greek studies, also his well-known *What Plato Said* (1933) and his shorter books on Platonism. Shorey attributed to the Greek thinker a rather simple and dogmatic philosophy, in terms of which the diverse and often elusive problems raised in and by the dialogues were solved readily and made to comport with each other—if they were not dismissed as irrelevancies to the main doctrine. It was a valiant and learned attempt to make Plato a philosopher, but only by settling upon him a closed system postulating two worlds with little to connect them; this effort was supported at the cost of minimizing parts of all the dialogues either as bits of negligent playfulness or as insignificant deviations from the principal arguments. Shorey and the British writers Lewis Campbell, John Burnet, A. E. Taylor, and others exerted a joint influence upon scholars on this side of the Atlantic, but here a quite different movement has flourished as well, one taking the dialogues as unique masterpieces not necessarily conforming to standards of thesis-proving treatises decorated with literary touches. They consist instead of elements philosophical and artistic, unified in a peculiar way, for the resulting structures contain no parts not exerting important effects upon each whole. A reading to bring this into prominence would consider the characteristics of a speaker or setting, any historical or literary references, any overt action such as merely changing one's seat, as contributing to the overall meaning of the dialogue in hand, and with that to the corpus in its entirety. Here the American tradition commences little earlier than Richard McKeon's detailed teaching first undertaken in the 1930s, when he also made an effort to show how the individual dialogues all suggest, without literally stating, an *open* system of extraordinary subtlety and power.

Professor Schmid quite evidently belongs to this latter group of critics, which, while holding in common certain very broad principles of interpretation, is nevertheless composed of individuals who frequently differ widely from each other in their readings of Plato (and, it goes without saying, other philosophers too). With the recent emphasis upon the closest possible ties between what participants in the dialogues say and what they are, the responses by these modern scholars to the extra subtleties brought out by this assumption and this method must be personal, original. Dr. Schmid has taken full advantage of this latitude, going his own way, adding several fresh matters for discussion—I shall mention them shortly—in what I am inclined to call depth dialectic. With the ground that it breaks, his study is worthy of most careful consideration.

The *Laches* has never been one of the most widely noticed among Plato's writings, and many of the previous commentaries, painstaking or impressionistic, have been disappointing by reason of their determined search for statements from which a kind of gist, a precis, could be extracted. The author of this book establishes a sense of a whole consistently interacting with its parts, so that every line of text becomes essential in its own way to the entire dialogue conceived as argument, dialogue, and ethicopolitical testament. He goes in four directions, and he goes further than anyone with whose writings on the *Laches* I am familiar. First, he devises and follows elegant outlines of the work that bring out twofold and threefold functional relations between the leading terms in every segment. Second, he shows how each phrase, each transition, each shift of attitude, is essential to a dialogue conceived not only as argument but as give-and-take of exhortation and dissuasion. Third, he draws attention, repeatedly and insightfully, to the best-established facts of the military and political history of ancient Athens, binding these to the concerns of two generals and their newfound companion, Socrates. Finally, he introduces a number of references to modern warfare and its literature. The *Laches* thus becomes a tract for its own times, albeit an odd one; but these times have a way of stretching to more than two thousand years.

This commentary recognizes that meanings are everywhere in the elements of the discourse, that every portion of the argument, from word to sentence to passage to section to the composition as a whole, has its own kind of meaning, or, more likely, its multiple meanings, and that those on one level of synthesis cannot be carried over lock, stock, and barrel to another. There have been specialists in Platonic studies: etymologists scrutinizing words and phrases; logicians and dialecticians examining propositions, proofs, disproofs; rhetoricians specifying the cumulative psychological effects of passages both long and short; and lastly historians with their summaries of the dialogue, lodging it in some well-prepared niche in society or in the historical evolution of ideas. Summaries of this latter kind necessarily omit Plato's finer shades in the queries, objections, definitions, proffers of synonyms, tentative agreements, reviews of the argument seeming or not seeming to replicate the text, supporting statements, mythic constructions, refutations. The traces of these are mostly lost, but they should be interpreted as carrying weight. This book pays close attention to them.

The responses to what is said and the apparent motives of the respondents are matters of rhetorical concern, not to mention the possible impact of the dialogue upon the reading audiences into whose hands the text might fall. Every gesture recorded, every exclamation or shout, insult, oath, every attempt to join the conversational circle or leave it, every quotation from a poet, every blush and mark of feeling—all these are intended by Plato to be genuine images of responses within the dialogue's framework. At the same time they are to be aids to the reader for marking phases in the arguments, breaks between sections, disconformities, changes in epistemic value, and transitions that the speakers are mostly aware of but which the reader, as a secondary participant, may not immediately recognize. The rhetorical focus in a Platonic dialogue, as in a play or novel, is always first of all on the characters present and then indirectly on the greatly extended and largely unpredictable readership that his texts have enjoyed but for which Plato could no more than tentatively plan.

Connecting the many assertions and challenges of the speakers, hearers, and readers implies that the works cannot be taken as ingenious exercises, fragile edifices that a sophist could demolish without ado. Although nearly every dialogue has its minor characters, not much more than mere names, those who are prominent are accorded capacities, prejudicies, experiences, reactions that remove them from the bland ranks of the frequent medieval designations of Master and Pupil of later dialogues, or of Thomas Hobbes' "A" and (as anyone may guess!) "B." To this aspect of the dialogue, Dr. Schmid has given close consideration as well.

Third, there are the ethical and political and military issues, and these he minutely analyzes. Plato evidently kept in mind both the facts of Athenian history, for example, facts pertaining to Thucydides the general, and also its literary accounts and images in Thucydides the historian. Laches and Nicias, with all their prestige and authority, are drawn against a rich background of their battlefield experience and of Homeric traditions of which their consciousness is by turns clear or vague and secondhand.

Fourth, it is Dr. Schmid's own focus that is perforce twofold: Concentrating mainly upon classical Greek sources, he also makes his reader clearly aware of currents of opinion regarding military discipline, emotions, and decisions in our own day, issues not remote from those of ancient times. Contemporary views, although they do not use Plato's word *andreia,* introduce its handiest English equivalents, or near-equivalents, courage, manliness, bravery, and relate these to a host of others such as boldness, practical judgment, caution, duty, and many more, much as the *Laches* manages to do in its short compass. This dialogue is among many other things a two-pronged debate between three men, one of them an erstwhile common hoplite, a heavily armed foot soldier, the other two general officers who have held commands in the past and will doubtless do so in the future. The fate of every Greek *polis* in the tumultuous fifth and fourth centuries rested, of course, upon leaders such as these two generals, who like many others were active in civic life as well. Plato had to choose his participants carefully, for victors in war are presumably confirmed in their opinions, less willing to explore and modify their formulas for winning, even in serious discussion with a master of dialectic. The habitual losers, the totally inept field commanders, could hardly be consulted, for the plurality of ostracizing shards would have removed them from Socrates' own beloved Athens—had not their lives been cut short already. Laches and Nicias, however, have in the past won some battles at the time of the dramatic date of this work and have become honored citizens in the full Greek sense of energetically taking part in public life and office. They are, for all we know, brave and decent men to whom the training and leading of soldiers such as Socrates could be entrusted by the great city they serve. And because for all *they* know they will be winning new battles in the future, they are well selected to be spokesmen for ideas, traditional or enlightened—ideas that might stand firm yet can be called into some doubt. It is an assumption, but a sound one, that Plato knew thoroughly the eventual defeats of the two generals—defeats so grim, so unnecessary, so disgraceful—as well as their shortcomings that brought these about, causes resting upon their severally inadequate conceptions of the main virtue upon which success in war must depend. So Plato could put into their mouths intimations of this shortsightedness as well as anticipations of the men's consequent downfall, hints whose true significance only readers of the dialogue, not the generals portrayed, could fully assess.

No violinist has extracted all the meanings and substance from César Franck's *Sonata in A Major.* The *Laches,* like its more than two dozen companion dialogues, has many tiers on which interpretation must take place, and one doubts that however strenuous the exertion, no elucidation can clarify all the ambiguities, straighten all the twists, and lighten all the shadows of this or any of these extraordinary pieces. The evaluation of achievements here must be made by comparisons not with some perfection but with other attempts. On this count, I believe that Dr. Schmid must be given credit for a resolute, clearheaded, and novel effort to dispel what at first reading may seem like needless perplexities in the dialogue. Did Plato mischievously put them in the way of readers expecting a lesson rather than the requirement that they enter, so far as possible, into the dialectical fray itself? In point of fact, he offered a generous supply of aids for the unraveling of these puzzles; and the author of this commentary has picked up a great many of these aids to enable him to enter the circle of primary participants. In this he can also give valuable hints for reading elsewhere in the Platonic corpus. The efforts of Socrates to elicit a defensible, long-lasting definition from Laches and Nicias are put in a new light, so that he is seen as not only the preferred teacher of the sons of Lysimachus and Melesias and the informal instructor of the two generals but our own teacher as well—an important feature of most of the other dialogues as well.

Mention of Lysimachus and Melesias, who might be described as a pair of has-been aristocrats piously hoping their boys will become well educated, prompts me to confess that most of this foreword has been restricted to the second half of the *Laches,* with its debates between Socrates and the eponymous commander and then between Socrates and Nicias. As with the tantalizing *Phaedrus,* however, there *are* two halves, and these seem at first to be only incidentally related to each other. A philosophic inspection, however, shows that in both cases the halves are united by bonds firm enough yet not easy to perceive. How Plato accomplishes this is a fascinating problem, one that I shall leave to Dr. Schmid for his persuasive answer.

In a brilliantly satiric stage sketch by Mike Nichols and Elaine May, the latter says, in the person of a movie star a trifle short in her intellectual promise, "I think the Bible is something we could all do lots more of with." Even she, I suspect, could eventually be brought to see how this prescription applies to the texts of Plato, among which the *Laches* is one of the briefer works though not a lesser. The author of the present study shows well how pertinent is the dialogue to the moral struggles of our bewildering, unstable, often violent century, and our need for courage to face its heavy vicissitudes—courage especially in its completest form, the form that we must suppose that Socrates envisaged and himself exemplified.

Preface

T HE *LACHES* IS LESS sophisticated than other Platonic dialogues and has seemed to many readers a blunt work, not unlike its title character, containing but a few straightforward arguments about the relationship of virtue and education, endurance and wisdom. Thus one critic assigned it as the first of the definition dialogues on account of its "primitive and awkward form."[1] But this disparagement of the dialogue is based on ignorance. As recent studies have suggested, and this commentary will show in detail, the *Laches* is a work of subtlety and depth; it reveals, under careful scrutiny, the hand of Plato's genius. This incidentally was the most wonderful thing about submitting myself to the discipline of this study—it has made me see that amazing genius more clearly than before and inspired me to write on the dialogue a commentary that I hope will not be forgotten after two or three years, but might be consulted often by those interested in Plato and the virtue of courage.

But why turn to the study of an author who wrote over two thousand years ago and who lived in a society that in many respects was radically unlike our own? To this question I answer here with the personal conclusion that an essential part of the solution for our troubles must lie in the recollection of the ancient philosophical wisdom of Plato. Nor would Plato's genius be what it is if the problems of our times were simply alien to him and to his age. The enduring capacity of men for over two millennia to draw on the wisdom of the Athenian Greeks is due to the fact that theirs was perhaps the first society in human history to suffer the crisis of its moral, intellectual, and religious foundations. The ancient Athenians were the pioneers to explore the dangerous new world of humanistic culture, and they realized with the powerful, vibrant self-consciousness of youth that they were on the stage in a new act in the drama of human history. The *Laches* is admittedly a relatively minor work in Plato's and the ancient Greeks' revelation of the truth of that experience, but it is the only work he offers us devoted especially to the virtue we seem most in need of understanding.[2] This is not to say that other works of the ancient authors do not also call for our attention, such as Euripides' *Heracles,* but in the *Laches* we find the beginning of a path that leads us upward toward the ancient wisdom—a wisdom that found its fulfillment not in science but in the action of a whole human life.

No translation of the dialogue has been offered because a perfectly good, literal version is available, thanks to James Nichols in Thomas Pangle's collection, *The Roots of Political Philosophy.*[3] The translations of passages offered here derive from Nichols, unless otherwise noted. It will become obvious in the course of the commentary that I fully agree with the necessity of a literal translation, if one is to understand the Platonic dialogue. Many translations of the *Laches,* as well as of other dialogues, do not do this, leaving the Greekless reader both hard put to carry his analysis beyond the surface, and easily victim to misunderstanding. In the *Laches,* for example, Laches at one point speaks of the "virtue" (*aretē*) shown him on the battlefield at Delium, but this word is translated in the Loeb Classical Library edition as "valor." As a result, the English reader loses the point that Laches naturally speaks of courage as equivalent to virtue. In the same edition, the Greek terms *phronēsis* and *sophia* are both translated as "wisdom," though the literal English equivalents are "prudence" and "wisdom," and one of the most important subthemes of the dialogue is the relationship between the two. There is even a problem with the word *andreia,* which in the title of this book is translated as "manly courage," though it generally is rendered simply as "courage" in the body of the work, with "or manliness" sometimes being added to remind the reader that, for the ancient Greek, *andreia* is linguistically and conceptually related to being an *anēr,* a "real man." But the prejudgments that color the modern idea of courage may be among the most formidable obstacles to understanding the *Laches* and perhaps to understanding what courage really is. Since names are the first aspect of meaning, confusion on names must create all but insurmountable difficulties for one who wishes to discover Plato's meaning, and so every effort is made in this study to attend strictly to what Plato said, on the way toward understanding what he meant, for the sake in the end of knowing what is true.

Finally, I owe a great deal to many teachers and friends, particularly Robert S. Brumbaugh of Yale University, my undergraduate and graduate thesis adviser and Plato teacher, and Robert J. Anderson of Washington College, my lifelong friend and philosophical mentor. I would also like to acknowledge among my friends and teachers at Yale Morris Kaplan and Seyla Benhabib, Frederick Oscanyan and Rulon Wells; among those who helped me continue my philosophical life while in the military service, Alfonso Gomez-Lobo,

Hans-Georg Gadamer, who was like a father to me, and Stanley Rosen; Seth Benardete, Jacob Klein, whose study of the *Meno* has long been my model of scholarly excellence, and Richard Kennington; and Gregory Vlastos and Arthur Hyman, with whom I have had the privilege to study at National Endowment for the Humanities postgraduate seminars.

In addition, I owe a special debt of thanks to the editor of the Philosophical Explorations series, George Kimball Plochmann, whose sage advice has undoubtedly made this a better book than it otherwise would have been; to Curtis L. Clark, Teresa White, and Mara Lou Hawse, my editors at Southern Illinois University Press, who saved me from other errors I would have fallen into; to my colleague and chairman at the University of North Carolina at Wilmington, James J. Megivern, for providing financial support to help defray the costs of copying; and to Margaret Bailey, our departmental secretary, who transcribed much of the original text onto computer disk and helped me many times when I was baffled by the machine.

I also wish to thank most dearly my wife, Catherine, and our children, Karl, Leo, and Mary Elizabeth, for their love and support of my philosophical activity. The errors in the work are mine; the good in it owes much to many.

On Manly Courage

I

The Historical Background

1.1 Introduction

BOTH THE *LACHES* AND its sister dialogue, the *Charmides,* are steeped in Athenian political history. The *Laches* takes place during a pivotal period in the course of the war with Sparta, probably in 423 B.C., two years before the signing of the Peace of Nicias, which ended the Archidamian War of 431–421, and it includes as Socrates' chief interlocutors generals Nicias and Laches, the two chief authors of that peace.[1] Thus the conversation is made to occur just prior to the moment when Nicias and Laches were at their politically highest point, which coincided with that of the Athenian Empire or at least of the post-Periclean Empire. As every ancient reader would have known, however, Laches and Nicias would within a few years be defeated and lose their lives respectively at Mantinea (418) and at Syracuse (413). These battles were two of the most devastating losses the Athenians suffered in the entire war, the defeat at Syracuse, in particular, being commonly regarded as dealing a mortal blow to Athens' hopes. The proud and confident generals Laches and Nicias would soon be dead; under their leadership a whole generation of Athens' young men would be slaughtered; Athens would lose the war; and Sparta would impose upon her the Thirty Tyrants, whom Plato said made the democracy look like a Golden Age.

It was also in 423 that Aristophanes' *Clouds* was first produced, the drama that Socrates in the *Apology* blames for the strong prejudices held against him by the jurors (19b-c). While Aristophanes' play and Socrates' trial and execution might not have been part of Athens' political history for Thucydides, they are an essential part of the background of the dialogues, since that execution by the city was an event no less momentous for the philosopher, Plato, than the rise and fall of the Athenian Empire was for the historian.

I

These remarks make it evident that we cannot understand the *Laches* without a knowledge of its historical context. At the very least, we must be familiar with the most important events and predominant concerns of political and intellectual debate of the times in which it is set, if we are to grasp the implications of its characters' actions and speeches. We can as little understand a Platonic dialogue such as the *Laches* if we do not know the relevant facts and issues in its background as we could a play written about America in the 1960s featuring President Lyndon Johnson or General Westmoreland or General Creighton Abrams, but were ignorant of their place in American history, or of the differences in points of view that separated liberals, conservatives, and radicals, or activists and quietists at that time. This is all the more true of the actions of the characters in the *Laches,* because Socrates makes prophetic allusions to Nicias' and Laches' later historical actions, and because the dialogue is structured, in part, on two great themes of debate in fifth-century Athens: first, the theme of the conflicting civic characters or constitutions of Athens and Sparta and the relation of those political regimes to civic virtue and human happiness; and second, the theme of the potential conflict between philosophical rationalism and the political community. Concerning the first, Laches is presented as sharing in the Spartan character type and outlook, while Nicias, at first strongly identified with Periclean Athens, proves in the end (as did Athens herself) to be a more ambivalent figure.[2] Regarding the second, an underlying question of the dialogue concerns the nature of the kinship or difference between Socrates and the various sophists alluded to in the dialogue. The "old charges," as Socrates calls them in the *Apology* (18b, 19b), could be reduced to the claim that Socrates and philosophy or sophistry—Aristophanes does not distinguish the two in the *Clouds*—played a decisive role, perhaps the most decisive one, in the intellectual corruption and demoralization of Athens, that the spread of philosophical or sophistic thinking was at the root of Athens' troubles. The *Laches* will have much to offer bearing on those charges, but to understand them we must understand what they entailed and what the reasoning was behind them.

In addition, the contemporary reader of a Platonic dialogue must make another, more complex, kind of effort at historical understanding. This is the effort to appreciate the very different presuppositions and concerns that dominated the world Plato wrote about and the one we ourselves live in—the difference we summarize by the contrast between the ancients and the moderns. Plato's world was divided into Greeks and barbarians, masters and slaves, aristocrats and free men; it was influenced by ways of thinking about social life alien to modern commercial democracy; and it was ignorant both of the biblical revelation and of the break with the society built upon that foundation that began with the political and scientific revolutions of the sixteenth and seventeenth centuries. We cannot really understand what Plato meant or said without understanding the basic categorial differences that separate his and our approach to things, especially, but not only, to political things. This is not to say that there do not exist or that Plato did not express truths that transcend the horizons and prejudices of the ancient world. Rather, in order to understand his truths, even to recognize our own horizons and prejudices, we must be aware of his starting points, and this is difficult to achieve. Plato wrote for the ages, but the dialogues are set in historical time and must be understood in relation to that time.

This chapter reviews the place of the dramatic characters of the *Laches* in Athens' history. Sketches are given of their lives and of the basic intellectual conflicts occurring in fifth-century Athens with which the work is concerned. Above all, the chapter seeks to identify the interpretive and philosophical questions that arise when we try to understand the dialogue as a work deeply embedded in a historical context. The question of the overall perspective of the *Laches* on the events it depicts and alludes to will be addressed in the next chapter. That perspective, it will be argued, is neither tragic nor comic, nor is it simply one of ironic detachment.

1.2 Lysimachus and Melesias

The conversation represented in the *Laches* is initiated by Lysimachus and Melesias, the sons of the famous Athenian leaders Aristides and Thucydides.[3] Lysimachus and Melesias are themselves fathers and old men by the time of our drama. They are men of patrician Athens, of noble lineage and ancestral virtue. Their teenage sons, named in accordance with ancient Greek custom after their grandfathers, are also present.

Lysimachus' father, Aristides, was second in command at Marathon, the Athenian commander at Plataea, and the rival of the brilliant Themistocles among the leaders in the Heroic War against Persia. Renowned for his financial integrity and patriotism, he was given the remarkable epithet "the Just," singled out among all Athenian leaders for praise by Socrates in the *Gorgias* (526b), and selected as one of the eight "Noble Greeks" for biographies in Plutarch's *Lives*. Melesias' father, the aristocrat Thucydides, was also prominent, if not of Aristides' stature. He was heir to Cimon as leader of the conservative party (dubbed "the Few" by Pericles) in the next generation of Athenian politicians. During the 440s he led the unsuccessful opposition to Pericles' great building program, a program also criticized by Socrates in the *Gorgias* (517b–519d). In the *Meno,* Socrates cites Thucydides together with

Aristides as being among the Athenian leaders universally acknowledged as men of public virtue (94a–d).

In striking contrast, the historical record tells us next to nothing about Lysimachus or Melesias—their accomplishments, their lives seem less than nothing in comparison with those of their fathers, men of legendary, aristocratic virtue.[4] This contrast in fact motivates the discussion, as Lysimachus himself admits, for he and Melesias have had to face the bitter questions, why they seem to be so much lesser men than their fathers, why their families have suffered such a fall in fortune, and how they might ensure that their own sons, the grandfathers' namesakes, will be more successful than they have been.

In the *Laches,* Lysimachus and Melesias believe that they know the answer: Their fathers were neglectful and gave them an altogether too permissive, democratic education, letting them do as youths what they pleased and thus allowing them to become corrupted. Lysimachus and Melesias do not intend to let this happen with their own sons, and to prevent it they have established a Spartan-like regime of martial discipline and fraternity in their households. But now they are perplexed; an unknown someone has recommended that their sons also study Athenian military science, at least the form of martial arts known as *hoplomachia,* the art of fighting in heavy armor, so they have sought out the two generals and gentlemen, Nicias and Laches, to advise them on the matter. (*Hoplomachia* derives from the words *machē,* a fight, and *hoplon,* the heavy shield carried by the infantry soldier or "hoplite" in the closely knit ancient battle formation, the phalanx.)[5]

We may note in passing that Lysimachus and Melesias are also used by Socrates in the *Meno* to illustrate the problem of teaching virtue. (Thus they won a place, if comic-ironic, in ancient Greek history after all.) However, Socrates says there that Aristides and Thucydides did seek to provide their sons with a good education, but it was to little or no avail. He concludes that if the sophists cannot teach virtue, and if the gentlemen cannot teach it to their own sons, apparently it cannot be taught (93a–94e). It is interesting that Socrates does not confirm the explanation that Lysimachus presents here, though he also neither denies that Lysimachus and his father share the same nature nor asserts that virtue is a function of nature rather than of education in the form of scientific instruction or habituating practice. The *Laches* will consider all three of these potential sources of virtue.

In addition to the comparison between the famous fathers and their nobody sons, the mention of Aristides and Thucydides also invites comparison of their virtuous lives and accomplishments with those of Nicias and Laches, the latter-day heirs of the conservative party, Nicias actually being the head of the Athenian government at the time of the dialogue (see 197d).[6] Of the statesmen

Aristides and Nicias, Plutarch recounts stories of each one giving up important commands to their political rivals, Themistocles and Cleon. But in Aristides' case, the action is part of a noble pattern in his life, his unique willingness to sacrifice both private gain and political ambition on behalf of the public welfare—for which he was rewarded with ostracism by the democratic public, owing to envy of his virtue. Concerning Nicias' actions, on the other hand, particularly his decision to give over command of the important Pylos expedition to the untried and irresponsible Cleon (who had questioned Nicias' patriotism), Plutarch concludes that Nicias "was a man content to betray the common good at the price of his own safety" (*Lives,* "Nicias and Crassius" 3.3).[7] The lesser pair, the politician Thucydides and the military man Laches, are also associated by parallel though somewhat comic events in their lives. Both, it seems, may have been brought up by political rivals on charges of the abuse of office for personal financial gain, and both may have suffered, in court, an attack of speechlessness, becoming unable to defend themselves against their sophistic accusers (see *Wasps* 947).[8]

Representatives of Athens' Golden Age, Aristides and Thucydides can be contrasted to *all* of Athens' political leaders in the post-Periclean era, of whom the historian Thucydides makes the decisive judgment: "More on a level with one another, and each grasping for supremacy, they ended by committing even the conduct of state affairs to the whims of the multitude" (*The Peloponnesian War* 2.65).[9]

The natural comparison of Aristides and Thucydides with Nicias and Laches thus invites us to ask the fundamental political question that must have puzzled any Athenian looking back from the fourth century B.C. upon the events of the fifth: Why did the city fall from the virtuous heights of Marathon to the shameful depths of the Sicilian defeat, the Thirty Tyrants, and Socrates' execution? Laches himself refers early in our dialogue to the "terrible fall" of Athens (181a), and although this reference is to the immediate post-Delium period, it surely would raise in the minds of Plato's early readers the question of the much greater fall of Athens' empire that was to come. But why did the glory days of Athens come to an end? Why was Athens defeated by Sparta? Why were the sons and grandsons of the Marathon fighters apparently far lesser men than their fathers?

The historical question regarding the causes of Athens' fall is an important part of the background for virtually all of the Platonic dialogues, particularly those that center on education and the nature of democracy, on the one hand, and those that center on education and the influence of sophistry and philosophy, on the other. It is no secret that Plato's Socrates raises critical questions about democracy as a form of government and social order, especially the question of whether or not democracy is prone to a lack of civic courage and self-discipline, with the consequence not only that it is less able in war, but also that it is effeminate, unmanly in its notions of justice and wisdom. These questions about the character of democracy lead Socrates and his students, then and now, to the radical question posed in the *Republic,* whether the only real solution to the seemingly innate flaws of democracy is not that it be replaced by the rule of a wise tyrant or tyrants, or by a constitutional aristocracy. While the *Laches* merely touches on these issues, it does expose some of the fundamental vices to which the democratic mind can fall prey. To the great question of Athenian history, Why the fall from civic virtue? part of Plato's answer would seem to be that democracy itself undermines civic courage and does not replace it with anything that can long withstand adversity.

As for the second, more universal political-philosophical theme considered in the Platonic dialogues, we noted in section 1.1 that the "old charges" expressed by Aristophanes amounted to the claim that sophistry or philosophy undermines belief in and respect for the traditional authority of religion, nation, and family—the old complex of social duty and awe. For us, as heirs of modern science and the Enlightenment, such charges are quickly dismissed as reactionary, but they are considered with the utmost seriousness by Socrates, for whom it is by no means obvious that the answer is simply "no" to one of the preeminent questions of classical political philosophy: Is truth-seeking reason opposed to civic virtue? Nor is it by any means obvious to him that sophistry and philosophy have not essentially the same corrosive effects on social order and civic happiness. Again, these issues are addressed indirectly in the *Laches,* fundamental, structural tasks of which will be to indicate how reason might be allied with manly civic virtue and how philosophical wisdom, which need not be socially harmful, might be distinguished from sophistic wisdom, which is.

1.3 Nicias

The second speaker in the *Laches* is Nicias, who, as we noted, is the head of government or the unofficial president in Athens at the time of the dialogue and who will soon conclude, with Laches as his ally, the famous Peace of Nicias, which brought to a close the first half of the war that Thucydides recounts in his *Peloponnesian War.*

Nicias' place in history is controversial. Thucydides says, after describing Nicias' death at the hands of his Syracusan captors, that he, "of all the Hellenes in my time, least deserved such a fate, seeing that the whole course of his life had been regulated with strict attention to virtue as commanded by law"

(7.86).[10] But Nicias is condemned by Plutarch, and the moral judgment of him by modern historians has been even more severe. His name alone was omitted by his fellow countrymen from the memorial erected in honor of the generals who fell in Syracuse.[11] Nicias suffered in his lifetime the most extreme peripety of fortune, from the glory of highest honor and office and wealth, at the time of our dialogue, to a shameful, violent death not ten years later.

Two traits stand out in Thucydides' portrait of Nicias.[12] The first is caution, carefulness, the attempt to secure his goals safely and keep himself from harm—in short, prudence in the ordinary sense of the word. This is a quality closely associated with the conservative, Spartan virtue of *apragmosynē*, which sought well-being in leisure and privacy (contrasted by the Corinthians to the characteristic Athenian life of intense public activity or *polypragmosynē*), though Nicias' caution is also associated by Thucydides with the characteristic Athenian intellectual virtues of military science and forethought (see *Peloponnesian War* 6.13; also 3.51, 6.10–11, 20–23, 96–103, 7.61–64). On the decisive question of Nicias' motivation, however, Thucydides makes the following judgment in connection with his account of the events leading to the Peace of 421: "Nicias, while still happy and honored, wished to secure his good fortune, to obtain a present release from trouble both for himself and his countrymen, and hand down to posterity a name as an ever-successful statesman; and he thought that the way to do all this was to keep out of danger and commit himself as little as possible to fortune, and that peace alone made such keeping out of danger possible" (5.16).[13]

Nicias' caution was the object of sharp wit on the comic stage, his very name (spelled with a *k* in Greek, *nikē* meaning "victory") lending itself to the Aristophanic coinage *mellonikian*, "to delay victory," in the *Birds* (640). But Nicias' strategic military-political caution now seems to most a virtue in comparison with the aggressive policies endorsed by his chief rivals in Athenian government in the post-Periclean era, the brutal Cleon, who had urged the execution of the Mitylenians after their revolt against the empire in 428, and Socrates' beloved, the amazingly versatile and clever Alcibiades, who proposed what we know would be the fatally daring Sicilian adventure in 416–415.[14]

Thucydides presents two speeches by Nicias in the Assembly to dissuade the Athenians from the attack on Sicily (*Peloponnesian War* 6.9–14, 20–23). He argued first that the expedition was dangerous and unwise, and then that it could not succeed unless vastly increased in size. But Nicias profoundly misunderstood his countrymen, who "fell in love with the plan" (6.24). The young did not want to seem afraid and were seduced by Alcibiades' arguments to attempt it—he reminded them that their fathers had built the empire by daring, not caution and that it still had to grow to survive—and the old were then inadvertently convinced by Nicias' arguments greatly to increase the magnitude of the invasion force, "as it was held that he gave good advice, and that the expedition would be the safest in the world" (6.24). With the possible exception of Thucydides' comments regarding Nicias' death, these are probably the most ironic words in the entire *Peloponnesian War*. After Alcibiades was recalled on charges of impiety, and after the aggressive Lamachus was killed in battle, Nicias would assume supreme command of Athenian forces in Sicily.

Regarding his actions in the campaign, Thucydides reports that Nicias repeatedly threw away opportunities and held back from decisive action, thus destroying the confidence of his army, earning the contempt of his enemies, and at the same time giving the Syracusans and their allies the strategic and tactical advantage of defining the conditions of combat (6.63). When it was finally too late to gain victory, again he moved too slowly, delaying and finally rejecting no less than four times the decision to withdraw, at least one of those times explicitly because of his fear of what the Athenians would do to him if he returned home with a defeated army (7.48). Even at the very end, with his army dying around him, Nicias may have been most intent on saving his own skin (7.85–86).[15]

Knowledge of these events would certainly have raised serious doubts for Plato's ancient readers concerning the appropriateness of this man for a dialogue on courage. Was it not his cowardly hesitation that led Athens to her most terrible military defeat? Was he not the man who as much as anyone was responsible for the fall of the empire and the nightmare of the Thirty? Did he not die a coward's death? The reader would wonder how such a man as Nicias could have any insight into the nature of courage. Why, then, make him one of the participants?

The second trait that stands out in the historical Nicias is his piety. We learn from Plutarch that Nicias made daily sacrifices, kept a diviner in his own home, and constantly sought out omens for guidance on matters of public and private affairs. In Aristophanes' *Knights* it is the pusillanimous but pious Nicias who gives the skeptical, daring Demosthenes the idea to use a fake oracle to save the city from Cleon. Now it might at first seem that piety is at odds with the trait ascribed above to Nicias, caution, and there is a certain tension between these traits. For real piety, we divine, would show itself in a lack of concern for the future or in an unconditional acceptance of God's providence, whereas prudent caution and foresight call on human self-reliance and reason to provide for future well-being and to master future fortune. But our opinion in this matter is influenced by the larger historical and conceptual differences that separate the ancient and modern worlds. As Saint Augustine observes in the *City of God,* the ancient pagan conception of piety sought for its reward in this world and expected that the gods would show their will to believers through overt signs that the diviners could interpret; conversely, Christian piety does not expect God to reward the faithful with good fortune or exhibit his will through unusual natural disturbances.[16] Thus there seems to be a closer relationship between ancient piety and prudence than there is between piety and prudence as they would rightly be thought of today.

These differences aside, there is nonetheless a real similarity between the way in which piety is generally viewed by rationalists in modern society and the way it was viewed by most rationalists in ancient times—namely, as a fine thing for old women, but not for grown men. To the kind of humanistic rationalism exemplified by that quintessential Athenian, Pericles, virtue to no small degree implies enlightenment, i.e., liberation through natural science from fear of the gods and of the unknown. Nicias' piety is in fact unique among Athenian leaders in Thucydides' *Peloponnesian War,* though it is a trait he shares with the people, and according to Plutarch it is one of the sources of their trust in him, just as Alcibiades' manifest impiety was a source of their mistrust toward him. But it is hardly obvious that Nicias' humble piety is a virtue in comparison, say, with Alcibiades' proud, Pericles-like rationalism.

The historical Nicias' piety unquestionably proved harmful at Syracuse, where it played an untimely role in the entrapment and annihilation of the Athenian army. For after various setbacks had made it imperative that the Athenians withdraw, and after the other commanders had finally persuaded the reluctant Nicias that this was the last opportunity to escape with their forces intact, at the very moment when preparations were complete for the withdrawal, there was a nocturnal eclipse of the moon, and Nicias, frightened along with the majority of the soldiers by this event, refused to consider departure until they had waited the thrice nine days prescribed by the soothsayers (7.50). It was perhaps Nicias' single most important decision in the entire campaign, since as a result the Athenian forces were, in Thucydides' words, "condemned to stay." The decision also occasions one of Thucydides' rare judgments, when he remarks that Nicias "was somewhat overaddicted to divination and practices of that kind." From then on, an atmosphere of doom settles over the narrative until the terrible end, with its scenes of slaughter and agony and Thucydides' shocking judgment that this was the "greatest deed" in Hellenic history (7.87).

It is perhaps not surprising, then, that Socrates refers explicitly and, apparently, critically in the *Laches* to this decision, when in the course of his examination of Nicias' definition of courage he emphatically declares that "generalship . . . is the mistress rather than the servant of the seer's art, because it knows better what is happening or about to happen in the operations of war; whence the law ordains that the general shall give orders to the seer, and not the seer to the general" (198e2–199a3). What *is* surprising, however, is the apparently *ad hoc* character of the remark. As we shall see in chapter 5, it is not at all obvious what the allusion is doing there or exactly how the reader is to understand the relation between the Nicias of the dialogue and the Nicias of history. This puzzle is compounded by the fact that for most of the *Laches,* particularly in his opening speech (181d–182d) and in the inquiry with Socrates (196e–199e), Nicias seems to be a spokesman for human foresight and Periclean rationalism, an association reinforced by his relationship with the sophist Damon, who was known to be Pericles' mentor (discussed in section 1.6). But then, under the pressure of Socrates' questioning, Nicias' rationalistic definition of courage as "the knowledge of what is to be dreaded and dared" gives way, and at the end of their inquiry Socrates induces Nicias to agree that it is in the one comprehensive virtue of "taking due precaution" (*exeulabeisthai*) of gods and men that courage is to be found (199d–e).

Thus Socrates appears to teach Nicias at the end of the dialogue that traditional prudent or self-regarding piety and justice, not rationalistic wisdom, is virtue. But does Socrates mean what he is saying? Certainly, Christians such as Saint Augustine may believe that courage must be founded in piety and righteousness, but can the same be true of ancient courage? We recall that the ancient rationalists opposed manly daring and self-reliance to pious servility. And was not Socrates' would-be lesson in speech to Nicias concerning prudent piety contradicted by the action to which Socrates had just previously alluded, namely Nicias' superstitious folly in the Syracuse harbor?

Whatever the answer to these interpretive questions may be, the presence of Nicias in the *Laches* also brings to mind enduring philosophical questions about the relationship between the virtue of courage and the virtues of prudence and piety. The Nicias of history seems to have been a man in whom the traits of piety and prudence were opposed to courage. Is it possible that the virtues of courage and prudence *naturally* belong to different character types, that they are *naturally* opposed? (Thomas Hobbes thought they were.) Perhaps the courageous man must seem rash to the cautious, the prudent man unmanly to the brave. And how are both these traits related to moderation, another virtue often attributed to the historical Nicias, but never to his rival Alcibiades, whom no one found fault with for lack of courage or daring or the ability to play the people like a flute? The more we know about Nicias, the man of history, the more questions we have about the well-known Socratic doctrine of the unity of virtue.

1.4 Laches

The central figure in the dialogue, Laches, also played a leading role in the Peloponnesian War. Why the dialogue is named for him and not his more famous colleague Nicias will be discussed later in this study.

Thucydides reports that Laches was commander of the first Sicilian expedition in 427–426, but his solid results only whetted the appetites of the Athenians, who always wanted more, blamed him for not getting it, and so enlarged the expedition and appointed new commanders in the spring of 425. Not a wealthy man like Nicias, Laches fought bravely, side by side with Socrates, as a hoplite in the Athenian defeat at Delium in 424. Shortly afterward, Laches began to appear as a leading associate of Nicias in the conservative peace or appeasement party. It was Laches who moved the acceptance of the one-year truce in 423 (which would have occurred shortly after our dialogue), and Laches was Nicias' chief supporter in negotiating the more famous peace concluded in 421. But Nicias and his friends could not hold the peace against Alcibiades' machinations and the innate imperialism of the *dēmos*. First, Alcibiades cleverly effected an alliance between Athens and Sparta's Peloponnesian rival city, Argos. He then set in motion the military actions that eventually led to the battle of Mantinea in 418, in which Laches was a general of the Athenian forces that fought with the Argive coalition against the Spartans, when the allies were defeated and Laches was killed. This was a far more important battle in the war than is generally reckoned, because a Spartan loss would very likely have ended the war, with Athens victorious.[17] The Spartans had never recovered from the debacle at Sphacteria in 425, which had cost them heavily in prestige and power and perhaps above all in self-confidence. But with the victory at Mantinea, and the way it was achieved, "The imputations cast upon them by the Hellenes at this time . . . were all wiped out by this single action; fortune, it was thought, might have humbled them [i.e., at Sphacteria], but the men were the same as ever" (5.75).[18]

Laches also appears, thinly disguised, in Aristophanes' *Wasps,* first staged in 422, when Cleon was at the height of his reputation, owing to his skill or good fortune in Pylos against the Spartans, and just before his death at Amphipolis later that year. The *Wasps* tells of a pious father named Philocleon ("Love-Cleon") who has come to believe that the life of the juror is happy and powerful. In the course of the play his impious son Bdelycleon ("Loathe-

Cleon") gradually persuades him to a different and better way of life. At one point in the cure, Philocleon is allowed to have a private trial in his home, in which a dog named Labes, from the same deme as Laches, is charged by Cyon ("Dog"), from the same deme as Cleon, with stealing some cheese and then not sharing it. When Labes is attacked by his accuser, he is speechless, and Aristophanes' stand-in Bdelycleon compares him to the politician Thucydides, who likewise was rendered speechless by two sophistic word warriors in a political trial. So Bdelycleon himself presents Labes' defense, saying he is a good old dog, that he has fought the wolves and suffered hardship for the defense of Athens, that he should not be condemned for his inability to speak, and that he should, even if guilty, be forgiven on grounds of his lack of music education (942–59). By a ruse, Bdelycleon gets his father to vote for Labes' acquittal, and Labes goes free, at first to the dismay of Philocleon, caused in part by his fear of divine retribution. (The real Laches was probably never brought to trial, or if he was, he was acquitted. This is not to say the whole experience would not have been bitterly shameful.)

It would be natural but quite wrong for us to think that Aristophanes had no other purpose in the *Wasps* than to make his audience laugh. In 425, in the *Acharnians,* he had announced his bold intention of "talking justice to the Athenians" (645), and the year before the *Wasps* was produced he had attacked Socrates' own injustice, that is, sophistry or philosophy, in the *Clouds.* Likewise, the explicit aim of the *Wasps* is to "talk justice," by defending the rule of law against the corrosive effects of politicians such as Cleon and ordinary thoughtless people, who were using the courts for private gain and threatening the city's well-being with their immoderate criticism of her soldiers, the latter being the very men the city had to trust in for her protection and freedom. This is a charge that takes on substance as we study Thucydides' *Peloponnesian War,* noting how many Athenian generals feared for their lives and reputations, including Demosthenes, Alcibiades, Nicias (at least three times), and perhaps even Laches. More than one astute observer remarked on the corruption of the legal system under the democracy during the war (see Aristotle's *Athenian Constitution* 27.4–5). Men such as Laches—proud, loyal, straightforward men of action—are defenseless against the shyster lawyers and word warriors like Cleon; they need the help of wisdom (Aristophanes) to rescue them—and the city—from harm. There is, perhaps, a parallel to all of this in our dialogue. Although our title character is articulate and witty, while the dog in the *Wasps* says nothing, Plato's Laches also proves to be less verbally able than his rival here, Nicias, and is reduced in the end to sputtering and angry silence. Like Labes in the *Wasps,* our Laches also lacks the wisdom to defeat his sophistic enemies, and needs help—but of Socrates.[19]

Incidentally, Aristophanes' central target of injustice in the *Acharnians* had been Lamachus, characterized as the martial spirit incarnate, who thought of war as an end in itself, not as a necessity for the sake of peace. Lamachus was the general who would be appointed, together with Nicias and Alcibiades, to command the Sicilian expedition of 415–413, whose simple, bold plan of attack was an immediate all-out assault, and who died fighting gloriously, if somewhat foolishly, in Homeric-style individual combat early in the campaign (6.49, 101).[20] Lamachus is paired with Laches toward the center of Socrates' inquiry with Nicias, where Nicias says that he would not deny the ascription of courage to either Laches or Lamachus or many other Athenians (*Laches* 197c).

The trial motif found in the *Wasps* is also an underlying theme in the Platonic dialogues. Of course Socrates never brings legal charges against anyone, but he generally brings the implicit moral or philosophical charge against his interlocutors that they risk harm to themselves and others through their errant conceit of wisdom. In the *Laches,* these charges are made as directly as they ever are when Socrates suggests that Nicias and Laches might be causing great harm to Lysimachus and Melesias, if their advice to them about their sons' education is not truly based on knowledge (see 186b–c, 187b). The significance of the Socratic elenctic ("refutative") investigation in revealing the soul of the interlocutor then is discussed by Nicias, who says that when you wrestle with Socrates you are compelled to give an account of *yourself* and of the manner of life you have lived (187e–188a). Thus the *Laches* as a whole is a kind of trial, and as we shall see, it is not without its comic elements.

Laches' supreme public trial, however, took place on the battlefield at Mantinea. Thucydides tells us that the Argive forces and their allies, including the Athenians, who had the largest contingent among the allies, when they first caught sight of the Spartan army, wisely took up a "strong and difficult position on a hill," from which they would need to move only if they wanted to (*Peloponnesian War* 5.65). But the Spartans, seeing the enemy's strength and advantage, stopped their attack on the hill and retreated back into the plain. At this point the allied troops became impatient and demanded that they be allowed to pursue the retreating enemy. The generals—including Laches, who as the senior of two Athenian commanders would have had an important voice in the decision—at first hesitated; they did not want to quit their secure position, not least because they were expecting soon to be joined by a large Elean force and would then have greatly outnumbered the Spartans. But as they could not persuade the men, the allied commanders relented, bowing to the popular will; the next day the allied army moved down and fought the Spartans on level ground, where they were defeated and the Athenian forces barely escaped a massacre (5.65–73).

The small details of the battle are interesting. When the allied army moved down the hill, the Spartans were completely surprised—more so than any Spartan army in memory—but nonetheless they fell into position without a word, obeying their commander "in accordance with the law" (5.66). Thucydides goes on to explain how in the ancient battles between phalanxes there was a tendency for the armies to extend on the right wing, each man moving somewhat to the right to secure protection behind his neighbor's shield. To guard against the encirclement of his left wing, the Spartan commander attempted a clever maneuver, though it failed completely. As the battle progressed, the allies fought ably, and the Spartans were "utterly worsted in respect of skill." But this advantage in skill did not matter: the Spartan forces in the middle simply battered through the Argive and Athenian forces opposing them, and thereby "showed themselves as superior in point of courage" (5.72). Saved by their courage and military discipline—and by the allies' impatience and bad judgment—the Spartans won a decisive victory and ended forever the threat that the allied forces had posed to their Peloponnesian hegemony.

It has already been noted in section 1.3 that Socrates makes a prophetic allusion to Nicias' pious but foolish decision to delay the escape from Syracuse on account of an eclipse of the moon. He does much the same thing toward the end of his inquiry with Laches relative to the battle at Mantinea, asking that general if the man who endures in war and is willing to fight because he knows "that others will come to his aid, and that the forces against him will be fewer and weaker than those who are with him, and when he has besides the advantage of position—would you say of this man, if he endures with such wisdom and preparation, that he, or a man in the opposing army who is willing to stand up against him and endure, is the more courageous?" (193a4–9). Laches replies that it is the man in the plain, not the man with good ground, who is more courageous, and he is forced to contradict himself and conclude that courage must then be foolish, not prudent endurance. Of course Socrates' descriptions of the prudent soldier on the hill and the enduring man on the plain below correspond exactly to the actions of Laches and the Spartans at Mantinea.[21] On the allies' side there were the many bold, imprudent troops who questioned the courage and even the patriotism of their generals, thus shaming and frightening them, against their better judgment, into rashly leaving the safety of high ground and taking a risk they would not have taken had they resisted and acted out of prudent calculation. On the Spartan side, by contrast, though "bested in respect of skill, they showed themselves superior in point of courage"—just as Laches' man of unskilled endurance seemed more courageous, after all, than the prudent soldier on the hill.

But the difference between the Lacedaimonians and the allies was not only that the Spartan troops were braver. The difference was also that the Spartan troops had been educated in and disciplined by the law to obey their king, while the allied troops thought they should themselves decide what was best.[22] Again the lesson of ancient Greek history seems to be that Athens' defeat was ultimately caused by the natural vices of democracy. As for Laches, it would seem that in real life, as in the dialogue, he had not learned that the path of courage and honor must *follow,* not violate, prudence, if one is to gain the victory. But how does one learn or teach such a lesson, before it is too late?

1.5 Socrates

From Lysimachus, Laches, and Nicias we ascend to Socrates, the fourth main speaker in the dialogue. Socrates is about forty-five years of age at the time of this conversation. He fought bravely the year before at Delium and will distinguish himself again the next year at Amphipolis, where his feats of physical endurance are to become the stuff of legend. We should picture him as a warrior and a stonemason, a man of rock-hard muscle and piercing eye— not as a round-bellied gentle satyr or a pale-skinned, continent old weakling.[23]

Now with Socrates we encounter a new aspect of the dialogue, namely the fundamental question posed by the historical Socrates' own life, public trial, and execution, the problem concerning the relationship of reason and philosophy to civic virtue and the city. This problem was first clearly posed by Aristophanes in his unforgettable attack on Socrates as the arch-sophist in the *Clouds.*

We may summarize Aristophanes' charges against Socrates as follows: Socrates corrupts the young by teaching them the art of speech, which includes the ability to make the morally worse argument appear stronger; that is, he teaches the skills of persuasion combined with the intellectual habit of considering with complete disinterestedness the arguments both for and against civic virtue. And Socrates corrupts the young and is impious, for he studies nature openly and does not hide his doubts concerning the reality of the gods the city believes in, but the law rests upon trust in that reality. On a still deeper level, Socrates threatens the city by teaching by example the complete indifference of the autonomous life of the mind to justice and the interdependent life of man in society. Philosophy, because it directs the hammer of reason against the convictions that form the foundation stones of political society, is profoundly dangerous to that society. If philosophy is to survive at all, it must hide its teachings both from the pious, greedy commoners and from the skeptical, ambitious young aristocrats; it must conceal its truths in the interest of wisdom itself for those who care about wisdom itself. Writing in 423, Aristophanes does not cite the argument that Socrates makes his students would-be tyrants, though it is evident that he believes this, too.

Aristophanes' charges were essentially repeated by Hegel and Nietzsche over two millennia later, and they must still be taken seriously. Plato's contemporary readers may be too ready to remember that Socrates' students included Plato and Xenophon, who were never political leaders, and forget that they included Alcibiades and Critias, who were. Of course one may simply view these charges as reactionary and praise Socrates, together with other philosophers persecuted by the Athenians, such as Anaxagoras and Protagoras, as witnesses and martyrs to the cause of reason and human progress. From that perspective, it is the task of autonomous reason to lead men from superstitious fear of the gods and ignorance of nature to science and the arts that enhance human freedom, rationality, and material well-being. But Plato's Socrates nowhere identifies himself with such a philosophy, and his response in the *Apology* and other dialogues to the Aristophanic charges is very different. He clearly takes it for granted that he must prove that he does not corrupt the young by teaching them disrespect for the law and that he is not impious. He presupposes, in short, that piety and justice or respect for the gods and Athenian law are expected of all citizens, and he sets about to prove that he has in no way violated the city's expectations in these matters.

Plato's Socrates offers two kinds of arguments in his own defense. The first kind of argument is dialectical: he questions his accusers, attempting to show that they do not know what they are talking about and that he is not guilty of the charges. These arguments, to say the least, are not convincing. Rather, we may say he succeeds in showing that he holds a view of moral responsibility that would undermine the entire legal system if it were widely adopted, and that he holds a view of the gods such that he can speak of them in terms at the farthest extreme from religious awe. Nonetheless, he insists that he is the most pious of men, because he has offered his life in service of the god (he does not say Apollo) who called him to question men in regard to their wisdom. It is the conclusion of others who observe these conversations that Socrates is wise, but he knows only that he knows nothing. Socrates admits, however, that this way of cross-questioning the leaders of society has fostered young aristocratic imitators, and the many who have been refuted by him or by his imitators hold him responsible.

The second kind of verbal argument that Socrates offers comes in the form of his exhortatory speeches, in which he praises the philosophical life of virtue and truth and prudence, and again proclaims that his life is that of a pious man, a servant of the god. Indeed, he is so pious that he would, out of duty to the god, have to defy the Athenians if they ordered him to cease philosophizing, though he also implies he would defy them anyway, simply because "the unexamined life is not worth living for a human being" (38a). We may consider the *Crito* an addendum to his defense, for in that work Plato shows Socrates making a powerful case for obedience to the law. (Though he leaves behind, in an otherwise tightly sewn argument, one loose string that if pulled long enough might unravel the whole garment; see 51b and compare *Apology* 29c–d.) We should then consider the *Republic* as a further addendum, since Socrates offers there, on the basis of ostensibly rational arguments, a theology that supports the law against sophistic arguments like those made by the Unjust Speech in the *Clouds*. The most important addendum on the matter of Socrates' piety, however, is found in the *Phaedo,* where he offers utterly convincing rational proofs of the immortality of the soul, and thus provides us with the basis for the new form and foundation of piety that he had only hinted at in the *Apology* with his talk of the perfection of the soul.

Socrates' arguments have convinced generations of Plato's readers that Socrates was a pious and just man and that the attachment to virtue or perfection is the proper human goal in life. But for most of Plato's readers, Socrates' most convincing arguments rest not on his words but on his actions, for these bear witness to the truth that he does not study nature, he does not accept money for teaching, he never fails to honor the gods at public ceremonies, and far more than most men, he has the highest regard for the law, as shown by his defiance of unjust orders when threatened with death (see 32b–d). Is that not the ultimate test of principle, that one be willing to die for it?[24]

But there are many things that Socrates says in the *Apology* that make us— and may have made the Athenians—wonder if he is as law-abiding and pious as he claims, or if they were being duped, that is, if he was being ironic in the supercilious, nasty Theophrastian sense. Certainly his fellow citizens decided that Socrates' daring rationalism was not fundamentally conducive to but was destructive of patriotism and piety and that he was responsible for the moral corruption of those many antidemocratic youths who were his imitators (23c, 33c; compare also *Euthydemus* 304a; *Republic* 498a, 539b). So Plato can assume that neither the old nor the new charges against his mentor have been wholly refuted in the *Apology,* and he must develop his defense further in his other dialogues. As we shall see, the *Laches* offers a defense of Socrates, based in large part on the alliance that he makes with Laches against Nicias and his teacher Damon. But this defense will not be altogether satisfactory, precisely because it does not clearly articulate, much less prove, the existence of a horizon beyond the city, even as the dialogue itself raises issues making it evident that the true nature of courage cannot be understood unless one breaks through the horizon of the city and envisions a more brilliant and more enduring source of death-defying action. In short, the *Laches* will not offer a conclusive defense of Socrates, though it will make a highly interesting contribution to such a defense.

In addition to this defense of Socrates against the charge that reason in his hands is essentially opposed to civic virtue and the common good, there is the other side of the coin, specifically the curious matter of the amazing liberation from fear, even the fear of death, that Socrates claims for himself in the *Apology* (28e–29b; also *Gorgias* 522d–e). Is it in the power of reason or philosophy to liberate men from the fear of death, or indeed of any other things we might suffer in this world, but about which we cannot really be sure they are evil? If it is, there is at least this direct connection between philosophy and virtue—that philosophical reason can free men from the most powerful of passions, free them to act in accordance with what is right or noble or good, if that is what they will. Socrates also says in the *Apology* that he does not rest his courage upon public opinion as to what is honorable and what is shameful, and this raises another kind of question about the relationship between reason and feelings. Socratic rationalism seems to be a radically powerful force, if it can remove from a man not only the most conventional fear, the fear of public ridicule, but also the most natural fear, the fear of death. We naturally wonder if it is entirely good to cure men of these fears, if indeed he can. How do his dialectical and rhetorical teaching methods effect these remarkable changes?

Moreover, Socrates' position—not only in the *Apology* but already in the *Protagoras,* whose dramatic date cannot be put later than 433—seems even stronger than the claim that reason can liberate one from social and natural passions; it actually seems to be that philosophy is moral enlightenment, that virtue simply is knowledge, that reason leads man to know the good, and that the state of real knowledge or philosophical wisdom is such that to know the good is to do it. In this regard, the doctrine of the *Phaedo,* that wisdom or prudence is the root of all virtue, seems merely to develop explicitly what is already implicit in Socratic deed and even word in the *Apology,* when he denies that he will ever fear death or any other unknown evil, or the loss of worldly goods, and correspondingly he asserts that since he knows it is wrong to disobey his superior, be he man or god, he will not (29b–e). The surface interpretation of the *Laches* also supports this doctrine, since the result of Socrates' inquiry with Nicias suggests that the apparently different virtues are in truth just the one virtue of wisdom or prudence, i.e., "the knowledge of good and evil" (199c–e), though a premise of the whole inquiry in the *Laches* is that courage is one of the parts of virtue, parts that may compose a whole but are nonetheless distinct (190c–d, 199e). But since the logic of the argument seems to lead to this conclusion, it would appear more reasonable—and more in accord with what we as readers of other Platonic dialogues know is Socrates' avowed method—to reexamine the common prejudice that courage is a part of virtue, that the virtues are not one. And indeed, if we did that, might we not come to the doctrine of philosophical virtue that we find in the *Phaedo,* the doctrine that true courage finds its source in Truth Itself, in the Eternal Ideas?

These speculations take us far beyond the horizon of the *Laches.* In our dialogue there will be but two fundamental positions to consider regarding the essence of courage. The first is suggested by Laches' original definition, that courage is a matter of civic will and honor (190e), and by his subsequent remarks that manly courage is different from but related to the other virtues, especially the political virtues of justice and prudence. This conception, as we shall see, is the most basic notion of courage examined in the *Laches.* The second fundamental position is introduced by Nicias, that courage is a form of wisdom or knowledge (194e–195a), which Socrates forces him to conclude implies the radical unity of virtue. (This part of the *Laches* is comparable to the latter part of the *Protagoras.*) It was noted in the last paragraph that this conception might be thought to represent the Socratic-Platonic wisdom-perspective that together with the related doctrine of the immortality of the soul is developed in the *Phaedo,* and in fact one may interpret some parts of the *Laches* as suggesting this idea of courage. But it will be argued in chapter 5 that the *Laches* also gives us good reason to conclude that it does not offer an examination of the *Phaedo* wisdom-idea, nor does it give us any reason to think that idea is true. To the extent that the *Laches* suggests any positive doctrine on the nature of courage, it seems to support the view that courage is distinct from the other virtues but related to them by means of the ordering virtue of prudence. It does not give us good reason to conclude that this is Plato's last word on courage, however, and as we shall see, this account of courage is put forward in the dialogue in a way that makes it clear it is a second-best, not truly sufficient human virtue.

1.6 Stesilaus and Damon

Among the characters there are, finally, the three sophists named but not actually present in the *Laches:* the martial arts trainer Stesilaus, the teacher of harmony Damon, and the master of exact speech Prodicus. Each of these men points us to important aspects of the sophistic movement and the larger historical phenomenon we now call Periclean Humanism.

STESILAUS AND THE SCIENCE OF WAR

As with the other minor figures, we know virtually nothing about Stesilaus apart from what Plato tells us; indeed, he is so much in the shadows that he might never have existed at all. Nor does Stesilaus appear directly in the *Laches*; the dialogue begins, "You have contemplated," indicating that the participants have witnessed Stesilaus' performance and self-congratulatory speech about the virtues of studying *hoplomachia* with him, of course for a fee. No one even proposes to question him about the value of his skill, but what he represents is obviously important: the claim to expertness and virtue that he offers to teach young men. We might compare him to an oriental karate master who would give an exhibition at a large suburban mall to advertise his new martial arts academy, urging the fathers that this training will make better men of their sons. The fathers are not sure what to make of it, if it is so valuable for their boys to study.

To understand fully what Stesilaus represents, we must place him in a large historical context, one that includes both the humanistic political movement associated with Pericles and the rationalistic intellectual movement assigned by Plato to the sophists. Stesilaus' specific role in the dialogue is to be the symbol, as it were, of sophistry in military things, the little professor of military science, the man who claims to teach virtue through the study of the arts of war. This is the view of the relationship between *technē* and war that Nicias develops in his major speech at 181d–182d, and the account Nicias presents there is clearly akin to the views that Pericles expresses in Thucydides' *Peloponnesian War*.[25] Thus while Nicias argues that the study of the arts of war leads to "the whole art of generalship," with the implication that in this way human intelligence can master the fortunes of war, Pericles argues that the Athenians are bound to be victorious, thanks to their superior experience, which has brought them to the art of seamanship and thus also to daring in that key arena of the war, whereas the Spartans do not have this skill, must be overcautious, and hence will not be able succeed (1.141–42). In this, and in a later speech, Pericles argues that skill and foresight lead to the discernment of opportunities and dangers, with the result that such a man knows when to be bold and when to be cautious, and thus he is able through his intelligence to master fortune, even in the unstable realm of war (2.61–62). This specific understanding of the relation of technical skill and intelligence to war plays a major role in the inquiry on courage in the latter half of the dialogue.

Moreover, what Pericles maintains is true of the Athenian navy concerning the development of virtuosity and the mastery of chance is what the sophistic movement, led by Protagoras, Anaxagoras, Democritus, Damon, and others, maintained was true in virtually every field of human endeavor, including that of political life.[26] Aristotle reports that it was during these years of the Periclean ascendancy, the fifteen years or so before the war, when the Parthenon was built and Athens was at her peak of glory and empire, that the arts and sciences were fully emancipated to serve the various human needs and desires in Athenian society (*Politics* 8.6). This was the first great flourishing of all aspects of human civilization, the one that set the standard by which history has judged all others since. (No such flowering of intelligence came about in Sparta, of course.) The pervasive influence of human reason in Periclean Athens could lead Plato to look upon the chain of command in Athenian life as beginning not with political leaders, but with thinkers such as Protagoras and Anaxagoras, who are the intellectual commanders of captains such as Pericles and Nicias, who in turn are superior to foot soldiers such as Stesilaus. But Plato's Socrates questions whether the realm of human life and politics does not for some reason resist the kind of expertness that can be achieved in relation to nonhuman nature, and whether the unfettered liberation of human intelligence to serve the appetites of the people is healthy for the city. At any rate, insofar as war is a human practice, the claim to mastery in the fortunes of war is precisely the kind of claim to wisdom that would interest Socrates greatly, not least because of its very real influence in the world of public affairs through the education of the young.

DAMON AND THE PROMETHEAN IMAGE OF MAN

The second sophist alluded to in the *Laches* is Damon, whose role here again underscores the silent presence of Pericles in the background of our dialogue, as well as the pervasive influence of sophistry in Athenian life. Plutarch reports that Damon "took refuge behind the name of music in order to conceal from the multitude his real power, and he associated with Pericles, that political athlete, as it were, in the capacity of trainer and teacher" (*Lives*, "Pericles" 4.1). This account is confirmed by the author of the *Athenian Constitution*, who reports that it was Damon who advised Pericles to increase the jury pay, which led both to his political ascendancy and the eventual democratic corruption of the law courts (27.4–5). Plutarch also discusses at length the influence of Anaxagorean naturalism on Pericles (*Lives*, "Pericles" 6), as does Socrates in the *Phaedrus* (269e–270a). Pericles was, then, a student of the sophists in music and politics, martial arts or war, and the science of nature or of the whole. Plato extends this influence of sophistry on Athenian politics to his Nicias when he makes Socrates say in our dialogue that Nicias also was a student of Damon and Prodicus (197d), and Nicias himself indicates that he is a follower of the sophists (200b), though Plato's Nicias is not associated with Anaxagoras and his familiarity with the martial arts seems to be largely theoretical. Note that if the historical Nicias did have Damon as his political teacher and mentor in wisdom in the manner suggested at the end of the *Laches,* then the real, no less than the fictional, Nicias would have been a thoroughly ambivalent figure, tied both to the traditionalists, who embraced piety and rejected rationalism, and to the sophists, who rejected that piety in favor of humanistic rationalism.

Perhaps even more important for our understanding of the historical background to the dialogue is the fact that Pericles and the whole humanistic political and artistic movement associated with him is in Plato's view so intimately connected with the sophistic intellectual movement that the two can seem virtually one (see *Gorgias* 462b–465d, 500d–503d, 515c–521d). Actually, the more one studies fifth-century Athens, the more obvious it is that the categories of interpretation scholars today bring to the dialogues—the conflict of philosophy and sophistry in particular—are not the terms that Plato's first readers would most likely have brought to them. For them, the fundamental antithesis would have been the one set out by Sophocles, Aristophanes, Thucydides, and Pericles and by the sophists themselves: the conflict between (1) the optimistic, proudly humanistic, and rationalistic view of life associated with Periclean Athens and the sophistic movement as led by Protagoras, who celebrates human knowledge with his slogan Man is the Measure, and (2) the pessimistic, moral, and religious view of life associated in Thucydides with Sparta and defended by the tragic and comic poets, especially Sophocles and Aristophanes, a view that seemingly found its latter-day defender in the older Plato, who, attending not to human knowledge but to human ignorance, offers the counterslogan God is the Measure.[27] Religious traditionalism and humanistic rationalism—these were the fundamentally opposed sides in the political and intellectual life of fifth-century Athens, as is strikingly indicated by the many trials of Athenian intellectuals on the charge of impiety. Indeed, as Socrates so unavailingly explains in the *Apology,* few of his contemporaries realize that he stands for something new and very different from what the sophists stand for. He is assumed to be a sophist, for hardly anyone distinguishes the two enterprises, and the greater part of his task in the trial is to try to indicate the two essential ways in which the philosopher differs from the sophist.

When we read the *Laches* in relation to this background, we cannot but be struck by the prominence given throughout the dialogue, and especially by Nicias, to the word *promētheia,* "forethought" (or "foresight"). The concept of forethought has a unique role in relation to the fifth-century Athenian Enlightenment.[28] Like other words, such as *gnōmē, pronoia,* and *technē, prométheia* is used by admirers and critics of Periclean rationalism alike to characterize the power of human reason to master nature and chance. But *prométheia* has a special symbolic association that the other words do not have: it points to the specifically secular image of man that Periclean humanism embraced.

In Aeschylus' *Prometheus Bound* the hero is the god who defies Zeus and gives mankind fire and the arts, and there it seems the god was meant to play an ultimately reconciling role between the emerging rationalist movement and religious tradition.[29] By the time of our dialogue, however, Prometheus could be seen as a symbol of human intelligence itself. This is how Protagoras interprets him (*Protagoras* 320c–328c).[30] "Prometheus," as Protagoras uses the name, is but the mythological title for the liberating power in human experience, the power that frees man not only from the forces of nature but also, and perhaps above all, from the superstitious fear of the gods. To Protagoras and the ancient humanists, then, *Prométheia,* or "Fore-thought," is not the name of a divine being who saves man through his gifts, it is the symbolic name of Rational Man as his own savior. Thus it connotes the whole Periclean ideal of the mastery of life through intelligence and skill, an ideal that silently discards any role for fear of or reverence to the divine in human maturity.[31] This, of course, is not just a philosophy of life peculiar to ancient Greece. It is the Promethean view of life that for the most part modern man has been brought up to share in, the optimistic view of history as an upward ascent through science and reason in a world without gods or divine retribution.

The looming presence in the background of the *Laches* of men such as Damon and Pericles, together with the preeminent role that the word *prométheia* plays in the dialogue, raises in the mind of the educated reader the kinds of criticisms that Sophocles, Aristophanes, and Plato made of the humanist ideal. Does not the reliance on human will and reason alone somehow rupture the fundamental order of things, the order that places man not only above the beasts, but below the gods? Does not Promethean humanism arrogate to the human what belongs to the divine, inflate human pretence, and pave the way to self-destruction? Must we not pull back from the brink to which impious daring has brought us, and exercise fundamental modesty or *sōphrosynē,* fundamental self-knowledge, before the altars of Apollo and the other gods?

And yet, who would deny the greatness and manly virtue of the Periclean-Promethean vision? Not the historian Thucydides, arguably the strongest mind of his or any other time to ponder human things. Nor can anyone seriously deny that Athens' greatest epoch occurred not during the pre-Marathon regime of old-fashioned virtue, but during Pericles' imperial reign. A few would say, not even Socrates would deny the truth of the Promethean vision.[32] For how can there be any going back from the life of autonomous reason, the life of liberation from subjection to nature, superstition, and the self-ignorance of human freedom and dignity? Surely the old hopelessness—the fatalism of traditional piety, the uncritical acquiescence in custom and in the inscrutable will of the gods—is no longer adequate to what man is and can be? Surely the old gods that make us afraid are dead? Everyone knows that the fearful, the humble, the pious all perish: must we not go forward bravely, boldly, proudly, as men who walk this earth alone, and not pretend that life is less relentless than we know it to be?

What is to be done? How are we to choose between these ways of seeing the world? Although the *Laches* does not confront directly this fundamental question or these fundamentally conflicting views, they are just as much part of the historical background to our dialogue as are the historical facts of the lives of Nicias and Laches and Socrates. We will not be able, nor should we wish, to avoid some reflection on what the dialogue offers in response to them, as we attend to the role of sophistry and the various uses made of *promētheia* in the course of Socrates' conversation with the failed old fathers and the two great public men.

1.7 Prodicus

In closing our historical survey, a few words are necessary about Prodicus, citizen of Ceos, master of linguistic analysis and precise speech, whom Socrates himself, in several dialogues, claims as his teacher. Prodicus is philosophically the most interesting of the three sophists named in the *Laches,* and we know much more about him than we know about the others.[33]

Like Gorgias, Prodicus gave both epideictic or public display speeches and private teaching, for which he earned a great deal of money. The most famous of these speeches was the homily "The Choice of Heracles," the moral of which was to choose the hard life of virtue, not the easy one of pleasure, a moral sufficiently in accord with Socrates' own view that Xenophon puts it in his mouth in the *Memorabilia* (2.1), and Plato singles it out for praise in the *Symposium* (177b). But Prodicus is best known for his linguistic studies. Socrates attributes the "knowledge of names" to him in the *Cratylus,* indicating that this is "one of the greater parts of knowledge" (384b).

Prodicus' method is to identify pairs of similar words that are blurred in ordinary usage and divide them neatly into two distinct meanings so as to convey the insight inherent in the natural meaning. For example, Socrates attributes Nicias' distinction between "fearlessness," which does not imply forethought, and "courage," which does, to Damon and through him to Prodicus (197d). In the *Laches'* sister dialogue, the *Charmides,* Socrates attributes Critias' distinction between "making," the good of which lies outside the process, and "doing," the good of which lies in its effect on the agent, to Prodicus (163b–e). And similarly, in the *Protagoras,* the humorously drawn Pretentious Professor Prodicus makes a series of stiff but philosophically interesting distinctions: Socrates and Protagoras should "debate," not "quarrel"; he and the others should listen to them "in common" (hear them out), but not "equally" (uncritically); then the speakers will earn their (appreciative) "esteem," not (merely verbal) "praise"; and the listeners will gain (intellectual) "enjoyment," not (merely sensuous) "pleasure" (337a–c). Prodicus is even credited with recognizing two of the more important distinctions in Socrates' philosophical lexicon, "will" (rational or prudent desire) as opposed to "desire" (irrational or imprudent desire), and "being" versus "becoming" (340a–b). Obviously, Prodicus' characteristic style of marking significant conceptual distinctions and identifying them with distinct words is a dialectical practice that Socrates uses often (e.g., *Euthyphro* 12a–c on fear versus shame; *Republic* 333a on alliances versus partnerships; *Gorgias* 462c, 463b on empirical knack versus art), so it is not surprising that he would, even if ironically, call himself Prodicus' student in this respect.

To appreciate Prodicus' role in the *Laches,* we must return again to the theme of virtue and education, and in particular to the nature of philosophical education. Plato depicts Prodicus, like all the great sophists, as making claim to teaching virtue (*Protagoras* 357e), but whereas it is obvious that Socrates rejects this claim from the other sophists, it is not so obvious in the case of Prodicus. First of all, Prodicus' attempts to identify precise discriminations among words seems to have been based on the principle that language may correspond to an objective reality or nature, contrary to the Protagorean doctrine of relativism and the corresponding linguistic theory that names are purely conventional (see *Cratylus* 386a–390e). Thus on the level of method, Socrates can see Prodicus' art of bringing rest to the use of names as an essential first line of defense if one is to defeat Protagoras' henchmen, the word warriors Euthydemus and Dionysodorus, who sought to set them in constant motion (*Euthydemus* 277e). Without Prodicus' capacity for grasping and holding precise and significant conceptual distinctions, without "the correctness of names," no one has a chance against them, and therefore it would seem that Prodicus teaches an absolutely necessary intellectual skill or virtue, which even Socrates cannot do without (see *Protagoras* 340a; *Phaedrus* 265d–

266b). In addition, there is the matter of "The Choice of Heracles" in which Prodicus, contrary to Protagoras' other students, seems to teach virtue and reject hedonism in the most direct and obvious way.

On the other hand, Socrates and Prodicus do not appear to agree at a deeper level of analysis. For example, they disagree on the proper usage of *deinos,* a word that plays an important role in the *Laches* (see *Protagoras* 341a–d). Is something *deinos,* "terrible," also capable of being "good"? Socrates seems to have thought yes (Sophocles in the "Ode on Man" in the *Antigone* agreed), but Prodicus did not: Prodicus appears to lack the Socratic sense of the potential duplicity or ambiguity of things (see *Cratylus* 437a). Prodicus' comic rigidity and lack of a sense of self-limitation also shows up in his empty boast that he alone had discovered the proper length of speech, neither short (Socratic, dialectical style) nor long (professorial, rhetorical style), but "just right" (*Phaedrus* 267b). In the end, Socrates clearly rejects the view that the knowledge of things is to be derived from names (a view that, fairly or not, he assigns to Prodicus), and he even more clearly rejects Prodicus' approach to speech making in educational contexts. We can, at least in part, see why, when we consider the two products of Prodicus' teaching art that Plato exhibits: Nicias, the notorious coward, who makes a fine distinction concerning courage, and Critias, the notorious profligate and tyrant, who makes an equally fine distinction concerning moderation.

Socrates treats Prodicus comically in both the *Apology* and in the *Cratylus,* where he makes sport of the difference between the one-drachma course, which he could afford to take, and the fifty-drachma course, which he could not, suggesting that the influence may not have been so great after all (384b). Certainly, Prodicus could convey in his lectures many important, and perhaps insightful, conceptual distinctions, and with these tools and the methodological model in hand, an apt student might avoid the verbal pitfalls set by Euthydemus and other such hunters. But would the professor's philosophical vocabulary lessons or his moral admonitions be of much avail when the student's own mettle was under fire? Had the student really been taught virtue, even intellectual virtue, by Professor Linguisticus? Or did Prodicus provide anything more than a collection of inspired categories to accompany his homily on virtue, which even he may not have believed in? (See *Protagoras* 358a–b.) The *Laches* will suggest that the answer is no to all of these questions.

2

The Literary Form

BOTH IN THE *REPUBLIC* and in the *Phaedrus,* Socrates offers extensive criticisms of tragic and comic poetry and of writing in general. His criticisms focus not only on the substantive teachings of the poets and writers of prose, but also on the forms in which they are presented. These criticisms make up the background against which we must understand the literary form that Plato employs in the dialogues. This chapter will discuss certain problems that Plato saw in writing truly philosophical literature and some of the techniques he used as an author who intended not merely to please or persuade or instruct but actually to teach people to think by means of the written word. In the process of examining the literary form of our dialogue, it will become evident that the *Laches,* far from being "primitive and awkward," is in fact a work of great artistic subtlety and depth.

Socrates' criticisms of poetry in the *Republic* concern both the moral fitness of the message of poetry, discussed in books 2 and 3, and the pedagogical and epistemic value of poetic creation, discussed in book 10.[1] In those earlier books, prior to the discussion of philosophy itself, he ignores questions concerning the knowledge transmitted by poetry; his focus is on the habituating imagery and exemplars of behavior that are presented in poetic art, and he and his interlocutor Adeimantus are interested primarily in censoring the messages of tragic poetry. The moral basis of Socrates' criticism of poetry is that the protectors of the Just City are neither to fear their own death more than slavery or shame nor to love their own friends more than they love honor or what the law commands. But poetry teaches the undue fear of death (386a–387c), unmanly pity (387c–388e), and perhaps worst of all, impiety (379a–380c). From the perspective of Justice, the tragic sensibility is morally deficient, since it undermines patriotism, courage, and civic religion. Rather than dry up the selfish, rebellious, and effeminate passions, it waters them and makes them stronger (see 387c, 388d; also 606d). The good aesthete makes a bad citizen.

In book 10, Socrates shifts his criticisms to a different aspect of the problem that he has with poetry. His great concern is that poetic imitation "maims the thought (*dianoia*) of those who hear it" (595b4). First he argues that the poet is at three removes from reality or truth, for he tries simply to depict the visual appearances of things, such as those made by human craftsmen, which are themselves physical copies of the true, eternal beings made by God. Then he replaces the triad of makers: God, craftsman, poet, with the triad of knowers: user, craftsman, poet. It is the one who knows how to use things, who knows their goodness or value, who alone knows them properly. Presumably the one who knows the ultimate purposes of things is somehow analogous or equivalent to God, who is or makes the Ideas or original natures of things. Be that puzzling as it may, the more obvious question of the whole passage is how to relate this criticism to the discussion of philosophy conducted earlier, in books 6 and 7. There, Socrates divided the ways of knowing into four, not three, levels, the first being fantasy or dream; the second common sense or belief; the third thought, especially mathematical deductive thought; the fourth insight, where the Ideas, with the culminating Idea of the Good, are known. Clearly, one level is missing in book 10, namely that of mathematics and deductive reasoning, of *argument*. Clearly, this is one fundamental defect of poetry: it seduces the listener into the lowest, uncritical mode of knowing, the mode of self-identifying, emotion-charged fantasy, the mode in which the soul is swayed by the power and beauty of the musical word to dwell unthinkingly in the world that the poet creates, because it is so pleasurable—so pleasurable, so true, somehow, to the way things are or ought to be, that the listener does not think to ask the poet for proof that what he says is true.[2] Thus the function of mathematics in the education of the guardian is to turn his mind from fantasy to studies that will train him in rigorous thinking and to reveal to him the most immediately recognizable eidetic structures in the nature of things—the prelude and inspiration to the dialectical, philosophical studies that are to follow. Poetry does not teach the mind and the man to "follow the *logos*," but without this habit of mind there can be no true enlightenment, no discovery or self-deepening in the invisible reality of the Ideas. (These comments are not meant to imply that Plato sees no necessary place for poetry in the educational process. To note only the most obvious point, poetry, unlike the mathematical sciences, addresses the question of what life is for.)

Socrates also offers criticisms of poetry, rhetoric, and writing in general in the *Phaedrus*.[3] The dialogue begins with Socrates' and Phaedrus' discussion of a speech meant to seduce its listener sexually, and this is followed by a long, marvelous myth that Socrates tells about the soul. This myth comprises the main rhetorical aspect of Socrates' teaching in the *Phaedrus,* insofar as it is needed to remind Phaedrus of his own soul's deep longing for truth, a longing covered up by his fascination with beauty. Afterward, Socrates and Phaedrus engage in a serious conversation about the nature of good speaking and writing. In the process, Socrates tells two other myths, one explaining how some men became subhuman through their imprudent passion for music, the other suggesting that the art of writing and the reading of writing may do more harm than good, as written works have a tendency to corrupt the power of memory, convince the reader that he possesses knowledge he does not possess, and above all—like beautiful but majestically silent paintings—fail to provide the means whereby the reader who genuinely seeks to know can question the presented knowledge and test its truth. The best a written work can do, it seems, is remind those who already know of what they know (274b–275e).

While the *Phaedrus* never directly addresses the questions of what this "reminding" involves or what kind of writing would best satisfy this reminding function, Socrates does lay down some rules of good speaking that, he indicates later, can also apply to good writing. First, the speaker must know and aim at the truth, not merely at probability or what will conform to the beliefs of the audience, as was the practice of the rhetoricians (259e–262c, 272d–274a). Second, the speaker must know the various types of souls, discern the type of soul his auditor possesses, and address that auditor with the type of speech that is appropriate to his type of soul (268a–272b). Socrates says also that the speech must be composed as a kind of living whole, with a head and feet, a beginning, a middle, and an end, each of its parts fitting into the whole (264a–c, 268c–d). In relation to this point, he appeals to the "law of logographic necessity" (264b7), namely the aesthetic principle commanding that there be nothing accidental in the work, but that everything be necessary at the place where it occurs. The Platonic dialogue is based on this beautiful or beautifying falsehood—on the denial of chance.

Now when we reflect on Socrates' rules, it is clear that the first and third pose no special problem for either the would-be good author or the would-be good speaker. Both must possess knowledge of their subject matter and strive for truth in presenting it, and both must compose their works as wholes with no inappropriate parts. But the second rule does pose a seemingly insurmountable problem, insofar as the author cannot talk to and question his reader so as to ascertain his type of soul and address him with the appropriate type of speech.

Correspondingly, the reader cannot address whatever questions he may have to the author, by way of clarification or criticism or further investigation. So in addition to the basic matter of possessing true knowledge about human souls, the would-be good author must solve two other problems of communication or form if he is to create a written work of real merit: first, the work must allow the author to test the souls of his readers and address the right kind of speech to each, knowing in particular "to whom it should speak and to whom it should say nothing"; and second, the author must allow the reader to question the answers the author provides, so that the knowledge he offers might be "written in the soul of the learner, and can defend itself" (276a6).

Plato intended to create a form of philosophical literature that would not be liable to the moral, pedagogical, and epistemological criticisms Socrates makes of poetry and the written word in the *Republic* and the *Phaedrus*. Certainly the dialogue form does not lend itself to being treated as a simple statement of Plato's opinions; even if we think of Socrates as Plato's spokesman, it is clear that Plato does not present us, in aporetic dialogues such as the *Laches* or the *Charmides,* with conclusive opinions about the subject matter under discussion. Furthermore, it is soon evident to the slowest-witted reader that Socrates' manner is not at all simple: he is, in a word, ironic, obviously playful, and possibly thoroughly deceptive (at least in his claim of ignorance and perhaps in more). So even if we are tempted to treat him as Plato's spokesman, that claim and his very manner restrain us from doing so. And yet many readers are content to do little more with the dialogues than read them as if Socrates were simply Plato's spokesman and then criticize the opinions or arguments he seems to offer, or else, like the cicada men in Socrates' myth, treat the dialogues simply as works of philosophical entertainment, that is, as dramas composed to give us pleasure rather than to lead us toward truth. Neither of these approaches will do. We must understand the Platonic dialogues on their own terms, as an attempt to resolve the criticisms their author had his Socrates make of poetry and the written word as a means of education.

2.2 The Platonic Dialogue as a Response to These Criticisms

How, then, does the Platonic dialogue itself address the kinds of criticisms that Socrates makes of poetry, rhetoric, and the written word in the *Republic* and the *Phaedrus*? Perhaps the most obvious matter concerns the doctrinal content of the teaching that Socrates gives, particularly in the *Republic*. The explicit call for censorship over writing and art that arouse illicit passions, the pointed insistence on a more vigorous role for the state in governing moral development, the rejection of permissiveness both as a matter of the letter and the spirit of the laws at work in the land, the recognition of the need for violence, the courageous will to restrict liberty on behalf of reason and justice—these are all part of the morally tougher stance toward vice that Socrates takes in the dialogues, in contrast to the lax or tolerant attitude of the democrat.[4] Furthermore, the dialogues themselves show remarkable restraint in their depiction of human conduct. There is not a single instance of fear of death in the Platonic dialogues—with the exception, of course, of the fourteen hostages in the *Phaedo,* who are rescued by the new Theseus-Socrates from that fear. There are no instances of shameless behavior in the Platonic dialogues—or only a couple—and Socrates specifically rebukes several characters for their unseemly behavior.[5] And there is only one instance of impiety in the dialogues, where Socrates expresses some doubt about the gods; he seems clearly and obviously to believe in gods who exist in harmony with each other, with mankind, and with the cosmos (see, for example, *Gorgias* 507c–508a).[6]

As for the other criticism, Socrates himself offers the theoretical foundation that he finds lacking in the poets and other writers. The essence of the whole *Republic* might be said to be the new theory of the soul that Socrates develops there—including the basic, tripartite theory of book 4, the extended theory of the philosophical soul in books 5 through 7, and the consequent theory of bad souls in books 8 and 9, not to mention the rational proof of the immortality of the simple soul, as well as the myth of the Choice of Lives and the reincarnation of the soul in book 10.

But it is in regard to the more formal matters that the Platonic dialogue has justly acquired its claim as the preeminent genre for philosophical literature. In marked contrast to Homer and the poets, Socrates resolutely "follows the *logos,*" and his whole way of being in the dialogues is to examine opinions, to test them, to elicit and develop arguments, and to seek the principles and also the implications of those arguments. This is not to deny the coexistence in the dialogues of myths giving imaginative form to conceptual positions that Socrates and his interlocutors take under consideration. But the point, which contemporary English-speaking scholars have brought to a new level of awareness, is that the Platonic dialogues are composed of literally hundreds of great and small, explicit and implicit arguments that cry out for our analysis, mutual comparison, and synoptic evaluation.[7] Unlike Homer, in relation to whom we can experience great pleasure just as empathetic listeners, we must make an effort to follow Socrates' reasoning if we are to enjoy and eventually understand the dialogues. Unlike Homer, who pulls us unselfknowingly into the flow of his musical dreamworld, Socrates stops us and asks: "This is the logical conclusion, is it not?" Unlike the poet, the philosopher does not wish for us merely to see and to feel; he wants us to think.

And yet it is possible to memorize arguments, no less than it is possible to memorize the conclusions of arguments, or simply memorize the beautiful sounding words of poetry, without asking oneself why they are beautiful, what beauty is, whether the conclusions are true, or whether the proofs are sound. The *Phaedrus* makes us intensely aware of this problem—of how to discriminate among its readers between those who want and those who do not want to seek truth, those who merely want opinions or entertainment and those who look for knowledge itself. There is the related problem of how to draw the potentially philosophical reader not merely into following the movement of thought as imitated by the characters in the dialogue but into initiating the movement of thinking himself (or herself), to provoke reflection culminating in self-consciousness and self-reflexivity (the kind that asks questions of the dialogue and thus leads to self-examination), to questioning one's own beliefs about the topics addressed in the *Laches* or other dialogues: the good life; the relation of virtue to knowledge; the noble, the useful, and the good; the place of philosophy in a just society; the nature of the human soul. The dialogues address this complex problem in two principal ways. First of all, there are mathematical keys to at least some of the Platonic dialogues that open the text to the discerning reader, allowing him to discover aspects of it that remain closed to those who ignore the mathematical signs. (The role of mathematics in the structure of the dialogues, particularly of the *Laches,* will be discussed in the next section.) Second, the Platonic dialogues present both the actions and the speeches of the characters, both drama and argument, *erga* and *logoi,* and these are composed in such a way as to reflect upon each other and point toward something that neither displays by itself. These features of Plato's literary art invite our participation in the life of the mind that the dialogue is intended in every way to imitate, without violating the principles of political restraint that, Socrates teaches, must limit the freedom of the just man, even the just poet. Thus we are led to critical reflection on the drama and arguments of the dialogue, to contemplation of the questions it raises, to making its thinking—be it on the nature of education or courage or prudence—our own. But none of its teachings are obvious: we must work hard to expose them; we must seek to find the truths that are concealed. As we raise questions, helped by the various signs that Plato leaves along the way to indicate where to look, we are taken ever deeper into the soul of the work, and we begin to experience the very quality of movement toward truth that it imitates. Thus the dialogue form in Plato's masterly hand overcomes almost all of the criticisms of poetry and the written word that Socrates offers; it becomes a perfect form of art.

2.3 The Mathematical Key

The surface of each Platonic dialogue is a continuous sequence of conversation and drama leading to a conclusion, which turns out, in the aporetic dialogues, to be the conclusion: We do not know the meaning of the concept under investigation. Questions are asked, examples are given to illustrate points, allusions are made to other situations or to mythological figures, conceptual distinctions are introduced, arguments are developed, the characters fall occasionally into contradictions, and the inquiry must begin anew, sometimes not without dramatic incidents of temper or surprise—but it all moves more or less fluidly along. Thus it is easy to suppose that what you see is what is there: an intellectual drama with its lesson more or less on the surface, its teachings in the arguments Socrates makes, its conclusion the one that contemporary readers of Plato tend to suppose is the merely provisional, early, Socratic conclusion that "we know that we know nothing"—a conclusion that will be replaced in the soaring middle dialogues by Plato's philosophic vision, though apparently he fell back or went forward into a more sophisticated critical perspective in his later works. This impression, however, is misleading. All of the Platonic dialogues are crafted to serve the political and philosophical-educational goals discussed in sections 2.1 and 2.2. All the dialogues employ literary techniques intended to insure that only those of a philosophical nature will have access to Plato's deepest thoughts. One of the two most important of these techniques is the use of mathematical signs to point the way to questions and answers not made explicit on the surface. Some of these signs can hardly be missed; others are much more difficult to locate.

The basic mathematical key to Plato's dialogues consists in the simple matter of number, of counting, of forming groups under kinds that can then be compared to other groups. It is important, in studying the dialogues, to count up and keep track of the number of characters, how often certain words are used, which item in a series falls in the middle, what analogies are suggested by parallel groups, how the work is divided up in terms of structure, and so on. We may note two small examples of this technique: first, the fourteen friends present in the prison who make evident to the careful reader Socrates' role in the *Phaedo* as the new mythological hero who will find his way through the labyrinth of arguments and defeat the fear of death, and second, the comparison we are invited to make in the *Republic* between the three levels of reality or truth suggested by the discussion of poetry in book 10, as well as the four levels of knowledge identified in books 6 and 7. The fact that one level is missing indicates there is a dimension of reality and a way of knowing that the later discussion is suppressing.

In the *Laches,* the key to the mathematical substructures is not the triad (although there are important triads), or four or the central position in a series or the fifth in a series or groups of seven, but the simplest count of all, the lowly business of adding one and one to make two.[8] Pairing or grouping of twos occurs in relation to characters and other details of all kinds. In fact, pairing is so common in the dialogue that when something appears on its own, without a paired character or word, it is singled out for special attention.

We have already noted one example: the characters in dialogue are typically paired, such as Lysimachus and Melesias; their two sons; Nicias and Laches; the pairing of fathers and sons in general, including Socrates and his father; Lysimachus and Melesias and their fathers Aristides and Thucydides; Nicias and Laches and their sons; and by implication the past and present, and the present and future generations of the Athenians. Other characters just named are also paired, including the musicians Agathocles and Damon; the poets Homer and Solon; Damon's two teachers, Agathocles and Prodicus. And there are other pairings as well, notably Laches and Lamachus, and, most important, Laches and Socrates. But in the early part of the dialogue, the predominant pairings are Lysimachus and Melesias, and Nicias and Laches. Socrates stands alone in comparison with them, a somewhat alien figure brought into their community of inquiry only after it is revealed that he is indeed a friend and shares a common interest with them. We recall, however, that Socrates can be paired with the sophists, though in our dialogue he is contrasted to Stesilaus, as regards their conduct in battle, and to Damon, as a teacher of virtue.

In addition to the pairings of the characters, which, as we shall see, can be interpreted to reflect the structure of the dialogue as a whole, there are many, many specific details of terminology, examples, kinds of distinctions drawn, and even specific actions that occur in pairs. For example, just within the field of education and knowledge there are many pairs employed, including: (1) two kinds of attitudes toward education, the one that exhibits care, the other that does not; (2) studies (*mathēmata*) and practices (*epitēdeumata*); (3) genuine or useful studies and fraudulent or useless ones; (4) the art of war and the art of tragic poetry (this distinction paralleling that between Sparta and Athens, that between gymnastics and music, and even that between action and speech); (5) between education that is aimed at the virtue of the soul and education that is not; (6) between knowledge acquired by discovery (*heurein*) or by learning from a teacher (*manthanein*); (7) between knowledge demonstrated by its product (*ergon*) and knowledge demonstrated by its ability to give an account (*didonai logon*).[9]

There are also many examples given in pairs, or things mentioned twice, or words used just twice. To follow up on one theme, Socrates gives Nicias two examples to show that education concerns the soul: first, medication for the eyes; second, a bridle for a horse. He later pairs sight with the eyes (and also hearing with the ears); distinguishes the knowledge of the two horses in a chariot from the knowledge of the charioteer; and discusses the art of horsemanship a second time. In relation to words that are used, just two pairs of characters, Lysimachus and Socrates, and Laches and Socrates, use the word "just" (*dikaion*); two characters, Lysimachus and Socrates, use words related to "shame," Socrates pairing it with "harm" (Laches avoids using the word "shame"); two characters, Lysimachus and Nicias, use words related to "memory"; two characters, Laches and Nicias, condemn the quality of "boldness" (*tolma*), Nicias for its imprudence, Laches for its opposition to common opinion; two characters, Socrates and Laches, are the only ones who use the word "soul" (*psychē*) or words related to "nature" or the word "god" (*theos*); two characters, Nicias and Socrates, use words related to "forethought," *promētheia* itself being mentioned only twice (words related to *dianoia* are also used only by these characters, one each); Nicias is associated with *philotimia*, Laches with *philonikia*; wisdom (*sophia*) is attributed to Nicias just twice, once by Socrates, once by Laches; the contrast of *logos* and *ergon* is mentioned just twice, by Laches and then by Socrates, as is the contrast of *logos* and *noein*; distinctions are drawn between cavalry courage and infantry courage, those who fight pain or fear, desires or pleasures, standing or turning back, prudent and foolish endurance, getting instruction (*didaskesthai*) and learning (*manthanein*), the knowledge of things that are to be dared and of things that are to be dreaded, the seer's knowledge of what is to be but the wise-courageous man's knowledge of what is better, those who look to others and those who look to themselves, and the prudence (*phronēsis*) that is befitting a statesman and the wisdom that is taught by the sophists. And again, these pairings call our attention to some words used only once, or only by a single character, e.g., "law" (*nomos*) and "piety" (*hosiotēs*) just once each by Socrates; "prudence" only by Socrates (though Nicias speaks of prudent things); "beneficial" (*ōphelimon*) just once by Nicias (though Socrates speaks of what is "harmful," *blabera*). Neither *erōs* nor *philosophia* appear in the *Laches*.

We also note that Socrates cites just two poets, Homer and Solon; he mentions Homer twice, citing each of his two major works, quoting two lines from the *Iliad*; of the oaths, only two are not by Laches and only two are not "by God"; Laches twice gets angry with Nicias; Socrates insists twice he will not release Laches from his share in their side of the argument; and both the fathers and the sons are to go to school with Socrates at the end.

Cumulatively, the overwhelming presence of such sets of twos can be neither unimportant nor accidental; they send far too powerful a message to be ignored. So it is not surprising that the technique of doublets is also evident in relation to the structure of the dialogue as a whole and that it offers one key to interpreting its meaning. We shall consider the divisions that can be made of the dialogue later in this chapter. The most obvious division of the movement of the conversation starts from the pairing between the attention to education (*paideia*) and becoming in the first half, and the attention to courage (*andreia*) and being in the second. A less obvious but also important division is into two parts of seven sections each, which contrast conventional and philosophical deliberation. In section 2.6, we shall examine a pairing that lends itself to an especially interesting interpretation of the teaching of the *Laches,* the pairing Socrates makes, himself with Laches, each one, together two, reminding us of the Homeric phrase, "Where two go together."[10] This pairing forms the literary basis for the single most influential modern scholarly interpretation of the dialogue, the Bonitz thesis. We shall also introduce at that time some of the main reasons for rejecting the Bonitz thesis as a satisfactory guide to the interpretation of the *Laches*.

2.4 The Play of Word and Deed

A second methodological key to the interpretation of a Platonic dialogue has to do with the relationship between its speech (*logos*) and its action (*ergon*).[11] We are enjoined to attend to this relationship in the *Laches,* whose title character calls for the true "Doric harmony" in which each one genuinely reflects the other (188d). When we attend to this relationship in a Platonic dialogue, an inner dimension of the work begins to come into view. The interaction of drama and argument points to features we would not otherwise notice, such as hints in Socrates' speeches or those of other characters that indicate reservations about the conclusions that have been reached, or that suggest themes or problems ignored in the discussion, or that cause us to reflect on the symbolic dimension of the narrative. As characters come to be revealed through both word and deed, and as opinions are themselves commented on by events, the dialogue begins to take on a three-dimensional quality, when before it had all seemed superficial. These reflections draw us into the philosophical quest. Finding more in the play than we expected, we are charmed into taking its questions and now obviously incomplete answers more seriously; we ourselves are brought into the thinking process—precisely what Socrates had argued a work of true rhetoric must do. (Incidentally, Plato is by no means the only ancient author to employ this technique in his writing. It is also characteristic of Aristophanes, and even of Thucydides.)

Recognition of the signal importance of the *logos/ergon* theme in Plato goes back a long way. The poet Chaucer knew of it in the Middle Ages: "Eek Plato seith, who-so that can him rede, The wordes mote be cosin to the dede" (*Canterbury Tales,* Prologue). In modern times, the theme of the interaction of drama and argument was first developed almost two centuries ago with Friedrich Schleiermacher, who wrote: "If anywhere at all, it is here [in Plato's philosophy] that form and content are inseparable."[12] Much later, Paul Fried-länder in the 1920s made a powerful case to refuse to separate the dramatic form and argumentative content in the study of the Platonic dialogues, though his work is marred by inadequate analysis of the arguments and a somewhat superficial approach to the philosophical issues. On the other hand, it is only in the past decade or two that English-speaking scholars have taken this theme seriously in their approach to Plato's teaching; for the most part, even the best of the analytic scholars ignored it.[13] But times are changing, thanks in particular to the arrival in America of German Jewish emigrés who combined the requisite philosophical and political basis for understanding Plato's dialogues. Today, English-speaking students of these men are beginning to work what amounts to a renaissance of classical scholarship that is attuned both to the distinctive form of Plato's philosophical literature and to the ways of thinking that characterized classical political philosophy; the acuteness and sensitivity to detail they have brought to the study of Plato has begun to influence even the most technical analytic scholars.[14]

The actual interplay of *logos* and *ergon* varies from dialogue to dialogue. But one can find at least four distinct ways in which the mimesis of action is used to contribute to the meaning of the dialogue.[15] One of these is the ethological or character-revealing mime, in which the speaker shows himself not only in speech, but also in action, and we are called upon to compare the two. As we shall see, ethological mimes are important in the *Laches,* in relation both to the title character and to Nicias. A second way in which action reveals teaching or at least comments on argument is the doxological or opinion-revealing mime, in which the falsity or rightness of an opinion is commented on by the behavior of the speaker. In the *Laches* this device is especially important relative to Nicias. A third kind of mime found in the Platonic dialogues, but one that has only a minor role in the *Laches,* is the mythological mime, such as the myth of Theseus and the minotaur in the *Phaedo* or the myth of recollection in the *Meno.* In these dialogues, the drama presents, interprets, or replaces a myth, sometimes with a new myth (such as the one about Theseus-Socrates). Finally, a fourth kind is the thematic mime in which the action imitates or represents a thematic point of view that Plato is taking in the dialogue. This kind of mime is prominent in the first part of the *Laches* and in the interaction among its three primary characters.

Moving from drama to argument and back again, the Platonic dialogue creates a wonderful suspension of mind in the reality of the play. But Socrates tells us that writing should not exist for its own sake, as autonomous poetry or autonomous science. Rather, it should exist for the sake of the quest of truth and civic virtue; it should exist to help us attain excellence—all without threatening justice or freedom. This is what the form of the dialogue is intended to achieve. The outer surface is intended to shield its inner questions and teachings from undiscerning readers, and to turn them back upon the opinions that preserve the common good. The dangerous interior is revealed only to one who begins to *participate* in the life of the mind that the dialogue represents, who reflects both imaginatively and conceptually on its drama and arguments, who contemplates both its explicit and implicit questions and answers, who makes its thinking—be it on the nature of education or courage or wisdom—his own. As we noted earlier, however, none of the dialogue's real teachings are obvious: you must work to dig them up, seek to find the truths that are concealed. But if you ask questions, helped by the various signs Plato leaves along the way to indicate where to look, you are taken into the mind of the work; you experience the activity of ascent and descent toward truth that it imitates.

The contemplation of *logos* and *ergon* together helps to open two other doors. One of these is an interpretation of the dialogue based on the metaphor of the Divided Line and the related parable of the Cave that Socrates tells in the *Republic*. The other is an interpretation of the overall poetics of the work, in terms of tragedy and comedy and of what is especially relevant to the philosopher, irony. Now let us turn to some of the overall interpretations of the *Laches* suggested by its outward structure and action.

2.5 *Two Interpretations of the Structure of the* Laches

At first reading, it may not be obvious that the *Laches* is composed in terms of a definite structure, but as one examines the content of the discussion with the doublet structure in mind, the deep binomial division of the work comes into view.[16] Lysimachus even does us the favor of announcing when the center of the dialogue occurs (189c8), the central speech being the one given by Socrates just afterward (189d4–e8). This doublet structure is as follows:

I. Problem of education (178a1–189d5)

  A. Deliberation concerning *hoplomachia,* the art of fighting in heavy armor (178a–184d)

    1. Origin of the deliberation (178a1–181d7)

      a) Fathers' plea for advice (178a1–180a5)

      b) Socrates is brought into the discussion (180a6–181d7)

    2. Leaders' conflicting advice (181d8–184c8)

      a) Nicias' speech: praise of *hoplomachia* (181d8–182d5)

      b) Laches' speech: attack on *hoplomachia* (182d6–184c8)

  B. Discussion concerning education and the soul (184c9–189c5)

    1. New standards established in the discussion (184c9–187d5)

      a) For making decisions (184c9–186a2)

      b) For judging teachers (186a3–187d5)

    2. Responses to Socrates' way of examining opinions and souls (187d6–189d5)

      a) Nicias' attitude toward it (187d6–188c3)

      b) Laches' attitude toward speeches (188c4–189d5)

II. Search for a definition of courage (189d5–201c5)

  A. Introduction and Socrates' examination of Laches (189d5–194c1)

    1. Introduction (189d5–190e3)

      a) Socrates and Laches are to discuss virtue (189d5–190c7)

      b) The inquiry is to concern courage only (190c8–190e3)

    2. Socrates' examination of Laches (190e4–194c1)

      a) Laches' first definition (190e4–191e12)

      b) Laches' second definition (192a1–194c1)

  B. Socrates' examination of Nicias, and conclusion (194c2–201c5)

    1. Examination of Nicias (194c2–199e12)

      a) Laches' and Socrates' examination of Nicias (194c2–197e10)

      b) Socrates' examination of Nicias (197e10–199e12)

    2. Conclusion (199e13–201c5)

      a) Laches' and Nicias' views of each other (199e13–200c1)

      b) Everyone agrees that Socrates should teach them all (200c2–201c5)

In addition to the more obvious doublet structure, the *Laches* can also be articulated in terms of a comparison between what might be called a vulgar or merely persuasive deliberative conversation and a philosophical deliberative conversation.[17] On this view, the dialogue is composed with another kind of doublet structure, in which seven parallel parts of the first deliberation, begun by Lysimachus and ending in an *aporia,* compare with seven parts of the second, begun by Socrates and also ending in an *aporia*. The overall outline of the dialogue using this schema would then be as follows:

Rhetorical (178a1–184c9)	*Philosophical (184d8–201c5)*
1. Preface by Lysimachus (178a1–179a1) Subject: conventional conditions of advice	1. Preface by Socrates with Melesias (184d8–e10) Subject: philosophical conditions of advice
2. Speech by Lysimachus (179a1–180a5) Subject: reasons for seeking advice	2. Socrates and Melesias (184e11–186a2) Subject: reasons for consultation
3. Nicias, Laches, and Socrates enter Lysimachus' community (180a6–181c9) Subject: conditions for trusting an advisor	3. Nicias and Laches enter Socrates' community (186a3–189d4) Subject: conditions for trusting and recognizing a knower
4. Socrates' speech (181d1–7) Subject: terms for Nicias, Laches, conditions of knowledge	4. Socrates' speech (189d5–190e3) Subject: terms for the rest of the dialogue, conditions of knowledge
5. Nicias' speech (181d8–182d5) Subject: advice regarding the art of fighting	5. Laches and Socrates (190e4–194c1) Subject: definition of courage
6. Laches' speech (182d6–184c8) Subject: advice regarding the art of fighting	6. Nicias, Laches and Socrates (194c2–199e2) Subject: definition of courage
7. Lysimachus and Socrates (184c9–d7) Subject: *aporia* based on disagreement among experts	7. Nicias, Laches, Socrates and Lysimachus (199e13–201c5) Subject: *aporia* based on self-contradiction of speakers

The various elements in both the straightforward doublet outline and this more subtle one will be discussed later, in commenting on the dialogue itself. It is worth noting by way of introduction to that commentary that the second analysis offers a more natural articulation of the work than the one based simply on doublets, though they correspond roughly to one another. But this articulation makes it evident how, beginning from a perfectly natural starting point for deliberation, first a conventional, democratic discussion community, and then a philosophical inquiry and philosophical discussion community can emerge. Again the *action* of the dialogue suggests items that the *speeches* do not. The *Laches*, more than any other aporetic dialogue concerning the virtues, offers a kind of introduction to Socratic philosophy in general, showing us not only how it is, but how it comes to be, as a result of the kind of failure to which conventional deliberation is prone (see section 3.5).

In addition, the *Laches* also lends itself to a division in three parts of seven sections each. This analysis, which will prove to be a natural variation on the second division mentioned above, is as follows:

	Part One *178a1–184c8*	*Part Two* *184c9–189d5*	*Part Three* *189d6–201c5*
1. Conditions for deliberation:	178a1 experience, reputation, good will	184c9 art of soul therapy	189d6 knowledge of what is better
2. Subject matter:	179a1 *hoplomachia*	185b9 art of soul therapy	190c8 virtue, courage (what it is)
3. Securing the community of inquiry:	180a1 Nicias, Laches and Socrates join Lysimachus	186a3 Socrates asks Nicias and Laches about soul therapy	190e4, 194c2 Socrates asks Laches and Nicias about courage
4. Conditions for knowledge:	181d1 age and experience	186a3 teachers or students	190c6 giving an account
5. Speeches/ inquiries:	181d8 Nicias' advice	187d6 Nicias on Socrates' method	190e4 Laches' account of courage
6. Speeches/ inquiries:	182d6 Laches' advice	188c4 Laches on word and deed	194c2 Nicias' account of courage

	184c9	189d5	199e11
7. Conclusion:	Lysimachus asks Socrates to vote	being is prior to becoming	Recognition of ignorance, all ask Socrates to teach

On the three-part analysis, a distinction must be made not only between vulgar or common and philosophical deliberation, but also between deliberation concerning production and things that come into being, as contrasted to deliberation concerned with the being, the nature of a thing and things that are. This distinction is sometimes blurred in the *Laches,* which makes the reader wonder whether Plato realizes that his characters are blurring the distinction. The discovery that the distinction between the kind of knowledge that is concerned with "becoming" (or "becomings") and the kind that is concerned with "being" (or "beings") is built into the very structure of the dialogue should lay such doubts to rest and alert the reader to learn precisely what role this distinction plays in the dialogue. As we shall see in chapter 5, it seems to play a major role in pointing us in the direction that further inquiry must take, if we are to discover the basis of true courage.

2.6 The Bonitz Thesis

Writing over a century ago, Hermann Bonitz proposed an interpretation of the *Laches* that has served as a starting-point for scholarly discussion ever since.[18] Bonitz argued that Socrates himself seems to allow for the importance of endurance to courage (194a) and that he does not simply refute the definition of courage as knowledge, but rather indicates that if that were all there is to courage, it would be complete virtue (199e). Because the dialogue does not explicitly rule out either the element of Laches' second definition, "a kind of endurance of the soul," or the element of Nicias' definition, "a knowledge of what is to be dreaded and dared," Bonitz concluded, the true definition lay in their combination: "Wir brauchen nur die unbestritten gelassenen und dadurch als giltig anerkannten Sätze zu verbinden, um darin die vollständige Definition der Tapferkeit zu haben."[19] ("We need only combine the remaining, uncontested and in that way recognized as valid sentences, in order to have the complete definition of bravery.") Thus it would seem that the secret teaching of the *Laches* on the nature of courage is that courage is "a kind of endurance of soul, oriented by the knowledge of what is to be dreaded and dared," i.e., wise or prudent endurance, as Socrates himself suggests in discussion with Laches (192c).

There is a good deal of evidence in support of the Bonitz thesis in the dialogue. Both in relation to the characters and in relation to the dramatic action, the play seems to point to the definition of courage as wise endurance.

In particular, several commentators on the *Laches* have noted that the treatment of the characters appears to support the Bonitz thesis.[20] Of the characters, Laches seems to be identified in the dialogue as a man of action who lacks the corresponding power of clear speech: He knows Socrates by his deeds, but knows nothing of his speaking, he judges men and purported skills by their efficacy in action, he criticizes Nicias for studying with a sophist, and he offers the only definition of courage related to conduct in battle; but he also fails to defend his accounts of courage, he admits he is unaccustomed to inquiry, and he is unable in his examination of Nicias to prove that what Nicias says is wrong, though he strongly disagrees with it. Nicias, on the other hand, seems to be a man of speech, without the requisite power of action: Practically his first word is *dianoia* (180a7), he defines courage in relation to knowledge and says nothing of action or passion, he has studied with a teacher of "the knowledge of names," and he proves himself the abler man in his verbal contest with Laches; but no one praises Nicias for his deeds, there is a clear reference in the dialogue to his miserable failure at Syracuse, and his actions in the dialogue at one crucial point seem cowardly. This contrast suggests that what is needed is a man who will combine these two qualities and thus overcome their respective deficiencies—that the courageous man will be the one who combines Laches-like endurance with Nicias-like intellectual ability.

There are, however, problems with the easy identification of Nicias with speech or intellect, Laches with action or will.[21] The most obvious problem is that Nicias is in the end not a very good representative of *logos*. He stands up well against Laches, but collapses against Socrates, and in the process he fails to notice implications of what is being said, so that we wonder if he understands his own position. It is clearer that Plato means for us to doubt that Nicias is wise, rather than he wants us to deny that Socrates or Laches are courageous. If courage is to be understood as the combination of Laches-like endurance and some form of knowledge or intellectual virtue, it would not appear to be Nicias who possesses the needed intellectual qualities.

But this problem also seems easily resolved. The character who appears to combine both words and deeds is Socrates—praised for his deeds at Delium, able by his words to expose the inadequacies of both Laches and Nicias—and so what is needed, it would seem, is the right combination of endurance (like or perhaps somewhat better than that possessed by Laches) with the proper intellectual qualities (unlike, and much better than, those possessed by Nicias). Thus: "We can at least gather from the arguments in the text what a complete definition might look like. It would include reference to endurance (and perhaps other qualities of temperament like boldness) together with wisdom, understood as knowledge of good and evil. The arguments . . . thus confirm the conclusion we arrived at by examining the characters of the two generals as revealed in the dialogue."[22]

Approaching the dialogue in terms of the relationship of *logos* and *ergon* also provides support for the Bonitz thesis, particularly when we attend to the movement of the dialogue as a whole. Thus Socrates questions Laches and finds his definition of courage as endurance wanting, but he does not simply leave Laches to talk to Nicias, he insists that he and Laches question Nicias together. After Laches fails to refute Nicias, Socrates seems to go out of his way to insist that the inquiry he then conducts is a common inquiry in which he and Laches are partners (see 197d–e, 198b–199a). That inquiry, of course, results in Nicias' failure, a failure more complete, as we shall see later, than Laches' failure: while Laches at least initially is prepared to go ahead with the search, Nicias sees no need—he will go back to Damon tomorrow and Damon will give him what he needs (200a). But this, we know, is foolish, for Socrates would knock that down no less easily than he has knocked down this definition. Nicias' problems go deeper than the mere lack of right answers today. Again, the dialogue seems to suggest, by its action, a completeness that it lacks on the level of speech alone: it seems to suggest that while Laches-like endurance is necessary but not sufficient, the right answer, the true ideal, consists in its combination not with Nician but with Socratic-like knowledge or wisdom.

Despite this impressive evidence, the Bonitz thesis must be firmly rejected. It offers a tempting but ultimately superficial esoteric alternative to the exoteric aporetic conclusion of the work, the conclusion that "we have failed to discover . . . what courage really is" (199e11). The aporetic conclusion, not the conclusion Bonitz pointed to, is better supported by in-depth analysis of both the drama and the arguments of the *Laches*. For when we read the dialogue carefully, there are several considerations that neither Bonitz nor his current supporters have taken sufficiently into account. By way of introduction, three reasons for not embracing the Bonitz thesis are mentioned here, each to be developed in the commentary. First of all, there is the role of boldness or daring in the dialogue, a highly significant aspect of the discussion, virtually ignored by Laches. This abstraction from the quality of boldness or daring points to a deficiency in the inquiry that neither Laches nor Nicias nor Socrates, at least in any obvious way, supplies. Second, the central objection concerns the nature of the "knowledge of what is to be dreaded and dared" that is supposed to be combined with endurance. This knowledge is generally assumed to be the "knowledge of what is in one's true interest—i.e., knowledge of good and evil."[23] But the dialogue gives us no reason to think such knowledge is available, at least to human beings. Perhaps if such knowledge *were* available, it would constitute a supreme form of courage. But if the *Laches* suggests we do not know that, how can it be read to conclude that such knowledge, alone or in combination with endurance, is courage? Finally, the Bonitz thesis fails to appreciate the importance of the first definition in the inquiry, and in general it pays too little attention to the relationship between philosophy and the city. That relationship, however, is the key to the right understanding of the *Laches*. It is also the key to understanding what is correct, and what is mistaken, in Laches' wish for a Doric harmony of *logos* and *ergon*. We are intended in the end to discover what a Laches will never know: the best action may be simple and direct, but the best speech is not.

2.7 The Laches, *the Divided Line, and the Cave*

A third approach to the overall interpretation of the *Laches* relies on the model of the Divided Line in *Republic* 6, with its division into the four ways of knowing: (1) *eikasia* (imagining); (2) *pistis* (belief or acquaintance); (3) *dianoia* (discursive thought); and (4) *noēsis* (intellectual intuition or apperception). It has appeared to several scholars that these four ways of knowing correspond to the four main speakers in the *Laches,* Lysimachus, Laches, Nicias, and Socrates.[24]

Thus Lysimachus can be seen to be a character who lives in a world of *eikasia,* taken up with the images or shadows of real things and never attaining the level of actual experience or *pistis*. Indeed, Lysimachus seems to know little more of the world than what he has heard of it. For instance, he has heard of Socrates by name, but he has never met him; an unknown someone directed him to the exhibition of *hoplomachia,* which is itself but a kind of shadow-boxing or image of real fighting; he realizes that by comparison to his father he lacks achievements or real experience of the world, but he is hungry for fame for his son; even his memory seems incapable of holding any but the faintest impressions, and those disappear quickly (189c).

Laches, on the other hand, appears to be a character of real *pistis,* a man whose knowledge of the world is based on *empeiria,* experience. He is the one who has had experience of battle and speaks of his knowledge of Socrates in relation to it; he is the one whose test of an art or science is whether or not it works, for instance of a military science whether it works in battle, and whether or not the premier men of war, the Spartans, make use of it; he is the one whose own definition of courage is related to his experience of war; and he is the one who, Socrates himself suggests, would seem by his deeds to have some share of courage, though that is less clear from his words (193e).

On this model, Nicias may seem to be the representative of *dianoia,* the way of knowing related to mathematics or science. Nicias is the only character who uses the word *dianoia* in the *Laches,* using it in his first speech; he is the character who praises *hoplomachia* as a genuine study (*mathēma*), and in praising he speaks of it as the science that is the first stage in the whole art of war; Nicias is the character associated with the sophist Damon and the art of speaking; and it is he who defines courage as a form of science (*epistēmē*). Thus one scholar concludes: "His theories, hypotheses and mental concepts place him above the *pistis* of Laches, and closer to the level of *dianoia.*"[25]

Following the same pattern, Socrates would appear to represent the highest stage, *noēsis.* He is the one seeking dialectical knowledge of an *archē* or first principle, by testing the various definitions put forward by others; he alone seems to have fully left behind him not only the fantasies and conventional beliefs of the *polis,* but to be reaching for something comprehensive, a true knowledge of good and evil beyond merely hypothetical knowledge; he alone is concerned with the soul; and in the end everyone turns to him for guidance.

Perhaps the greatest attraction in using the Line as a guide to the interpretation of the *Laches* has to do with the relationship that Socrates draws between the Line and the natural path of *paideia* in the myth of the Cave in *Republic* 7. If the *Laches* develops, in terms of its cognitive levels, from *eikasia* (Lysimachus) to *pistis* (Laches) to *dianoia* (Nicias) to *noēsis* or true *epistēmē* (Socrates), then its path of inquiry would seem to imitate what Plato believes is the natural path of the mind as it quests for and attains truth.

Unfortunately, careful examination of the dialogue renders any straightforward interpretation of the *Laches* based on the Line highly suspect.[26] Lysimachus and Laches fit the model well enough, but it is less obviously appropriate to Nicias and Socrates. As was noted in the discussion of *logos* and *ergon* in the dialogue, Nicias proves to be a poor representative of a higher stage of knowing, and since the *Laches* ends aporetically, one is hard put to identify Socrates with the seemingly synoptic level of dialectical knowledge that is named *noēsis* in *Republic* 6, and later called *epistēmē* in *Republic* 7 (533e). Perhaps Socrates somehow prefigures the highest level of knowing, but in what way is Nicias a representative of thought?

If we are to read the Divided Line and the Cave into the *Laches,* it seems more appropriate to see Nicias as a representative of the sophistic *image* of *noēsis* or *epistēmē,* rather than as a representative of *dianoia.* On this view, Nicias does not represent a genuine mathematical or hypothetical-deductive way of knowing, though his way of thinking is somewhat similar to that. He does take certain premises or definitions on trust, namely those he receives from his sophistic teachers, and he is able, in his interaction with Laches, to apply his apparent knowledge somewhat, in the give-and-take of argumentative discussion. But what he possesses, on this reading, is very unlike the kind of real, if philosophically shallow, knowledge possessed by the mathematician.

Theodorus in the *Theaetetus,* for example, may not know how to prove the existence of the beings he supposes in his mathematical science, and from the standpoint of the *Republic* this means that his science is suspect, shadowy, unanchored in genuine *epistēmē* (510c–511e). But it is nonetheless real mathematical knowledge, which realizes the truths of mathematical beings. Theodorus has something more than mere opinions that he has acquired from someone else about mathematical things; he has knowledge that he has acquired by *understanding* those mathematical things and by having come to a precise knowledge of them in relation to their fundamental, albeit unexamined, principles (compare *Meno* 85c–d). In the language of myth, Theodorus has come to discover truths that were eternally present in his soul. They did not need to be put into him but were already there and were awakened by the sensations bringing him in contact with them. Nicias' knowledge, on the other hand, will not prove to be as securely fastened down, for the opinions he holds seem *not* to have been based on his own understanding of the things to be learned, *nor* do they seem to have been in his soul prior to having been told of them by his teachers. Socrates speaks with Laches of their apparent share in courage through their deeds, and he also refers to "Courage Herself," perhaps a reference to the Idea. But we have no reason to think from reading the *Laches* that Nicias has had any contact with the reality of courage, be it a reality encountered in his experience of others or in his own soul, or be it of an Idea that somehow transcends ordinary experience. Nicias' opinions about courage will prove to be like the wind-eggs Socrates speaks of in the *Theaetetus* (150c), abstractions without empirical or existential content for him, because he has never had any acquaintance with the realities to which they refer. Of course the same kind of thing would be possible regarding mathematics: one could memorize certain theorems or even proofs without understanding them. But then, too, the fact that the supposed knower had no real understanding of them would be revealed under questioning.

On the other hand, Nicias evidently represents an image of the highest kind of knowing, so high that Laches speaks of it as belonging to a god (196a). In his exchange with Laches, Nicias suggests that the knowledge or wisdom (he uses these words interchangeably) of his courageous man is something very unlike the technical knowledge of future contingencies that the seer might possess. He might also be supposed to suggest that his definition derives originally from Socrates himself, and Plato's readers know that Socrates seems to accept the same account of courage as Nicias gives in the *Protagoras*

(360d). Thus it seems possible that Nicias presents us with an image of the highest level of the Line and of the culmination of *paideia,* albeit a sophistic image, a false image.

Now if this is the case, two things should happen in the movement of the dialogue. First, since Nicias does not possess the level of knowledge that he claims to represent, he should fall from that level and the dialogue should descend to a lower one. This proves to be true. As we shall see in chapter 5, Nicias' understanding of the definition he advances is confused, and he cannot sustain an interpretation of it on the highest level. From the perspective of the Line and the Cave, the dialogue may be seen to reach its acme in the first part of the inquiry with Nicias, when he is responding to Laches' questions. In the second part of his inquiry, when he is responding to Socrates, his account of courage will prove to suppose a lower level of cognition and a lower level of ontological object than he had earlier, albeit unknowingly, represented. There is a real, upward movement to the mimesis of thought that we find in the *Laches*; but it seems to reach its height in the third, not the fourth segment of the inquiry, and Nicias falls from that height to a lower, more common form of reflection in the final section.

A second expectation readers familiar with the Line and the Cave might have concerning the *Laches,* if indeed Nicias proves to represent not wisdom but its false appearance, is that we might learn through him something about the dangers of leaving the cave of the *polis* and its conventional opinions, if it is not left on the path of real enlightenment, real philosophy. Nicias will prove to have been freed somewhat from the binding chains of conventional belief, custom, and law; his sophistic teachers may have liberated him, to some extent, from the world of ordinary civic trust. But Nicias' wisdom is fake, purely artificial, without real foundation, and he reveals some of the evils that can ensue for the polis and the individual who trusts in sophistic wisdom and its way of teaching. In this respect, the final segment of the inquiry can be seen as the appropriate movement by the philosopher back down into the cave of political life, a movement in which he must join with his ally, Laches, so as not to fall into the error of the sophist, who forgets the truths of everyday life in his eagerness to grasp godlike wisdom.

2.8 Comedy, Tragedy, and Irony in the Laches

Finally, there is the question of the kind of overall genre of literature or poetry to which the dialogue form belongs. To answer this question, the guide is again Socrates, who at the end of the *Symposium* compels the tragedian

Agathon and the comedian Aristophanes to agree that "the same man might know how to make both comedy and tragedy, be by means of his art both comedian and tragedian" (223d). We shall consider first the comic and tragic aspects of the *Laches,* and then the further question of whether its true perspective does not somehow transcend both of these views of life.

There is a good deal of the comic spirit in the *Laches.*[27] It is present in funny characters, like the forgetful old Lysimachus, funny speeches and images, especially by Laches, and funny scenes, in which the two powerful generals argue like emulous schoolboys. It is less obvious to the modern reader that the dialogue has the formal structure of Aristophanic comedy, particularly in the first part.[28] Thus:

1. Prologue: compare Lysimachus' introduction, 178a–180a.

2. Parodos, or entry of the chorus: compare Socrates' entrance, 180a–181d. The chorus generally is summoned by the hero to assist him, though it sometimes hears of his plans and comes to oppose him.

3. Agon, or formal debate presided over by the chorus: compare Nicias' and Laches' speeches, 181d–184c. The first speaker in the agon is the ultimate loser.

4. A succession of dialogue scenes: compare 184c–186a. This part of the play often includes a parabasis, or address of the chorus.

5. Parabasis, or address of the chorus to the audience: compare Socrates' speech 186a–187b. Socrates speaks to Lysimachus and Melesias on a topic of interest to him, teaching virtue.

6. Exodos, which often takes the form of a sexual union and/or feasting: compare the call for further discussion at 187d.

The formal pattern of Old Comedy can also be seen in the dialogue as a whole, with the second part of the work, the inquiry concerning courage, forming a second agon (189d–199e), followed by a more compressed succession, including a parabasis in which Nicias and Laches join in addressing advice to the audience that includes Lysimachus and Melesias, and the exodos, in which there is another call for further discussion (200a–201c).

The *Laches* also compares closely with the functional structure of the Aristophanic comedy.[29] This includes the following elements:

1. The phase of initial situation and conception in which we learn of the social problem or disorder that troubles the hero and of his Great Idea (in Aristophanes, a fantastic project) for putting things right. The analogy is Lysimachus' initial speech, which presents his Fantastic Idea to turn his sons over to the sophist Stesilaus for training in virtue, should Nicias and Laches recommend it.

2. The phase of struggle in which the hero and his allies meet with difficult-

ies in their efforts to realize the Great Idea. In the *Laches* this occurs in two stages: first the contest between the two generals, in which they take opposite sides, and then the further struggle, in which they try to realize a new Plan, to define courage.

3. The realization of the Great Idea, which is followed immediately by the final phase. In most Aristophanic dramas, the Great Idea succeeds in its aim, but in the *Clouds* the Great Idea is a disaster. In the *Laches,* the Plan also fails, since "we have not discovered . . . what courage is" (199e11).

4. The final phase or consequences that follow from carrying out the Great Idea. In the *Clouds,* this includes Strepsiades' discovery of the full depravity of Socrates' teaching, and then the happy reversal: he'll burn Socrates' school down and chase him out of town! In the *Laches,* the discovery of ignorance has as its consequence for the original plan that they do not know who the teachers of virtue are or what the boys should study. But here the reversal is completely happy: they recognize that Socrates is the teacher, the savior they seek; and the final scene envisages the boys' triumphant education in Socrates' school, "God willing."

In short, the *Laches,* as much as any Platonic dialogue, has all the elements, and the overall form, of comic poetry.[30] The comic heart of the play is the futile struggle of the two boasters, Nicias and Laches, to prove themselves worthy advisers, teachers, knowers of virtue. Their failure exposes their pretense to wisdom for all to see, and the audience can enjoy what Socrates in the *Philebus* (50a) calls the "mixed pleasure" of comedy—so long as we do not suppose the joke is on us.[31]

For the comedy of the *Laches* rests, at least in part, on our belief that we are not the fools that Nicias and Laches are. But do we not then presuppose that we possess the knowledge they reveal themselves to be lacking in? The happy ending of the *Laches* relies finally on the certainty that the elusive *Logos* exists, that the quest for the wisdom that mockingly eludes Nicias and Laches is available. And yet that is what the destructive element in the work denies. Is it so certain our wisdom is not just as bankrupt, our ignorance just as conceitedly concealed? After all, these men died badly, perhaps because they did not know what real courage is. The thoughtful reader will ask: Who am I to presume that I will not also die badly because I also do not know? More to the point, who am I to presume that I am not already living badly for the same reason? And is it not ignorance that leads to tragic error (*Alcibiades I* 117d)?

Thinking along these lines, the *Laches* may strike the thoughtful reader as more tragic than comic, at least if Laches and Nicias are considered its main characters.[32] The lesson of comedy is that we can overcome Fortune, clever and malicious as she is; the lesson of tragedy is that we cannot overcome Fate and Character. The comic hero rushes forward, slips on a banana peel, falls on his bottom, and, slipping and sliding, makes it to his feet again. But in tragedy the hero commits himself, realizes his powers, and it is not enough. Ultimately comedy reflects the joy of life, continuity, and rebirth, but tragedy reflects finality, grief, and death. There is little doubt that the *Laches* points forward toward the real, historical death and failure of its chief characters, and through them to the crash of their city. That future is somber, not funny.

To see the tragic aspect of the *Laches,* we need to see Nicias' and Laches' failures as predictive of their later failures, and we need to see the movement of the dialogue, particularly the elenctic inquiry, as imitative of their lives. This is entirely appropriate, however, if, as Nicias says, the Socratic elenchus reveals who the person is, not only what he believes in—his "whole manner and way of life" (188a). Thus Socrates' challenge can be seen to establish the tragic rhythm as the dominant form of elenctic inquiry, for through it the interlocutor's thought and character are put on trial, and in that trial his tragic error or flaw (*hamartia*) and self-blindness are revealed. The movement of the trial-inquiry thus conceived is growth, which reaches a point of crisis the character cannot surmount. In that cognitive peripety the man's claim to knowledge is reversed and he should realize that he does not know what he thought he knew, his claim to virtue is destroyed, the man is defeated, exposed, seen to be less than what he or anyone else thought he was. In the *Laches* the elenctic failure concerns the knowledge of courage, the knowledge of the one virtue, if any, that a soldier must possess. Thus the failures of Laches and Nicias in the *logos* raise the question of their fitness to command. In fact, their failures in the dialogue anticipate their later, tragically destructive failures in battle.

Moreover, Laches' and Nicias' most serious failures in the dialogue may be said to come not in the process of the inquiry, but in its aftermath. The result of this inquiry, in each instance, is the moment that imitates the tragic peripety, the reversal when the character discovers, "I did not know" what courage is. What follows is the decisive moment in the Socratic process of teaching, the opportunity for recognition, for taking this discovery to heart and seeking to learn what it is that one is missing, for beginning to examine one's beliefs and actions more thoroughly, that is, for beginning a philosophical life. For the two generals in the *Laches*, this was the "Heraclean crossroads" in their lives, the opportunity to begin a process of self-examination that might have made all the difference. But at this crucial moment both men failed,

Laches being diverted by his competitive feelings, Nicias going back to reliance on Damon.

And thus Laches and Nicias not only fall short of virtue, they also fall short of tragic stature. For an essential aspect of tragic stature is the achievement of tragic insight, of recognition, and where that heightened stature of wisdom gained through suffering is missing, there can be no real tragedy. Laches and Nicias fall short of real tragedy, not only because they are often ridiculous, but because they do not have the depth of mind and character to see themselves naked in the mirror Socrates has held up to them. Each one of us, as members of the philosophical audience, can see who they are. They fail, however, to see themselves.

We began our discussion of the the poetic structure of the *Laches* by considering Socrates' statement in the *Symposium* that art should combine tragedy and comedy, and we have seen decidedly comic as well as tragic aspects of the dialogue. Certainly, Socrates' stripping of Nicias and Laches and their scurrying for clothes is, if not beautiful, grandly comic, and just as certainly their failure in the dialogue to recognize their self-blindness, as well as the prophetic references to their own, and, through them, Athens' future fall, gives the work a tragic dimension. Nonetheless, the *Laches* is neither a tragedy, nor a comedy—the future is too dark for the one, the characters end by being too small for the other. What then is it?

The one relevant term that Plato's readers, ancient as well as modern, can agree upon is "irony."[33] The mode of irony pervades not only the speeches of Socrates and his deeds but the dialogues themselves, which view the tragicomedy of life ironically, standing somehow above and detached from it all, just as Socrates is said by Alcibiades to relate to his interlocutors ironically, through a different kind of mask (*Symposium* 215a–217a). Yet this mode of detachment is not the same as that which we find, say, in Saint Augustine's view of the fall of Rome. It is not simply the vision of things human *sub specie aeternitatis*. There is a fundamental difference between two very different kinds of irony that we discover in the dialogues.

The one kind of irony is the simple irony that the Greek audience was familiar with from tragic and comic poetry. In this irony, the hero says one thing, but without knowing if his words mean something very different—a fact understood by the audience, whose members share in the perspective of wisdom, knowing the reality, while the actors, noble or all too human in their terrible or funny simplicity, move in ignorance, caught in the world of appearances. This kind of irony is found in the *Laches*. As members of the audience of our dialogue, we see the two generals in the mode of direct, present action, in a drama of freedom and thought; but we, like Socrates, share in the privilege of prophetic wisdom and know what they are bound to do, their fate: the former is appearance, the latter reality, and we by our knowledge are freed, while they, like most men, by their ignorance are enslaved. The comedy in it lies in the seriousness with which they parade their ignorance as wisdom, the incongruity in the opposition between them, claiming to know, and the hero, claiming in all seriousness (with his fingers crossed for us to see) that he does not know. The whole tragedy of ignorance and folly is a joke that less willful and determined men would abandon for the examined life. Even Socrates' own trial and death is just a glorious tragic joke. We see it all, *sub specie aeternitatis,* and we scarcely know whether to laugh or cry. Why are men such fools? Why do they not understand?

If we read the dialogue this way, however, we have missed *the* distinctive feature of the new, modern, Socratic irony. For as Alcibiades says emphatically, Socrates laughs not only at "them," but at "all of us" (216e). It is true that we are meant to see in Nicias and Laches two men caught in the power of Fate and Character; we see *why* they will do what they will do, why they are not free to do otherwise. But we are not meant to be involved in the *Laches* only as witnesses to the actions of characters on a literary stage; we also are meant to be involved as participants in the quest for the meaning of courage. So long as we become involved in that inquiry, we are excited by its progress and are not indifferent to its outcome. As the inquiry makes its ascent toward the truth, we cannot but feel that we ourselves are moving out of the cave of thoughtlessness toward the sunlight of clear vision. So when Laches' and Nicias' definitions fail, we too fail; and unless we believe that we have discerned a secret answer hidden beneath the surface of the dialogue, we must be confounded by the aporetic conclusion: we also must feel the flushed face of embarrassment when Socrates suggests that Courage Herself is laughing at us. Nor can we take solace from the hope that Socrates will lead us to the answer tomorrow. For us, there is no Socrates, there are only the dialogues, and they give us no direct answer. Are we, perhaps, caught up in ignorance no less than are the interlocutors?

The distinctiveness of Socratic irony is that it is deliberate. Socrates presents himself through dissimulation, taking the position of the knower—while we, as part of his audience, are often unsure if we are any better off than his hapless interlocutor. His is a double or complex irony, in which the uncertainty is turned back on the audience, in which the speaker knows he is speaking ironically but leaves it unclear to others what the true meaning is. The tragic irony was moving; even comic irony is amusing; but the Socratic, the genuine philosophical irony is discomfitting, irritating, bewitching. Like the interlocutors, we come to believe that Socrates must know the answer, that the dialogue must contain the secret. We do not know why he is playing with us, but we have come to realize we cannot stop now. The Socratic, double irony is the gentle goad, the gadfly's sting, without which we might not recognize our own need for inquiry, for philosophy.

3

The Origins of the Inquiry

3.1 Lysimachus' Plea for Advice (178a–180a)

AS IN SEVERAL OTHER Platonic dialogues, the speeches in the *Laches* begin after the participants have witnessed a sophistic exhibition.[1] Thus Lysimachus' first words are: "You have contemplated [*Tetheasthe*, observed] the man fighting in armor, Nicias and Laches." From the start, we are in a world in which the action of war is a seeming constant of human life, the question of how to gain an edge a matter of vital interest. From the start also, we are in a world in which the imitation of reality by the arts, no less than reality itself, is the subject of intense deliberative thought.

The discussion begins not with wonder about war and the virtue of courage, but with the fatherly concerns of the two old aristocrats, Lysimachus and Melesias, about the education of their sons and the welfare of their family names. Still, as we shall see, these practical concerns are not unrelated to the theoretical ones of the second half of the dialogue. The first half presents us in its content and in dramatic form with the origins of the second half, with the reasons why there is a question, not only for these particular individuals in this time and place, about the nature and virtue of courage.

Lysimachus' opening speech is divided into two main parts, the preamble being concerned with the conditions for the deliberation (178a1–179a1), the rest with the subject to be discussed, namely whether the sons of Lysimachus, Melesias, Nicias, and Laches should study *hoplomachia*, fighting in heavy armor (179a1–180a5).

Lysimachus introduces his speech by flattering Nicias and Laches, noting that he and Melesias trust them as advisers not only because they are sufficiently knowledgeable, but because Nicias and Laches, unlike other men, will say what they really think (178a1–179a1). Lysimachus and Melesias may be naïve about what counts as "sufficient knowledge," but they are not complete fools. They have learned through hard experience that not all enemies show their colors clearly and that it is essential to be able to distinguish friends from enemies, before one forms a community able to deliberate collectively. We might suppose that Lysimachus has sophistic men such as Stesilaus in mind, men who stand to profit by telling you not what they believe, but what you would like to hear (compare *Gorgias* 462b–465d, 482d). Yet one cannot but also be reminded of Socrates and his duplicitous, ironic manner of speaking. Might not a friendly adviser choose not to tell his opinion, because the adviser knows he does not know what is best, or because he believes the advisee would not understand his words correctly, or because he wants to help the advisee form his own opinion on the matter? (As it turns out, Lysimachus also is mistaken about the two men: one of them will try to hide his real opinion later in the discussion.)

Continuing the suspense a bit, Lysimachus goes on to state the overall reason why he and Melesias have invited Nicias and Laches to the show of fighting in armor (179a1–b6). Lysimachus introduces his son and that of his old friend, respectively Aristides and Thucydides, and explains that as fathers they care a great deal about the boys' education. The old men have resolved to give them the proper upbringing so that they "become the best" (*genointo aristoi*). Knowing that Nicias and Laches also have young sons, and knowing that they do, or should, share the same concern about their education, Lysimachus and Melesias thought to join with them about it. We already see in these remarks Lysimachus' clever, if not altogether successful, attempt both to save face for himself and Melesias and to enlist the two prominent generals in their service.

The most striking features in this part of Lysimachus' speech are his repeated emphasis on the care (*epimeleia,* 179a5, 8, b5, e6; compare also 179b1, 4, d3, 4) he and Melesias have for their sons, that the boys become the best, and the contrast he draws between this aristocratic approach to the education of the youth and the negligent democratic approach.[2] For Lysimachus, as for the aristocratic Greek tradition in education going back to Homer, *paideia* in its primary sense is not mere training or studies; originally it meant the formation of character, not unlike what is called liberal education today.[3] But the task of aristocratic *paideia* was not intellectual liberation from the bondage of false beliefs or false desires, it was to instill in the young men of prestigious families images of noble actions and the will to imitate them. The Homeric motto for the aristocratic ideal is found in the *Iliad:* "Always to be the best and be superior to all others" (6.208). Among the models held before the youths were the great warriors and statesmen of the past, especially of one's own family.[4]

Thus the quest for recognition was also for many young noblemen a quest to fulfill their own identity, their natural birthright. And the Homeric motto was still very much alive in fifth-century Athens. However faded and decadent the aristocracy had become, the conversation of the *Laches,* including the Socratic inquiry on the nature of courage, occurs only because there still are gentlemen in democratic Athens who want their sons to become the best and who have the foresight to deliberate on how to achieve this.[5]

Lysimachus then approaches the more specific motives behind the invitation and, speaking freely, tells the interesting if embarrassing story of how it came about (179b6–e6). He and Melesias are raising their sons in the bracing military discipline of the Spartan *syssitia* (common meals), and evenings after dinner they tell the boys tales of their ancestors' noble deeds (*kala erga*) in war and peace.[6] Unfortunately (this is the comic turn in his speech), Lysimachus and Melesias are ashamed that they have no such deeds of their own to point to, and for that they blame their famous fathers, who let them become spoiled in their youth while the fathers were busy attending to the affairs of others (see the discussion of their education in section 1.2). So now Lysimachus and Melesias have been forced to admit all this to their own sons, so that the sons will not themselves, like their fathers, end without honor (*akleeis*), but will become worthy of the noble names they bear. Into this setting came an unknown someone (Lysimachus later admits he has a bad memory), who told them that this was a noble study, so they thought they had better look into it.

This part of Lysimachus' speech is disturbingly revealing of his and Melesias' characters. Both men seem to lack the most elementary sort of a free man's self-knowledge, when they slavishly deny their own responsibility for their lives and actions.[7] They are shadow creatures not only because their names are not written on the walls of public memory: they are shadow creatures from within. Moreover, Lysimachus divides what is private from what is public in a way that his father surely never did. What Lysimachus calls "the affairs of others" are the very things the men of Marathon held were most their own: the affairs of the city, with which they identified their own being. Inwardly, as outwardly, Lysimachus and Melesias seem to live in a curious isolation from, and attachment to, public things. They are, at the same time, purely private men (the Athenian word for this, *idiōtēs,* having the connotation political idiot) and yet devoted to the images they see of honor and the public world.

On the other hand, Lysimachus and Melesias' *action,* in calling on Nicias and Laches for advice and telling them freely why they did so, is virtuous: prudent (foresighted regarding their sons' well-being), just (responsible), moderate (in recognizing their limits), and morally courageous. The deliberative inquiry begins because these two old gentlemen swallow enough of their pride to admit their need for help, and they risk being laughed at for asking for it. Knowing that they do not know, they turn their choice over to those whom they believe do know and are their friends. This would seem to be, if at the lowest level, a form of wisdom (see *Alcibiades I* 117e).

In closing his address (180a1–5), Lysimachus speaks of the "partnership" (*koinōnia*) Nicias and Laches are to have with him and Melesias. This word is contrasted in the beginning of the *Republic* (333a–e) with "association" (*symbolaion*), the latter word suggesting cooperative alliances intended for the private good of each, while partnerships suggest cooperative unions undertaken for the common good and beneficial to all together, because what is attained is shared in fellowship and not just enjoyed individually. It is hard for one to see on what basis Nicias and Laches or, later, Socrates would want to join in either alliance or partnership with them, however, since neither do they seem to have anything to offer that would benefit anyone else, nor do they seem to recognize a common good that transcends private interests. But if no such common good exists, why besides possibly meaningless old customs and family ties should the other fathers want to help the young Aristides and Thucydides succeed and become superior to their own boys?

In retrospect, Lysimachus' speech is reminiscent of the whole world of aristocratic life, as depicted above all in the Homeric epics.[8] According to that conception of life, the aristocratic youth is not so much an individual or a citizen as he is part of a family and a tradition, a tradition he must be educated in and learn to live up to, if he is to live up to his father's and his father's father's name. (See *Iliad* 4.370–410, 6.145–211, 466–81; *Odyssey* 1.207–23, 16.300–320.) But according to that tradition also, virtue is linked to social station and assigned by birthright: master and slave, man and woman, nobleman and commoner, all have their characteristic social functions and appropriate virtues, which are not the same. (This is evident throughout the epics; compare also the young Thessalian oligarch's definition of virtue in the *Meno* 71e; *Protagoras* 318e; *Alcibiades I* 124e; also *Gorgias* 484c–486d.) Thus the duty of the young nobleman or knight is to rule the city, a duty that includes as a central component the will and ability to wage war for the community, to protect his own and in that way win for himself immortal glory in the stories of future generations.[9] (Compare *Iliad* 6.440–46, 11.401–10, 12.310–28.)

It is not at all obvious that the old aristocratic ideal of honor and virtue would be relevant in the new world of the *polis* that emerged between 800 and 450 out of the Dark Age of ancient Greece, but it was: Tyrtaeus in Sparta, and Pericles in Athens, recast the Homeric aristocratic ideal of manly virtue in the new ideal of the patriot and citizen-soldier.[10] Particularly in imperial democratic Athens, the desire to be the best found a new space of appearance: specifically human life (*bios*) came to be understood as the life of the man of action, the man dedicated to *politeuesthai,* to "take part in political life" and thereby win a name for himself in the civic memory.[11] Virtually all of Athens' leadership in the fifth century B.C. came from the knightly class, including Miltiades and Cimon, Aristides and Themistocles, Pericles and Thucydides, Nicias and Alcibiades (but not Cleon or Anytus). Though the heirs of the landed aristocracy could no longer simply claim to "be" the best, they could still aspire to "become" the best in the struggle for political supremacy in the city.

Notice, however, that the emphasis in the virtue formula has changed, the Homeric-archaic functional model of virtue based on the proper social work (*ergon*) of the naturally best, knightly caste being replaced by a relativistic model based on victory in the city's contests, especially the *agōn* (contest) for rule.[12] This change in the social character of manly virtue might not lead to markedly different action on the part of the individuals involved, but it reflected the revolution in social structure that the democratic city had inaugurated, and it lay at the base of the crisis in thinking about virtue that began with the sophists and was brought to a new head by Socrates. Of all the themes introduced by Lysimachus in the opening speech of the *Laches,* the aristocratic ideal of manly virtue is the most basic and important in relation to the inquiry to follow, an inquiry concerned with the central component of that virtue, courage, and its relation to prudence and justice. The admiration for noble deeds and the desire "to become the best and be superior over all others and win immortal fame" was a driving force in the remarkable will of fifth-century Athenians to excel, and it proves to be a driving force in the action of our dialogue as well, but it is not certain that such a desire is altogether good. It also is curious that the first encounter with virtue in the *Laches* is through the eyes of a man who knows it only in the mode of fantasy, in the stories he tells of his ancestors and the desire he has for their fame. The play begins with a pair of images—a new, sophistic image of fighting and an old man's image of heroic virtue. Is the reader not meant to wonder about the relation of these images to present-day reality?

3.2 Socrates Joins the Discussion (180a–181d)

When the *Laches* begins, the old aristocrats Lysimachus and Melesias know little or nothing of Socrates. But by the end of the dialogue, Lysimachus and everyone present, including Nicias, the head of state, turn to him as the one who will save them all from their ignorance and lead them and their sons to a better life. Although we do not see in this section what it is about Socrates that makes them acknowledge his virtue or superiority, we do see what it is that makes them want to have him in their deliberative community.

President Nicias is the first to answer Lysimachus' request, confidently agreeing to give his own advice and suggesting his colleague Laches will do likewise (180a6–8). The slower-moving Laches says it is true, noting that Lysimachus spoke well when he said that public men imprudently neglect their private affairs, but Laches expresses wonder that Socrates—whom we now learn was standing by, listening with the others—had not been invited, given Socrates' interest in noble studies (180b1–c4). Nicias, not to be outdone, jumps back in to add that he, too, could speak on Socrates' behalf, as Socrates had advised him to have his own son Niceratus study with the musician Damon, who has proven to be the "most graceful" (*chariestaton*) of men and worthy in every respect as a companion for youths of that age (180c5–d3).[13] (It was apparently a fitting match: Niceratus would later become a rhapsode.) But Lysimachus is lukewarm: he allows that if Socrates has something good to say, he might do so, and then recalls that his boys had spoken well of a Socrates, whom he now realizes might be the son of his old friend Sophronis-cus; then, when the young Aristides, in his only speech in the dialogue, confirms this, Lysimachus swears by the goddess of the family that it is good to know Socrates is doing right by his father's name, but he still refrains from urging Socrates to speak freely (180d4–181a6). This reticence changes to enthusiasm, however, after Laches praises Socrates for honoring his fatherland by fighting bravely in the retreat from Delium (181a7–b4). Such praise is noble, beautiful, splendid, coming from such a man for such a thing, and now Lysimachus insists it is a matter of "justice" (*to dikaion*) that Socrates join them and spend time with him and preserve the friendship of their households and tell them right away: Should their boys study *hoplomachia* or not? (181b5–c9) Socrates is respectful but unwilling to speak first; bowing to traditional virtue, he says it seems most just that the older and more experienced men, starting with Nicias, speak before him, allowing that if he had anything to say against their remarks, he might try to teach and persuade them all, but they should speak first (181d1–7). (Note that these last words set the terms of the speech and the order of the speakers: Socrates is already in charge.)[14]

It is a dramatically effective scene. Lysimachus' ignorance of Socrates heightens the suspense, postponing and giving dramatic weight to his inclu-sion, as well as drawing out of the participants an apparently ascending sequence of praise. Just previously the old gentleman had spoken of his dream for the glory of noble deeds; now before his very eyes the honor-bestowing act occurs and a wondrous he-man of virtue appears. Yet the praise that allows, not to say forces, Socrates into the discussion never speaks of philosophy. One realizes, even at the end of this lengthy introduction, that he is being shown from the outside, the appearance he would present to an older, prestigious group of citizens who knew little or nothing of the life of the mind and who had not yet had their opinion of him shaped by Aristophanes' caricature. Socrates the son of Sophroniscus and Socrates the citizen of Athens appear, but the philosopher Socrates is still hidden, albeit under the cloak of a more respectable public image than the one he will soon acquire. At most one catches a glimpse inside that cloak, in Laches' reference to Socrates' interest in studies that are themselves noble.

It is also a wonderfully suggestive scene, not only as regards the characters of the participants but in terms of the whole structure of their relationships: Nicias, whose first word is "I" (*egō*) and who praises Lysimachus' "thought" (*dianoia*), is identified through his connection with Damon with the Sophistic Enlightenment; Laches, whose first word is "true" (*alēthē*), is identified with the old-fashioned self-forgetful civic-minded patriotism of the Marathon men, in contrast both to the present-day decadent aristocracy and to the modern political general Nicias, who prudently does not neglect his private affairs; Lysimachus, whose ignorance of Socrates and whose forgetful, archaic manner underscore his separation from the present-day public world, is now seen even more clearly as a man of the past. We are meant to look forward and up from Lysimachus to Nicias, who is placed ahead of, and somewhat superior to, Laches, but also from Laches up in wonder at the philosopher Socrates, who is placed above them all. Already Plato has Laches paired with Socrates, Nicias with Damon, a pairing and rivalry that will become basic to the movement of the dialogue as a whole.

Let us now consider the two things that bring Socrates into Lysimachus' deliberative community, his claim to "sufficient knowledge" and his trustworthiness in the eyes of Lysimachus. As regards his knowledge, there is first of all his reputation as a man familiar with musical things, with the education of boys, with noble, peaceful studies. But what makes Socrates' reputation and secures his worthiness to advise is Laches' praise of him for manliness in war: Socrates will get to vote in this aristocratic democracy because he was willing to fight, he was brave enough to fight well, and there is someone whom gentlemen can trust who tells about it. Note that this action presents, by way of a thematic mime, a principle of justice that in the ancient world was a historical truth, but that we have—with questionable wisdom—rejected in our society. This is the principle that makes participation in collective self-government dependent upon the willingness to risk life and limb for that collective freedom, the principle that links political rights and military service.[15] *Andreia,* "manly valor," is displayed here mimetically as the first virtue of the citizen, the first thing needful to be a member of a free community. Note too that in this dialogue, which ends with the aporetic conclusion that they cannot say and therefore do not know what courage is, Socrates is established at the very beginning as the man who most of all can lay claim to knowledge of courage. From the common point of view, the point of view of action, not talk, Socrates knows unquestionably what courage is, for he has proven that he has it where it counts—in battle.

There is another and very interesting aspect of Laches' somewhat extravagant praise of Socrates' virtue. For Socrates did not do at Delium the things we normally associate with military courage: there was no victory, he was not even involved in an attack, we never hear of his killing or wounding anyone, and, as Laches admits, the Athenian army suffered a terrible defeat (Thucydides reports that over a thousand Athenian hoplites were slaughtered). Rather than heroics of the sort associated with an Achilles or a John Wayne, Laches' praise of Socrates rests on the fact that Socrates did not lose his head in the gravest dangers and fling away his arms and run; rather, he prudently kept turning back on his would-be attackers in measured retreat, and in this way saved himself and Laches as much by his intrepid appearance as by his use of arms (see *Symposium* 220d–221b). This was not an act of boldness or the stuff of glory, which of course is not to say it was not courageous, and we must note that Socrates' actions saved not only his own, but also his comrade's life. But one must also see that unlike Lysimachus, whose head is filled with the fantasies of long-dead heroes' *kala erga* (fine deeds), the philosopher knows the grim realities of war: of fear and maiming wounds, of defeat and slavery and violent death. He knows there is more to war than *to kalon,* the noble.

The second characteristic that brings Socrates into Lysimachus' deliberative community would appear to be his *dikaiosynē,* his justice. As in the *Republic* and the *Euthyphro,* Socrates' participation in the conversation of our dialogue is not entirely voluntary. This is in contrast, say, to his participation in the conversations depicted in the *Charmides* or in the *Lysis.* He is pressured to join by Lysimachus, who says it is a matter of "justice" (181c2). To Lysimachus, Socrates is trustworthy because he is already a friend, that is, because his and Socrates' families have a bond of friendship established and secured by time and custom. Lysimachus believes it is Socrates' duty to help his friends, and to give them the advice they need, and indeed Lysimachus goes so far as to say that they should have all things in common (181a5–6). We are not convinced, however, that it is only this traditional conception of justice that for his own part makes Socrates willing to join in the conversation. We would

helping his comrades (as Socrates had done at Delium). The real utility of *hoplomachia* would seem to be to prepare the individual against harm from others rather than to serve the collective good of victory for the city or even his friends in trouble. Freedom and virtuosity in war, it appears, are practically equivalent, both serving the welfare of the individual.

After this, Nicias shifts to consideration of the noble. His fourth point commends this study for promoting the desire or appetite (*epithymia*) to learn more of the noble martial arts, everyone who learns fighting in armor desiring to learn battle-line tactics and then having become proud in these skills, driving on to the whole art of generalship (182b4–c1). Nicias completes his ascent with his fifth reason in support of *hoplomachia*, the unquestionably manly judgment that it is clear that every study and practice having to do with war is noble and worthwhile for a real man, to all of which the art of fighting in armor may be the introduction (182c1–4).

In the last part of his speech Nicias offers two additional considerations for studying *hoplomachia*. His sixth reason is the "by no means small point" (*ou smikran*) that every man would be made not a little bolder and braver (*tharraleōteron kai andreioteron*) than himself by this science (*epistēmē*) of how to attack and retreat (182c5–7). This is the first mention in the dialogue of *andreia*, and it is noteworthy that Nicias already here speaks of it in relation to science. It is also remarkable that Nicias does not seem to distinguish courage or bravery from boldness, and that he says that science makes one braver "than himself."[18] Thus it seems that art can alter nature.[19] Nicias goes on to pair the idea that knowledge makes one become more courageous with his seventh and final point, which he is "not ashamed" to add, that the art of fighting in armor makes you seem more terrible to the enemy because of your decisive appearance (182c7–d2). We wonder if *hoplomachia* is a real or spurious art, if it makes one really better, or only seems to (see *Gorgias* 462b–465d)—or does Nicias think that who one is depends, actually, on how one appears to friends and enemies?

Two things stand out in Nicias' address. The first is the same principle that was central to Lysimachus: what matters in life is victory in the city's contests, or individual honor and distinction (as contrasted, say, to service to the city). Thus Nicias speaks of the *epithymia* for honor-gaining studies, and no small part of his praise of *hoplomachia* consists in its role in promoting ambition (*philotimia*, 182b7), which can be seen as a form of courage, namely the boldness to seek high honors or noble things. There is a difference between Nicias and Lysimachus; the former, a prudent man, seeks not only to attain honor, but to avoid harm. In his general outlook, however, Nicias seems to agree with Lysimachus' narrowly private point of view: war is more an individual than a team sport; *hoplomachia* is most useful only when it is each man for himself, without regard for one's comrades; the question of how the noble martial sciences are to be used never arises; he values every study contributing to generalship and the martial life as noble and worthwhile, not only what actually helps him serve his city; he even uses for "enemy" a word that can refer to private as well as public enemies (which raises again the question of why a rational man should want to help his own son's rivals learn a useful skill).[20] Like Lysimachus, Nicias wants to become the best, and like Lysimachus, too, Nicias seems to care less about the common good than about his own bestness or superiority, and seems not to distinguish bestness from the reputation or appearance of it.

The second outstanding feature in Nicias' speech is his view of the relation of science to war, as contrasted with that of his rival here, Laches. As was mentioned in chapter I, several aspects of Nicias' speech correspond unmistakably with the views expressed by Pericles and associated with the Athenian civic character in Thucydides' *Peloponnesian War* (see section I.6). This is evidenced by Nicias' conception of a hierarchy of military science, by his praise of the military sciences as noble in their own right (that is, independent of their civic utility), by the important idea that through science men can master even the fortunes of war, and by what is for the inquiry to follow the even more important idea that knowledge or science can make a man courageous, change his character or nature. This technical conception of courage will play a major role in the philosophical inquiry concerning the virtue of courage that constitutes the second half of the dialogue. Obviously, the man who is skilled at the use of arms, or the general who is confident of his army's advantage, may be less fearful as he begins to act. But does genuine courage show so much in what one sets out to do as in what one does in facing real danger? Finally, the form of Nicias' speech is also suggestive. The repeated use, in its third part, of words related to learning; the fact that he cites no examples from the real world of empirics; the resulting abstract and thus philosophical or sophistical quality of the speech; the internal progression of the speech from body to whole man, to whole man in action, and thence to higher forms of knowledge, culminating in the noble ideal of the martial life; and the immediately following point that even courage is the product of science—all these show Nicias to be a man of mathematics, a man of Athenian science, a man of the Sophistic Enlightenment.

Thus we may feel that by the end of his speech we have already seen the real Nicias. He appears to be a daring, energetic man, ambitious for the noble, but not imprudent or unconcerned about suffering harm, a spokesman for

Athenian wisdom and all things military, a man who admires science and the musical. He does not seem to be a particularly modest or moderate man, but that is not obviously a manly virtue anyway.[21] More disturbing is the fact that he also does not appear to be concerned with justice. What we miss above all in his speech is anything like the Tyrtaean or Periclean conception of the free and good life as consisting in the love and service of the city, or even a clear concern for obedience to the law, such as we find in Socrates' speech in the *Crito*. Nor is there any reference to actual events or the real experience of life, or to any particular people. It is indeed the speech of a man whose primary terms of reference are *egō* and *dianoia*. Do we not already begin to suspect that Nicias is something of a fraud, a man who has unjustly ascended to the office of highest honor on the basis of his words more than his deeds, because of his wealth and good fortune and clever, self-serving prudence, rather than because he really is the best man, the man who deserves to be the president? Do we not also begin to wonder if he is a man who will pursue his own good and the city be damned, the type who would surrender the noble to escape harm? (As Plutarch charged was true of the man of history.) Or is Plato's Nicias perhaps a man of superior daring and intelligence, one whose nature is so extraordinary that he can disdain what the many call "just" and "honorable" and simply do what he believes is best? What will the course of the dialogue reveal about the man?

Nicias has asserted that the military sciences are noble in themselves, and that science is, or produces, courage; but he has said nothing about the just or noble use of the military sciences or of virtue (compare *Euthydemus* 290b–d).[22] It would seem that there may not be for Nicias a necessary connection between wisdom and courage, on the one hand, and justice, on the other. It would seem that, for Nicias, the confident warrior— armed with the fearful weapons of science—is noble, whether he aims at the victory of his city or not, whether he helps friends and harms enemies or not, whether he obeys the law or not. The mere fact that he was superior to all others in the contest of life would seem to make him, in Nicias' eyes, free and noble, make him "the best," and of course he would also be good, at least in the sense that he would be secure from harm. We do not know as yet how, in Nicias' view, the prudent concern for safety should be related to his aristocratic desire for honor, or if his views are secretly tyrannical. But he seems to us to be dangerously close to the view that justice and moderation are not necessary to the noble life, the life of manly virtue.

3.4 Laches' Harsh Attack on Hoplomachia *(182d–184c)*

Nicias' speech has seemed a fine performance, topped off with the depreca-
tory gesture toward his subordinate that he would be "pleased" to hear Laches'
criticisms. Then the rough old soldier steps forward and launches his attack.
In place of flowery rhetoric, hard logic; instead of mere words, the realities
of war; where Nicias' speech was optimistic and liberal, Laches' is biting and
sarcastic. We cannot imagine that Nicias is pleased, when Laches finally stops.

Laches is mocking right from the start, his repetition of *mathēma* and
manthanein and the truism that "it seems good to know all things" setting up
the main premise of his first and second arguments, namely that (1) if *hoplomachia* is not a real science, or is of little value, then it is not worthwhile to
learn it (182d8–e4). But he shows (2) that if it were a real science or of real
value, then the Spartans would study it, which they do not (182e5–183b7);
and in addition, he points out that if it were a real science or of real value,
then this Stesilaus and these so-called masters of arms would prove their mettle
in battle, but to say the least they do not do that either (183c1–184b1).
Therefore one must conclude (3) that *hoplomachia* is not a real science or is
of little value, and we should not waste our time on it (184b1–3). So much
for Nicias' argument that *hoplomachia* is useful. But if it is not useful, Laches
continues, then this supposed art will only make the coward bold and make
more evident what kind of man he really is; or if he is brave, such pretension
of science will incur envy, and only a man of wondrous virtue would escape
being made a laughingstock (184b3–c3). So much for Nicias' argument that
hoplomachia will make you be or even appear more courageous.

These are cleverly drawn, powerful arguments. They smash both lines of
Nicias' defense of *hoplomachia,* his claim that it would be useful in war and
his claim that it would make you both be and appear braver to your enemy.
Moreover, Laches' arguments rest on the strongest of evidence. In contrast to
Nicias, who spoke in generalities and cited no particulars, the plain-speaking
Laches deals in facts. Fact: The Spartans are the greatest authorities in the
world as regards everything pertaining to war, but they have not the slightest
interest in this so-called art (182b2–7). Fact: Not only do the masters of this
art avoid Sparta altogether, tippy-toeing around it as if it were sacred ground,
but none of these so-called "experts" have distinguished themselves in actual
war (183c3–5). Fact: This very "professor of war," Stesilaus, who puffs up
himself and his art with such great words, made an utter fool of himself in
battle, catching his *sophisma,* his "wisdom-weapon" in a ship's rigging and
getting himself dragged end to end, with the result that the weapon wielded
the warrior, not vice-versa (183c8–184a6). These are the deeds, the facts of

real life that we must deal with, and all the beautiful speeches in the world will not change them. We are impressed. Laches is a blunt man attached to practice, to experience, to reality—not to useless theories, to mere words, to the fantasies of sophistic art that may seem to make you better, but are in fact nothing but cosmetics. Nicias now appears to be a man after Lysimachus' heart, a man of seeming wisdom and seeming virtue, seeming martial prowess; but Laches is tough and direct, and he really knows what he is talking about.[23]

Laches also has nothing but contempt for Nicias' self-flattering claim that military art or science can make one bolder or braver and more fearsome before the enemy. First of all, boldness and courage are not the same. This science might make the coward artificially bold, but then when he was placed in danger, his real nature would reveal itself; thus the science that was to change his fear-filled nature would result only in that nature's being shamefully exposed, like the wisdom-weapon that tried to do two things at once, and beautifully, truly revealed its proud practitioner against his will (184b4–6). Laches believes that courage is a matter of who you are, your nature or character or will, not a matter of armor, of superior knowledge or skill. Like armor it might clothe, but it will not transform the man. Laches adds that such self-display of wisdom will only expose you to envy, and you would have to be a man of "wonderful virtue" to stand as one against the many who felt that way about you (184b6–c4). This important idea will be discussed later. Regarding Nicias' claim that *hoplomachia* introduces its student to the hierarchy of military sciences, including battle-line tactics and generalship, Laches is silent, reflecting the Spartan skepticism about the role of military science in the practice of war. One should note, however, that Thucydides tells a somewhat different story (see, for example, *Peloponnesian War* 2.89, 4.41, 6.69, 7.67). Human intelligence and technical skill play a significant and effective role throughout the course of the Peloponnesian War, though the Spartans are at first loath to admit it. In fact, one may argue that the Spartans win the war because they become Athenian in their practice of it.[24] Granted, these things are less obvious from the point of view of the ordinary soldier, the point of view Laches adopts. From the point of view of the hoplite in the battle line, it is not tactics and strategy, it is courage and discipline that decide who will conquer and who will flee. But should a general take this point of view?

Finally, Laches' and Nicias' speeches are also contrasted relative to what is noble. Whereas Nicias' eloquent, flattering speech appeals to the bold desire for high honor, the more modest Laches' harsh, condemnatory speech employs the cautionary rhetoric of fear, above all the fear of opinion or shame (*aidōs*). Laches alerts the fathers to the danger of dishonor, reminding them of the actual experience of shame—the burning shock of disgrace, the disorienting, painful self-awareness of being seen by others in a way that reveals me to be less than I want to be. Such shame, shame-as-disgrace, is the confrontation not only with my inferiority, but with my community's rejection of me, my community's ridicule of who and what I am, my exile, my exclusion from the community of the confident men of action, the knowledgeable men who run the city. Such shame is the shame of never becoming a man among men, or even worse, of having proved oneself to be less than a man, having had one's public being destroyed. Is there any greater evil than this to a man of honor such as Laches or, indeed, to any of us with the least sense of pride? Is there?[25]

Laches knows there is not. So the real power of shame lies in its taking on the warning role of discretion, caution, alertness to what may lead to shame, what your comrades and community will look down on and what may cost you face. Shame-as-disgrace is passive, unwilling self-revelation, but shame-as-discretion is active self-knowledge and self-respect, the moral knowledge of what is expected and what is condemned, and the moral control related to it.[26] Shame in this sense is the specifically restrictive potentiality of pride, the self-regarding, self-restraining, fearful aspect of the public man's sense of honor. It is the central element in the *Laches'* sister dialogue, the *Charmides,* the quality possessed by the beautiful young Charmides, the quality entirely lacking in his wicked uncle.[27] But it also has an important, if less obvious, role to play in this dialogue about courage and cowardice and teaching virtue to young men. Laches' earlier remarks revealed him to be a man of old-fashioned virtue, more concerned with the public than with his private good. The present speech, however, shows us what binds him to the public good: Laches' sense of shame is the link between his courage on the one hand and his moderation and justice on the other, the link conspicuously absent in what Nicias had to say. A man such as Laches could never betray the common good on behalf of his own safety; his sense of self-respect binds him to bravery more strongly than any fear of punishment, and he would rather die than be shown a coward.[28] If virtue can be taught, it would appear that shame might be one of the means that the true educator would seek to use. But Laches' speech also suggests how shame might lead a man such as Laches to neglect or even betray the public good. He seems more concerned with avoiding disgrace or defeat than with attaining glory or victory; and if he were forced to choose between his city's welfare and his honor, what would he do?

Whereas Nicias' speech presents characteristic Athenian values and the characteristic Athenian view of the relation between *technē* and courage, Laches' presents the Spartan view and Spartan values, such as are expressed by Archidamus in book I of Thucydides' *Peloponnesian War,* where he says: "We [Spartans] are both warlike and wise, and it is our sense of orderliness that makes us so. We are warlike, because self-control [*sōphrosynē*] contains shame as its chief constituent, and bravery is contained within shame. And we are wise, because we are educated with too little learning to despise the laws, and with too severe a self-control to disobey them, and are brought up not to be too knowing in useless matters—such as the knowledge that can give a specious criticism of the enemy's plans in theory, but fails to assail them with equal success in practice—but are taught that the schemes of our enemies are not dissimilar to our own, and that the freaks of chance are not determinable by calculation" (1.84).[29] Like Archidamus, Laches esteems those things that give men an advantage in the practice of war: his blasphemous, comic image of the fighters in armor circling Sparta as if it were holy ground not only mocks them, but tells us what Laches reveres, Spartan self-sufficiency. (Compare Nicias' Athenian praise of military self-sufficiency; the one thing they share is the highest regard for military virtue.) Like Archidamus, Laches has nothing but contempt for sophistry or empty learning or for the characteristic Athenian notion that military science can conquer fear, make one brave when that is not the kind of man one already is. In contrast to Nicias, Laches says nothing of studies that are noble for their own sake, and he explicitly repudiates the claim that art can alter human nature any more than clothes can change the naked body. Finally, Laches' concern with shame and his fear of public disgrace is distinctively Spartan too: it is *aidōs* that makes the Spartan soldier stand in the battle line and fight to the death, *aidōs* that makes him obey the law, *aidōs* that is the great motivating power in his conduct. Laches' emphasis on nature, the actual practice of war and the modest aversion to disgrace is as characteristically Spartan as Nicias' emphasis on art, learning, and the daring appetite for the noble is Athenian.

And yet the form of Laches' speech is anything but Spartan. For Sparta, like Communist Russia, was a country without comedy (or tragedy—unlike the Athenians, who do not neglect things musical, but excel in them, as Laches points out).[30] This is a last and by no means least point to consider. Why does Plato put this brilliant, comic speech in the mouth of the man whom Aristophanes will turn into a speechless dog? It will not anticipate later arguments too much to say now that the answer has to do with what the angry Laches represents, his role in the overall thematic mime of the dialogue. Laches presents us here with an attack, made by a traditional, old-fashioned public-spirited man, against the new order that Nicias represents. Indeed, the now aroused Laches puts Nicias himself into the company of the tippy-toeing, self-uptripping eloquent sophisti who expose themselves to ridicule by pretending to a wisdom they do not have. This attack on the fantastically ambitious Nician science or wisdom is not philosophical, but it is made in one of the highest modes of conventional rhetoric, the mode of comedy. It is the poetic equivalent of the ridicule and blame used by the city, together with the fear of punishment, to guide its citizens toward the noble and good. It is therefore the very kind of thing that Aristophanes would enjoy; he, too, delighted in exposing the undue love of honor and the undue love of learning. It is comedy in exactly the spirit that Socrates describes in the *Philebus*, where he discusses the ridiculous as the pretense to virtue and attributes laughter to the pleasurable, malicious sense of superiority we get in contemplating our friend's present or future embarrassment (see 47d–50e).

Nonetheless, there seems to be an important difference between Laches and Aristophanes. For the poet said that he attacked others in order to teach justice, but Laches' motives seem less pure. Laches appears to be attacking his old friend and ally for another reason, one giving the clue to something that has long puzzled scholars about Socrates' account of humor in the *Philebus*. For Socrates does not tell us there why, if the objects of the comic emotion are our friends, we bear them malice. Why do we triumph in their misfortune? Laches suggests here that the answer lies in envy. It would appear that even in relation to our friends, we may live in a state of rivalry and modest warfare: whereas tragedy may speak to that which makes friends even of enemies, the common suffering of mankind, comedy speaks to that which makes enemies of even friends, the common rivalry of all men for property and honor and rule (compare *Lysis* 215a).[31] Aggression, on this view, goes very deep in human nature. Laughter only helps relieve it and give it a nonviolent outlet. And that is in relation to our friends, so long as we assume they are harmless. If once we think them otherwise, we will not be so restrained.

3.5 Lysimachus' Aporia *and Socrates' New Beginning (184c–186a)*

Lysimachus follows Laches' advice, turns to Socrates, tells him their council is in need of a judge to make a decision, and urges him to vote. But Socrates ignores Lysimachus' request, asking him instead if he then will merely adopt whatever the greater number praise, to which the hapless Lysimachus answers, "Why, what else can one do?" This perplexed response, Lysimachus' *aporia*, marks the end of the first deliberative inquiry of the dialogue, the vulgar or conventional deliberation (see section 2.5). The second and philosophical deliberation is radically different in its aims, methods, and results, though these differences are not immediately apparent. In response to Lysimachus' first request for his advice, Socrates had asserted that if he had anything to say besides what Nicias and Laches said, he might try to "teach and persuade" them. His remarks in most of the remainder of the first half of the dialogue—

prior to 189e, where he begins his singular way of teaching—are intended to persuade the participants that they should reconsider their whole approach to this conversation. Specifically, he will try to persuade them that their standards of knowledge and decision making, even their assumptions about the subject matter, need to be reexamined. The discussion concerning the boys' education has been too narrow; they need to consider the purpose of education, the goal they are seeking to attain, if they are to evaluate the appropriate means.

Socrates answers Lysimachus by turning abruptly to the other father of the conversation, Melesias, and asking him if, in preparing the young men for a contest (*agōn*, Nicias' metaphor at 182a2), he would not prefer the advice of a man who had studied and exercised under a good trainer rather than the advice of the majority or even of all four of them (including Lysimachus, who had excluded himself from the council). Melesias agrees, and Socrates establishes his first principle, that it is by "knowledge" (*epistēmē*) that it is fitting to decide, not by "numbers" (*plēthei*), if one is to decide well. So they must determine if any of them is expert (*technikos*) in the subject they are consulting on, and if so, be persuaded by him, or if none is, seek one out (184d9–185a3; compare *Euthyphro* 2d–3a; *Apology* 20b; *Crito* 47a–48a).

It is instructive that Socrates must abandon Lysimachus to begin his own kind of deliberative inquiry. Certainly, we can appreciate why Lysimachus feels confused. After all, he did consult with men who seemed to be experts in things relating to the city's contests, men who had been victorious in attaining high office, generals who had won battles for the city. These masterful men seemed sufficiently knowledgeable to offer authoritative opinions, but then they completely disagreed. So it seems there is no knowledge of this matter, only opinion. Now if the decision is not to be reached by force, must they not take a vote? By turning to Melesias and beginning the conversation as if anew with him, Socrates deflects our attention from the apparently real dilemma that Lysimachus faces and calls our attention to Lysimachus' own inability to participate in the vote, an inability resting on his apparent lack of any basis from which to evaluate the reasons the two speakers have offered for their conclusions. Unlike Melesias, who knows the fundamental difference between amateurish ignorance and technical knowledge, Lysimachus lives *entirely* in a world of *doxa,* in a double sense of opinion and reputation, and is a complete *idiōtēs,* also in a double sense of one who leads ·an apolitical life and one who is an unskilled amateur (see *Alcibiades I* 119b).[32] Lacking any experience by which to judge for himself between conflicting opinions, Lysimachus must rely utterly on what people say, and since people say that both these men and Socrates know what they are talking about, he must regard their opinions as equal. Because he has no standards of his own by which to judge among the different opinions as to what is best, Lysimachus, the true child of complete democracy, makes the majority opinion his measure of what should be done, not realizing that he has no good reason to make this his measure, either. It is no accident that Lysimachus drops out of the conversation altogether a little later on. In a way, he was never in it, for he was never in a position to decide for himself on what they ought to do. The true democrat, who relies completely on what people say, can no more himself have a say than he is himself responsible for what he is. He needs someone else to rule for him; he is a natural sheep.

Socrates must attempt, therefore, to reestablish the claim of knowledge over and against majority will or mere opinion in the democratic city: he must reestablish the claim and reality of the ideal of *epistēmē* as the rightful basis of action in a conversational world that is dominated by *doxa* and *epithymia*. To establish his general principle (that it is knowledge rather than numbers that must be our guide), he must proceed persuasively, appealing to what even on a common sense level proves that real knowledge exists and that it is, when available, the only appropriate guide—namely the arts. He must conveniently ignore the fact that the authorities' disagreement may imply that no one has real knowledge in the matters they are taking into consideration (compare *Protagoras* 319b–d).[33] He must conveniently ignore for the present the democratic principle that authoritative knowledge of the good life for the individual and the city is not available.

Socrates' second principle concerns the object of the inquiry and what we may call the mood or spirit in which it is to be conducted. Having established that they must be guided by knowledge or truth and not conformity to popular opinion, Socrates goes on to ask Melesias if he thinks this is a small matter at issue in the discussion or if it does not rather concern their "greatest possession." Does the welfare of "the whole of their father's household" not depend on what quality of men the boys become, so that it must be said to demand much forethought (*promētheia*) from them? Melesias agrees it does (185a3–10). Here again Socrates is proceeding persuasively. By reminding Melesias that his "greatest property" is at stake, Socrates removes the somewhat drunken sense of safety that thus far has governed the deliberation and arouses sober or prudent fear in Melesias, convincing him that knowledge in regard to this matter is necessary and inducing him to forget or ignore the possibility that such technical knowledge is not available. Note that Socrates' rhetoric here appeals to Melesias' concern for his own and that for Melesias this is the good of his family or household, rather than the good of Melesias seen purely as an individual, or the good of his city. Melesias' horizon is that of property and his family's welfare. It is not merely selfish, but it is also not enlightened, or civic-minded. Note too that Socrates introduces forethought (foresight) here as an effort of mind intended to determine what one ought to be or become, rather than merely what one in the future *will* become or experience; it is to be an exercise of prudence or wisdom, rather than prediction. Socratic forethought, unlike the Promethean, raises the question of what it means to care for oneself (see *Protagoras* 314a-b, 361c; *Gorgias* 501b; *Alcibiades I* 128a).

Socrates then asks Melesias, if he wished to consider who among them was most expert concerning a contest, would he not pick the one who had studied and practiced and had had good instructors? Melesias, whose father trained him as a wrestler, agrees (185b1-5). But the more basic question, Socrates suggests, must concern what it is they really are consulting about. Nicias, puzzled by this remark, interrupts—for are they not considering whether *hoplomachia* is a good thing for young men to learn? Socrates responds with two examples. The first concerns medicine for sick eyes, the second when to bridle or tame a wild horse or colt (185b5-d4). These examples seem particularly apt as models for the therapy of the soul, though in the *Laches* Socrates never discusses explicitly some of the problems they suggest, problems concerning therapy for a part (such as the rational part), as opposed to the whole, of the soul and problems concerning the different kinds of therapies that might be needed for different kinds of souls in the city.[34] The general principle that Socrates draws from the two examples is that in each case the deliberation is not about the means but about the thing that is being deliberated over, about the eyes and the horse, about the end that one has in view from the start (185d5-7; compare *Lysis* 219c; *Gorgias* 499e). "Necessarily," says Nicias. It is fitting, then, Socrates continues, that we also consider if our expert is skilled in the treatment related to the end we have in view. But are we not considering this study for the sake of the young men's souls? Therefore we must determine if one of us is an expert in the treatment of the soul, and which of us has had good instructors (185d9-e6). Thus the Socratic deliberation reaches out to determine the aim of life, from the perception of which the appropriate means of education are to be chosen. This section of the dialogue ends with a second interruption, this time by Laches, the voice of experience, who is anxious to see good works added to good teachers as evidence for the claim of knowledge, and for now Socrates agrees (185e7-186a1; compare similar criteria in *Protagoras* 326e-328a; *Gorgias* 515a-b; *Meno* 90b-91b).

Just as the shift from Lysimachus to Melesias as dialogue partner seemed to be necessary for Socrates to establish his first point about knowledge, so the shift here from Melesias to Nicias seems also to be necessary to establish his second principle, which is that the subject matter of the philosophical deliberation is the treatment or care of the soul. For it is not at all clear that Melesias would have the least idea of what Socrates means by a "therapy of the soul" or the "virtue of the soul" (see *Apology* 29e; *Crito* 47d–48a; *Gorgias* 501b). But Nicias, we learn shortly, is familiar with the various enlightened ideas that Socrates and the other wise men appeal to and thus is friendly to this strange use of a word, whether he is familiar with the comparable use by the *physiologoi* or even by the followers of the ancient salvation religions such as Orphism or Pythagoreanism. (Socrates himself says at *Charmides* 156d–157c, the dramatic date of which is about nine years prior to the *Laches,* that he learned about the therapy of souls in a foreign country from foreign priest-doctors of the god who confers immortality, Zalmoxis.[35] These doctors, he reports, reject Athenian medical science because it ignores the whole. Of course this account is ironic, but it does suggest that Socrates may well have been influenced by the salvation religions and their ideas about the soul.)[36] Moreover, we have learned just previously that what is at stake for Melesias in this discussion is the honor of his father's household, but it is by no means obvious that the Socratic therapy of the soul will contribute to that. Whereas the expansion of the epistemological horizon of the dialogue from opinion to knowledge depends on the presence in the discussion of a man with genuine experience of *technē,* the expansion of its pedagogical and teleological horizon depends on the presence in the discussion of a man who seeks wisdom. There is some substance to the claim that Nicias represents a higher level of knowledge or at least desire than do Lysimachus and Laches (see section 2.7). At any rate, it is probable that if it were not for Nicias and his attraction to a more scientific way of thinking (whether or not he was also attracted to a salvation religion), the Socratic inquiry could not have begun.

This recalls the matter alluded to in our discussion of the structure of the dialogue, namely that the events of the dialogue themselves appear to mime or imitate the theme of the origins of the philosophical inquiry about virtue (see section 2.5). That inquiry would appear to have its basis in two or three fundamental elements. The first is the desire to be the best, for honor and superiority, together with the continuing presence in the democratic society of a class of men who have the money and leisure to take care that their sons become the best, but who realize that the traditional ways may no longer suffice to attain that goal. These men do not ask the philosophical question, What is virtue? They think they know what it is—to become winners in the city's contests for power and prestige. Their problem concerns the means to that goal, specifically the role of the new war sciences that now exist in the city (including the arts of speech that bring victory in the lawcourts and success in the assembly). So the fathers consult with two of the city's leading men as to their opinion on the matter.

Unfortunately, the leading men disagree completely. Their disagreement reflects the most basic differences of opinion in the world, differences associated with imperial Athens and scientific wisdom on the one hand and with self-sufficient Sparta and patriotic traditionalism on the other. Their disagreement even points to an underlying difference of opinion as regards what it is to be the best. To the one man, science has everything to do with virtue, and virtue is found in the bold, skilled, and therefore superior individual. To the other, they are completely separate, most so-called science being impractical pretense, and virtue is found in the brave, moderate gentleman who serves the fatherland. Thus the second basic element underlying the philosophical question about virtue would seem to be the conflict in the historical city between at least two comprehensive and contradictory ways of viewing the noble and the good.

To resolve this disagreement the aristocratic fathers turn to a commoner who was allowed to be a citizen in their community because he was willing to kill or risk his life for freedom and the city. There would not have been an inquiry, nor does an inquiry exist, in a community in which the leaders are all united in their basic opinions (as was true, for example, of Sparta, a city that also excluded the sophistic or enlightenment sciences). Nor would there be an inquiry here if the common man would decide and thereby establish the ruling opinion in the city. But this man resists the temptation to decide arbitrarily, to act simply to rule. Thus the philosopher presents us with a third indispensable source for the inquiry to follow: a man who cares so much about attaining knowledge (in relation to the wonder he experiences at contemplating the fundamental disagreements of opinion about virtue and education) that he is unwilling to trust in either of the authoritative opinions or to take sides with one of them so as to share in rule over the city.[37] It is this man who introduces into the conversation a concept of virtue that points beyond the differences of opinion between the cities or civic leaders about virtue, that transcends the conventions: the idea of natural or human virtue, the idea of the virtue of the soul. He introduces this idea to the many others by appealing to the influential few among them who admire things scientific (whether or not they are also attracted to a salvation religion). But he must begin his inquiry on behalf of the fathers who care less about the common good than that their own sons become the best by questioning the authoritative opinions of the leaders, including both those who seem closest to him in their desire for wisdom and those who seem closest to him in their willingness to serve the city.

3.6 Socrates' Speech and Lysimachus' New Request (186a–187d)

After establishing that knowledge is the basis for sound decision making, and that the subject matter of their deliberations must be the therapy of souls, and in the process also suggesting that the credentials for possessing that art would be having had good teachers or good works of our own to show, Socrates makes his longest speech in the entire dialogue, addressed to Lysimachus (186a3–187b7). Viewed dramatically, it may be seen as the pivotal speech in the *Laches,* since as a result of what Socrates says in it Lysimachus will ask Nicias and Laches if they will submit to Socrates' questioning and, after they agree, Lysimachus turns the entire responsibility for the deliberation over to Socrates. At that point, midway in the dialogue as a whole, Socrates leads the conversation from the seemingly more practical deliberation they had been engaged in concerning *hoplomachia* and *paideia* to a philosophical inquiry concerning manly courage.

Socrates' speech at 186a–187b is divided into three parts. The first (186a3–b8) makes the general point that all those present should offer their credentials for possessing the therapeutic art, be it in the form of good teachers or—if they had no teacher—in the form of "products," namely, what Athenians or aliens, whether slave or free, it is agreed became good because of them. But if they cannot say what teachers they have had or point to such products of their own art, they must bid Lysimachus and Melesias search for a teacher elsewhere and not themselves run the risk of harming the boys and suffering the disgrace of being accused by their friends. In the central part of the speech (186b8–d5), Socrates contrasts his own experience in regard to the art of therapy with the apparent situation of Nicias and Laches. Socrates claims he never has found such a teacher, though he desired one from youth onwards and lacked the money to be taught by the sophists (who claimed to be able to make him a gentleman). He opines, however, that Nicias and Laches must possess the ability to educate a human being, for they would not dare speak so fearlessly on what is beneficial or harmful to a youth if they did not trust themselves to know sufficiently, though he wonders at their disagreement. This is actually the first point in the *Laches* where Socrates' famous sarcasm or irony is unmistakably present, so much so that even Lysimachus seems to recognize it (see 187c5–d1). In the final part of the speech (186d5–187b7), Socrates requests Lysimachus to question the two of them on his behalf, to say who was the "most terribly clever" man they had heard concerning the rearing of the young. If they had acquired their knowledge by learning (*manthanein*), they should say who the teachers were, so that we may go to them and try to get them to care for our children, lest our sons turn out to be base and disgrace our ancestors (a harsh allusion to Lysimachus and Melesias). Or if Laches and Nicias acquired their knowledge by discovery (*heurein*), they should give a paradigm, someone whom through their care they made from being base to being noble and good. In his concluding remarks Socrates gives Nicias and Laches this warning: If they are only now beginning to educate, they must reconsider, lest they run the risk with their friends' children rather than with a Carian—that is, treat their friends' children like human trash (187a8–b4; compare *Euthydemus* 285b–c). He ends with the injunction to Lysimachus that he "not let them go" (*mē methiei,* 187b6). This phrase invokes again the wrestling metaphor employed repeatedly in this dialogue, especially in relation to Socrates himself (for instance by Laches at 181a7 and 184c6–7 and by Nicias at 188a2–3, where he uses it to characterize Socrates' manner in relation to his interlocutor; see also 186d6–7).[38]

Lysimachus' enthusiastic response to Socrates' thrice-uttered warning includes his own request, made three times, that Nicias and Laches allow themselves to be questioned by Socrates and that they give an account of their knowledge in the matter. Lysimachus also shows that Socrates did not fail to arouse his temper at what he now perceives as Nicias' and Laches' possible threat to his property. Thus he too pricks with the needle a bit, noting that he and Melesias had at the outset supposed, "as it seemed" (*hōs eikos,* 187c7), that Nicias and Laches had given serious consideration to these things. So if it makes no difference to them, would they not exchange their views with Socrates? For they too have young sons and they are all now consulting, as Socrates has well remarked, about the greatest of their things.

Each of the three parts of Socrates' speech at 186a–187b makes an important contribution to the development of the dialogue. First of all, and of greatest significance, Socrates manages to substitute for Lysimachus' and Melesias' original desire that their *sons* become the best a new goal, namely, "that their *souls* become the best" (*hoti aristas genesthai tas psychas,* 186a5–6). Although all the implications of this change are not yet apparent, Socrates hints at one potentially tremendous consequence in his discussions of what the soul therapist would do, if the virtue of the soul is not something tied to a given or natural social station. Thus he speaks apparently equally of Athenians and aliens, free and slave, as becoming "good" (*agathoi*), as if this were equivalent to "best" (*aristos*), and in the middle speech he refers to Nicias and Laches as being able to educate a "human" (*anthrōpos*) rather than a "freeman" (*anēr*)—another indication that there may be a notion of natural human virtue correlated with soul therapy not tied essentially to social station and birthright (186b3–5, d1). He blurs these points for now, however, by his references to becoming a gentleman, a "noble and good one" (186c4, 187a8).

The second most important development is presented in the last part of his speech, where Socrates discusses the *technē* that he says Nicias and Laches must have, to be fit to advise on the education of the youths, and the criteria they must fulfill, to prove that they possess the art of soul therapy (see 186d5–187a6). This part of the speech develops a theme that we also find in other Platonic dialogues, notably the discussions with Anytus in the *Meno* (89e–95a) and with Protagoras and Gorgias in the dialogues named for those gentlemen (*Protagoras* 319a–329d; *Gorgias* 448e–466a). There, as here, Socrates seems largely intent on raising the questions of whether the art exists and whether his interlocutors possess it. But his discussions of the so-called art of teaching virtue are everywhere so laden with irony that beyond the matter of refuting the claim of others to the art, it is difficult to say whether Socrates even believes such an art to be possible, much less whether Plato portrays Socrates as indeed possessing it. What is evident is that the claim to possess the art points to a still higher criterion of knowledge than any yet introduced.

In his speech here, Socrates thus appears to take the idea of an art of soul therapy quite seriously. He appears to accept both the main criterion of possessing an art that Nicias would accept, having had an established teacher, as well as the main criterion that Laches accepts, being able to show good products of your skill. But Socrates goes on to undercut both of these criteria. As regards the claim to have had a teacher in the art, he notes that although he "hungered" for a teacher of virtue from youth onwards, he never found one and never discovered the art himself (the word Socrates uses at 186c2 for his desire, *epithymia,* Nicias used at 182b5 in relation not to virtue but to honor). The only persons who even professed the ability to make him "noble and good" (i.e., a gentleman, someone virtuous by conventional standards) were the sophists, but they demanded payment for their services, so he could not try them out. Socrates also uses (at 186e4) the word *deinotatos* in relation to such teachers as Nicias and Laches may have heard lecture, a word that, as we have seen, was applied to the sophists and is laden with negative connotations (compare 182d2; *Protagoras* 312d; and the discussion in section 1.7). This reminds us of the fact that the sophists' claim to teach virtue was emphatically rejected by traditionalists such as Laches and by common opinion, which regarded their profession as being disreputable.[39]

The philosophical problem that Socrates' speech raises has to do with the relation of the longed-for soul craft to opinion. If the student claims that he has had good teachers, they must be known to be good themselves and to have taught him and others. But likewise, if he claims to have discovered the art himself, his students must be acknowledged to owe their goodness to him, as their teacher. Thus whether the claim to possess the therapeutic art is based on the teachers one has had or the students one can point to, the ultimate test of the artist's credentials would still appear to rest with popular opinion. But what if the bestness that the soul healer teaches is not at all clear to the many in the same way that victory in the city's contests or the truthfulness of commonly held opinions is clear? (Compare the account of the man who descends back into the Cave at *Republic* 517a with *Apology* 29d–e; *Gorgias* 481b–c; *Crito* 49d.) Despite his praise of art and apparent support for *technē*, not mere numbers, as the basis for sound decision, Socrates' speech actually shows that one could not know that one had the therapeutic art in question unless one also knew what bestness of soul is—that is, that one could not know that one had what made virtue *come to be* in a student unless one already knew what it *is*. But this implies that the standard of *technē* introduced in his discussion with Melesias does not, in itself, raise their deliberation beyond the level of *doxa* and "numbers." For that, for their deliberation to proceed on the basis of genuine *epistēmē*, it will be necessary to engage in philosophy. And so Socrates will readily bypass the discussion of Nicias' and Laches' claim to the art in question in the second half of the dialogue, going on instead to inquire, with them, about the nature of virtue in the form of courage.

Recalling the discussion of the structure of the dialogue in section 2.5, we can begin to understand how the entire section from 184d to 189d fits into the *Laches* as a whole. It presents not so much a part of the philosophical deliberation, as it does the rhetorical transition to it.[40] The later, genuinely philosophical deliberation or inquiry is the one in which a kind of knowledge not ultimately referring back to public opinion is at issue, a kind of knowledge that has as its object the way things are, not merely how they come to be. It is only in that later part of the dialogue that the question of a genuine art rooted in knowledge actually becomes relevant. Only then will Socrates envisage for the participants a being—the Idea of Courage Herself—that is the object of real knowledge. This part of the dialogue, by contrast, remains entirely in the Cave, that is, in the realm of opinion and becoming, where the ultimate good and being of things remains unexamined. That later, more fundamental discussion itself depends, however, upon the philosophical principles that Socrates establishes here, however shakily this may be.

There is one more point worth noting in Socrates' discussion of the *technē* of soul therapy. This point bears on the question of Plato's view of education and whether Socrates might not himself be a teacher, despite his protestations to the contrary here and elsewhere, most notably *Apology* 19b–23b. We recall that Socrates playfully claims, at the beginning of the *Charmides* (156d–157c), that he was taught by the Thracian priest-doctors of Zalmoxis, who knew the charms that cure the soul and induce *sōphrosynē*, psychic health. He emphasizes most strongly to the young *Charmides* that the treatment he has to offer requires an effort on the patient's side and that the patient must be willing to "submit his soul" to him. Now since Socrates' description of the art seems not to require that the teacher both know what virtue is and impart that knowledge to his students, it should be at least possible that even if Socrates does not possess the knowledge of virtue, he still could have a craft or at least a knack of soul therapy. Nicias at any rate will soon attribute some such art to him (187e–188b). But at 187a7–8 Socrates says that to claim validly to possess the art, Nicias and Laches would have to prove that they transformed their students from being base into being noble and good; and this may suggest that the perfect soul therapist, in Socrates' mind, would need successfully to treat all of his would-be students, that is, be able, like a shoemaker or carpenter, to produce again and again the right result out of his materials. If this indeed is Socrates' criterion for possessing the art in question, we would have here another reason for his not wanting to claim to have it. The kind of educational art Socrates may be said to possess relies upon the innate goodness of the eye to be restored to health, and upon the willingness of the student or patient to endure the teacher or doctor's medications. Even apart from the question of his knowledge, Socrates may wish to deny himself the title of "teacher" on the grounds that he is simply unable to work with all kinds of students (see *Theaetetus* 150b–151d). If one has that willingness and good nature, however, might he not be the teacher we seek?

Finally, there is Socrates' emphatic warning that Nicias and Laches run the risk of advising too freely if they lack the requisite art, and there is the bearing of this warning on Lysimachus' praise of Socrates' remark that they are consulting now about the greatest of their things. From a dramatic standpoint, the speeches of Socrates and Lysimachus now effectively transform the model of the discussion from the somewhat carefree democratic war council that Lysimachus established to what amounts to a trial in which Socrates plays the role of prosecutor, Nicias and Laches the defendants against the charge of recklessly and unjustly giving potentially harmful advice to their friends on the basis of less than sufficient knowledge. One is inclined to suppose these charges are lodged against the kind of thoughtless confidence that men of action typically show, a confidence resting on their many victories in the city's contests and the intoxicating flattery they receive for them, on their inevitably limited experience of what works and what does not, on what people think is true. Such thoughtless confidence typically derives from the equally thought-less trust that although they may win honor if their views are accepted, they will not suffer any harm, for nothing vital to them is at stake in a merely private, leisurely discussion about education. Such men and such a trial may seem comic, or tragic, or both (see section 2.8). But the main point that emerges from Socrates' speech is that their free and brave words may be foolhardy and unjust: they may fail to recognize the very real danger that they do not know what they think they know. This is not only about the teaching of virtue but about virtue itself and what human life is for; the danger is that their lack of thoughtful foresight about the good of the soul at stake in every deliberation reflects insufficient care not only for the youths involved, but also for themselves. Thus for Socrates the path to wisdom, if wisdom can be attained, must begin with forethought, and the root of forethought is proper fear—the fear that one may be directing oneself toward the wrong goal, that one does not see rightly the way, because one's vision of life is somehow distorted (*Protagoras* 314a–b; *Gorgias* 458a; *Charmides* 166c–d). At its root, this fear about one's way of life and thought seems to be inseparable from the true self-care that Socrates recommends at *Apology* 29e–30b, the care for the perfection of the soul. We shall see in the trial that follows, just how deep is Nicias' and Laches' care to "be the best."

As an afterthought to this discussion, it seems appropriate here to take cognizance of the fact that the Socratic testing and eventual refutation of Nicias and Laches presents us with the very kind of conduct on account of which he was charged with corrupting the youth (*Apology* 33c–d; *Meno* 94e–95a). What would Plato say to us in his defense? First, he would note that although Socrates questions public leaders in the *Laches,* he questions neither religious nor civil law, and indeed, he will uphold piety and moderation at the end of the inquiry. In the next place, Plato would point out, Socrates was specifically requested by the fathers to conduct this examination, and they urge him at the end of the dialogue to take on the sons as his students. Lastly, Plato would insist that Socrates does not harm the laws, he only questions the wisdom of the men who were elected to apply them; nor is such questioning itself in violation of democratic law (compare *Crito* 51b–c, 54b–c). Socrates' action is perfectly just.

3.7 Nicias' Response and Socratic Dialectic (187d–188c)

Nicias' and Laches' responses to Lysimachus' new request constitute the next two sections (187d6–189d3) in this transitional part of the dialogue. These speeches correspond both to the ones they had given earlier on *hoplomachia* and to the answers they will give Socrates in the philosophical inquiry in the second half of the *Laches* (see again the outlines of the structure of the dialogue in section 2.5). But whereas the earlier speeches were about the value of a particular study, these are about the value of learning in general and about their attitudes toward discussion with Socrates. As we have noted, their agreement here to submit to Socrates' questions has changed the conversational community from an assembly, composed of Nicias, Laches, and the two fathers, to the very different community of a courtroom in which Socrates is the district attorney prosecuting Nicias and Laches for ignorant counsel. And whereas these speeches express verbally the unconditional willingness of Nicias and Laches to engage in that dialogic trial with Socrates, it is in those later conversations that they express through their actions how willing or unwilling they really are. Indeed, Nicias and Laches do not prove to be quite as willing to inquire as they say they are. Their responses here suggest why that might be so.

Once again Nicias speaks first, noting that Lysimachus must not have known Socrates personally except, perhaps, in his childhood, when Lysimachus may have chanced to meet him with his father in Apollo's temple or some other gathering of the demesmen (187d6–e4). This comment might well have been evoked by Lysimachus' final suggestion that Nicias and Laches examine in common with Socrates, "giving and receiving an account from each other"; Socrates is not the kind simply to give or receive an account. Rather, as Nicias goes on to describe it, Socrates' manner in discussion is to lead the man with whom he is speaking round and round in a circle (compare *Euthyphro* 11b), until finally he must give an account of *himself*, of how he lives and how he has lived his past life, for Socrates will "not let go" (*ou . . . aphēsei*) of him until he has "put all his ways to the test" (187e6–188a3).[41] But if one suffers these things and does not flee from them, if one is willing and holds it worthwhile to "learn as long as one is living" as Solon says, necessarily he will be more forethoughtful (*promēthesteron*) for "his life ever after."[42] This is why Nicias' attitude toward Socrates is not unfavorable, as he goes on to explain (188a4–c1). For he is accustomed to Socrates and so is not offended by such ungentlemanly treatment; rather, he takes pleasure in it. He sees no harm, he says, in their being reminded of anything they have done or are doing that is not noble, and he really expected all along that with Socrates present their speech would be not about the boys but about themselves. Nicias concludes that for his part nothing prevents passing the time with Socrates, but they should see how Laches stands on it too (188c1–3).

At first glance, Nicias' account of Socrates' manner of discussion seems similar to other Platonic accounts of the Socratic art of refutation or elenchus, accounts depicting it as a highly personal method of teaching or healing, and the elenctic teacher or healer as the one who helps produce, in himself and others, psychic health or moderation, *sōphrosynē*.[43] He does this, above all, by removing from his interlocutor the disease of complex ignorance, which consists not only in not knowing but in the delusion and conceit of thinking that one knows, when one does not (see *Meno* 84a–c; *Sophist* 229c; *Laws* 863a). This kind of ignorance is common—almost everyone has it in relation to wisdom (*Apology* 21a–23b)—and it is the cause of the greatest evil in human lives (*Meno* 77e; *Gorgias* 479a–c). But the Socratic method aims to succeed where others might not because Socrates makes the student his own witness against himself, so that when he is refuted, he cannot deny that he did not know what he was talking about, a process Socrates likens to medicine in the *Gorgias* (477a; compare also 464b–465d, 472b–c, 505c). The result of submitting one's soul to such a *therapeia tēs psychēs* would seem to be the psychic health of the moderate man described in the *Charmides*: the one able to examine and discern what he himself and others really know and do not know (167a). The most comprehensive statement about the elenchus is found in the *Sophist*, where the Eleatic Stranger distinguishes two kinds of education, the old-fashioned method of exhortation and the new method of refutation, which aims at removing the conceit of wisdom: "[Noble sophists] question a man on those matters where he thinks he is saying something although he is really saying nothing. And as he is confused, they easily convict his opinions by bringing them together and putting them side by side, thus showing that they are contrary to each other at the same time in the same respect about the same things. When he sees this he becomes angry with himself and gentle toward others, and in this way is relieved of great and stiff-necked opinions about himself, this process being pleasantest for all to hear and the most secure for the one who suffers it" (230b4–c3). Plato's Stranger goes on to say that those who perform this *katharsis* or "purification" believe that a soul cannot profit from the knowledge that is offered to him unless the elenchus is applied, the man refuted and brought to shame (*aischynē*), thus purging him of the opinions that hinder the teachings.

Upon examination, however, one notices important differences between the account of Socratic dialectic as presented by Nicias and the account we find elsewhere in the dialogues. Above all, Nicias simply ignores the zetetic or inquisitive aspect of the Socratic method—the fact, as Socrates puts it in trying to allay Critias' contentiousness in the *Charmides*, that "I inquire with you always in regard to what is proposed because I myself do not know" (165b8–9). This is a point that Socrates is forced to elaborate on shortly afterward, when he exclaims that if he seeks to refute Critias it is primarily out of his fear that he concealedly supposed himself to know something he does not know. That is why he is examining the argument—mainly for his own sake, and that of his friends, for is it not for "the common good of almost all humankind" that each of the beings be revealed as it is? (166c–d)

Indeed, when Socrates himself describes his method it is always the zetetic, and not the elenctic, aspect that he places first. One must be committed above all to the search for truth and seek to refute the interlocutors' opinion only, or at least chiefly, in order to "follow the argument" and determine if the opinion expressed in it is sound, and if it is to secure it in the process by finding reasons in one's own thinking that will hold it "firmly fastened" (*dedemenon, Meno* 97e4; compare *Gorgias* 505e–506a, 508e–509; also *Crito* 46b). Nicias so far overlooks this aspect of Socrates' procedure that he significantly distorts it; rather than examining the persons' opinions (*doxai*), he makes it an examination of his life (*bios*); rather than exposing his false words (*logoi*), he has him exposing the persons' ignoble deeds (*erga*). But Socrates emphasizes again and again that if he examines his own or anyone else's life, it is through their opinions, their words, not through direct inspection of their deeds (see *Laches* 193e; *Euthyphro* 9e; *Protagoras* 333c, 348a; also *Phaedo* 99e–100a). Nicias' portrait of Socrates' method makes one wonder if he is not less directly acquainted with it than he suggests, or at any rate wonder why his view of it is so one-sided.

Similarly, Nicias' attitude toward conversing with Socrates seems at first to be free and willing, but a closer inspection raises doubts. Like the young musician in the *Lovers* (133c), Nicias misquotes Solon, substituting the word *manthanein,* "to learn," with the connotations of learning for oneself and intellectual learning (this word was also prominent in Nicias' earlier speech and mocked by Laches), for the correct word *didaskein,* "to instruct," the passive form of which is used by Laches (189a5) and includes the connotation of learning how to live, for instance, as a son is taught by his father to be a good citizen.[44] Does Nicias, like the young musician, think of philosophy as *polymathia,* the acquisition of ever more skills, information, noble studies? This would be consistent with his earlier speech (181d–182d), which expressed his regard for studies in themselves noble, even if not practical—an attitude in sharp contrast to that of Laches. So Nicias' desire for honor or learning is one reason for him to participate in the inquiry. But Nicias' view of learning and philosophy seems also to ignore the shocking and soul-turning part of Socratic *paideia,* the part that issues in the experience of *shame* at the discovery of boastful not-knowing, the part that is supposed to unchain the student from the bonds of contentment with opinion and release the passion to really know. Nicias says one must "not flee" (*mē pheugonta,* 188b2) Socrates' words, but he also says he "enjoys" and does not find it "unpleasant" to talk with him. These are words more consistent with the experience of those who observe Socrates' elenctic inquiries than of those whose souls are being stripped (see *Apology* 23c, 33c). Must we not conclude that Nicias' supposed experience of Socrates up to this point is merely that of an observer of, not a participant in, the elenchus, and that this is why he thinks it will be pleasant and not harmful? For the elenchus is pleasant to observe but soul wrenching for the one who genuinely submits to it, for to that one, as Nicias unknowingly but indeed correctly indicates, his *whole life,* not merely a fragment of his thought, is put in question in the end.

The curiously abstract and passionless character of Nicias' expressed attitude toward Socratic teaching is set in very sharp relief when we compare it to Alcibiades' experience of Socrates, as presented in the *Alcibiades I* and as he himself reports in the *Symposium.* In the former, in which he is a young man, he exclaims: "But by the gods, Socrates, I myself don't know what I am saying," *at which admissions he burst into tears (Alcibiades I* 116e, 127d).[45] And in the latter, as a man in his prime about to lead the attack that was intended to conquer the world, he says: "When I hear him I am worse than any wild initiate at the mysteries; I find my heart leaping and my tears gushing forth at his speeches, and I see all kinds of others suffering the same things. . . . Even now I still know that if I were willing to give him my ear, I could not endure him, but I would suffer the same things. For he compels me to to admit that, as incomplete as I am, I am not caring for myself, when I attend to the affairs of the Athenians. . . . And there is one thing that I have suffered in the presence of this one alone of all human beings, which no one would think is present in me—to be ashamed toward someone; I suffer shame toward this one only, . . . but when I go away from him I am overcome and enslaved by the honors of the many. So I run from him like a slave and flee, and when I see him again, I think of those former admissions and am ashamed" (215d9–216c2). *This* is the experience of shame one comes to see as the culmination of the refutative method of education—the very shame that Socrates himself says it is his goal to engender in the Athenians, that they abandon their former way of life and turn to philosophy (*Apology* 29b–30b). Why is there nothing of this in Nicias' account?

To formulate the question is to sense the answer. Is not the difference already evident? Alcibiades, as much if not more than any other figure save one or two in the Platonic dialogues in which Socrates has the leading role, is a nature of both overwhelming intelligence and *erōs.* He is one who would rather die than fail to attain the highest *kalon,* and thus he can be attached to the supreme nobility, the nobility of the hidden truth (see *Alcibiades I* 105a–c, 115d, 124b, 131d; *Symposium* 217a, 218e, 222a). Nicias, by contrast, already seems to be a very different kind of man, one who cares about his honor, yes, but one who is also very much concerned about what is pleasant and will cause him no harm. Whatever else we may learn about Nicias and

his willingness toward true learning in the remainder of the dialogue, his utter
failure to appreciate the zetetic and shame-inducing purposes of Socratic
inquiry and psychagogy suggest that we will not be shown a man with a
passionate love for freedom and truth. Nicias is no Alcibiades, nor even a
Glaucon or Callicles, and the inquiry with him will not probe as deeply the
mysteries of virtue and the soul as the ones Socrates conducts with them.[46]

3.8 Laches' Response and the Harmony of Word and Deed (188c–189c)

After Laches, too, agrees to submit to Socratic examination, Lysimachus
transfers all responsibility for the conversation to Socrates, and the first half
of the dialogue comes to a close. Once he is fully in charge Socrates makes
a new beginning, again changing both the topic and form of the discussion.
Originally, the scope of conversation was narrow but seemingly clear: Should
the young boys study *hoplomachia*? Then, after the generals had disagreed,
Socrates led them to realize that the discussion must be broadened to include
the nature of education and the criteria for knowledge of the therapy of souls.
But rather than cross-examine Nicias and Laches on their credentials in the art
of soul therapy, Socrates will instead propose that they inquire concerning the
nature of virtue, and together with Laches decides to focus on the virtue of
courage. In this inquiry, we are exposed to the power of the Socratic dialectic
to examine critically both conventional and unconventional opinions in the
interests of truth and justice, and to the effects of that dialectic on the participants, who have asserted their willingness to learn from Socrates. However,
as we have just seen, Nicias may be lacking certain qualities necessary to learn
what Socrates has to teach, and he will, as was noted earlier, be something of
a failure in the discussion (see section 2.7). Laches also reveals in his speech
accepting Socrates' challenge certain limitations to his willingness to learn,
though he displays other qualities that make him a more promising candidate
for the elenchus—as the limited success of his later participation in it will also
confirm.

Laches starts by saying he is "single-minded" concerning speeches, or
"double-minded" Nicias might say, for he seems a speech lover in this, that
when he hears real men speak on virtue or some sort of wisdom he becomes
gentle-minded and rejoices to see that their deeds live up to their words, but
is a speech hater otherwise. In Laches' opinion, a man is truly musical only
if he has tuned himself in the finest harmony, not on a lyre but in his life so
as to "live a concord of speeches and deeds," in the Dorian mode, which is
the only truly Greek *harmonia*. Such a man Laches loves to hear and Laches
trusts what he says; but in regard to someone in whom the two do *not* conform

(e.g., "wise men" such as Stesilaus), the more eloquent he is, the more he pains Laches and makes him angry, and so Laches is made to seem a speech hater (188c4–e4). These being Laches' general principles, he goes on to apply them to Socrates. He has no experience of Socrates' speeches, but he does of his actions, and in these he found Socrates to be a man worthy of the noblest, freest speech (188e5–189a1). For Laches also accedes to Solon's authority, but wishes to be taught (*dikaskesthai*) by worthy men, even if they are younger or without reputation (189a1–b1). Laches concludes by commanding Socrates to teach and refute him and learn whatever Laches knows. For Socrates gave him the kind of proof of virtue (*aretē*) that justice demands (189b1–7). (As was mentioned in the preface, Laches' use of *aretē* here is sometimes translated as "valor," which is what actually he has in mind, implying that for him virtue and valor are synonymous—something that is not true of course for Socrates, at least insofar as his remarks at 190c–e will suggest.)

The transition to the second half of the dialogue is then completed by Socrates, who observes that they cannot blame Nicias and Laches for being unwilling to continue, and by Lysimachus, who turns over his part in the inquiry to Socrates (189c1–d3).[47] In the process Lysimachus notes that he forgets everything if new arguments arise "in the middle" (*metaxu*). This announces that it is the center of the dialogue and also tells us that Lysimachus will forget the entire philosophical part of the inquiry! (See section 2.7 on Lysimachus as the representative of the lowest level of knowing, the level that we seldom remember.)

Laches' discussion of Dorian harmony gives the crown to his earlier Spartan speech in praise of men of action, in contempt of men of (mere) words. We recognize in him an image of the forthright soldier who stands nobly above disputatious chatter, a workman who handles the truth as he sees it and hates all duplicity.[48] This is the ideal of honesty and integrity represented in Homer by Achilles (see *Iliad* 9.312–13; *Hippias Minor* 364e–365b).[49] As readers of Plato we are also reminded of *Republic* 3, in which Socrates defers to Damon as the expert on musical harmony, though he himself establishes the point that there are two modes appropriate to just men, one imitating a man who is brave in warlike deeds and other violent work (the Dorian mode), the second for a man performing a peaceful, voluntary deed and who in a moderate, orderly manner is persuading or being persuaded or taught (the Phrygian mode; see 398c–399c). Laches seems well attuned to the first of these modes, but not nearly as well to the second. Nor is his purely Dorian tuning entirely consistent with the Homeric tradition, which not only condemned Thersites as the basest of all men in the *Iliad* (2.211–77), but also made Ajax, paradigm doer of deeds but weak in counsel, a far lesser hero than the brilliant Odysseus (see

9.443; also 2.166–210, 24.725–28). Laches is no cool persuader. He lacks the eloquent words to impress; he is too blunt to soften and please. He is what he is, and he wants others to be forthright also. But it is not clear that he can check his anger if once aroused.

Laches' words suggest that he may in one way be well suited to Socratic teaching, in another way not. For one necessary condition of the elenchus is that the interlocutor should present his real beliefs for examination, so it will be himself, no less than the words, that is tested.[50] But what is a "real belief" when it comes to notions of the virtues and the good life?[51] In the *Charmides,* Socrates suggests that a real belief is one that we hold because we have some relevant experience giving us reason to trust the belief as true. Thus he says that *Charmides* should be able to offer an account of moderation, because the moderation in him must give him some "perception" or "feeling" (*aisthēsis*) from which he can form his opinion (*doxa*), and after Charmides gives the answer truly reflecting his youthful sense of that virtue, Socrates comments on the "manly self-examination" that issued in it (160d–e). In such a case, the refutation does something more than merely embarrass the interlocutor with a dialogic checkmate; he is confronted with the fact that he cannot say what he thinks *must* be true. As one critic has put it, this serves to bring him "out of his individual arbitrariness into the common world of reason."[52] Another important feature of a real belief about the virtues is that it expresses a position that the speaker upholds as desirable. The speaker who merely says what he believes the others want to hear, who flatters (perhaps, as with Gorgias and Polus, to save face), or who strives simply to win, not to know (such as Critias and Protagoras and many others), avoids the practical commitment that makes the elenchus about oneself and one's own. But if the interlocutor offers his real belief concerning the very idea he cares most about, he may be open to the self-directed anger and shame that the Eleatic Stranger describes as the curative process in the elenchus, to the self-discovery that "I don't know what I thought I knew," and perhaps even to the philosophical quest for real knowledge, as against what he now can call mere opinion. A third characteristic that makes Laches receptive to the elenchus is his spirited, Socratic-like belief that it is wrong merely to speak "freely" when one does not know what one is talking about. Thus Laches can be indignant with those who pretend to a knowledge they lack, as now it seems may be no less true of Nicias than of Stesilaus. But then a man such as Laches, because he calls it what it is and condemns all talk not based on knowledge, and because when he talks about manly virtue he relies on his own experience—he does not bow even to Solon, most pious and moderate and just of all Athenian political sages—such a man can suffer the elenchus and become indignant with himself, and he may even come to see his way of life placed at stake in the conversation. This treatment is one that Laches, to some extent at least, really does suffer (see 193d–194b). The fact that Nicias, by contrast, does *not* suffer this experience when his words are refuted suggests that he did not put his real beliefs at risk.

On the other hand, Laches' words also suggest an attitude toward truth that makes one wonder if he will endure the philosophical challenge to his way of life.[53] His distrust of eloquence and all useless learning, his love of simplicity, his gymnastic neglect, not to say disdain, of music and private things including all *paideia*, his attention to the speaker's deeds rather than to his words, his manly self-certainty and commitment to the life of public action—these values are in vivid contrast to the Socratic life of patient inquiry, which is first of all oriented to discovering and knowing the truth for oneself and for those of one's friends who also are striving to find what is hidden beneath surface appearances. Just as Nicias' attitude toward Socrates was set in sharp relief by comparison to that of Alcibiades, so Laches' attitude toward the truly harmonious is set in relief by a comparison with Socrates' own stated views on self-harmony, views found in his speech to the notorious Callicles in the *Gorgias:* "For I, my good sir, would rather have my lyre or my chorus out of tune and discordant, or have many human beings disagree with me and contradict me, than that I, being one, should be in discord with and contradict myself" (482b7–c3). It is not that Socrates rejects the principle of constancy that Laches speaks of—he strongly approves of it (see, for example, *Apology* 28d, 35d; *Crito* 46b; *Gorgias* 488a). But the principle that Socrates adheres to requires more than practical consistency alone; it requires that Socrates *test himself* to insure that he is logically self-consistent, in his words and thoughts no less than in his words and deeds.[54] (This principle is rejected, incidentally, by Dionysodorus in the *Euthydemus,* and this is one reason he cannot be refuted.) Socrates describes this process in the *Hippias Major,* playfully contrasting his own self-dissatisfaction with the self-complacency of the sophist who never examines himself. But Socrates does and he must, for "I am called every kind of bad name by that man who is always cross-examining me. He is a very close relative of mine and he lives in the same house, and when I go home and he hears me give utterance to these opinions he asks me if I am not ashamed of my daring to talk about a beautiful way of life, when questioning makes it evident that I do not even know the meaning of the word 'beauty'" (304d1–8; compare *Cratylus* 428d; *Euthyphro* 9e; *Charmides* 167a; *Gorgias* 458a–b; *Republic* 382a–b).[55] Laches is of course "harmonious" in a way that the terribly clever Hippias, who claims to know everything, is not. But Laches is no less single-minded than Hippias when they are both compared to Socrates' double-minded "two-in-oneness"; the intellectual conscience that guards Socrates from ever speaking or listening perfectly freely seems not to live in Laches' house.

Guided by experience, trusting in men who prove themselves in action, Laches is not easily fooled by sophistry or eloquence or even reputation or age, but he also does not examine his opinions or those of men like him to see whether they might be wrong. Because he looks directly at men's deeds, he is blinded by the light of the city in which those deeds must appear, the light in which action seems to be a trustworthy guide to virtue, the light in which virtue and science or wisdom seem clearly to be measured by the common good, the light in which the soul is concealed. But the apparent consistency of public things is an illusion, as the action of the dialogue has already suggested and the inquiry that is to come will make patently clear. The deed that seems noble may not be good; the virtue that is not wisdom may not make one the best; the truth perceived by the common eye may be superficial; and the courage we attribute to men such as Laches may not be courage at all.

4
The Inquiry with Laches

4.1 Transition to the Inquiry

THE FIRST HALF OF the *Laches* has been dominated by private desires. Two old and failed aristocrats, who have sought to uphold the family name, appealed to two of the leading men of the city for advice concerning their boys' education. But these latter two, the central characters in the drama, prove to give fundamentally conflicting advice. Another man is then invited to join in the deliberation, a man not at first recognized by the fathers who began it, but who is recognized and honored by the central characters for his military and musical (educational) abilities. This newcomer is a philosopher, it turns out, one who distinguished himself from the others by modestly claiming a lifelong unsated desire to know or obtain the good of the soul. He alerted the old family men to the dangers threatening their property, if they simply follow the will or opinion of the majority, rather than base their action on what is fitting in accordance with knowledge (*epistēmē*). The first half of the *Laches* ended with the family men consenting to have their leaders tested on whether or not they really know what is good for the whole of their houses.

The second half of the *Laches* is dominated by the contest for victory and honor among the leaders, and by the quest, initiated by the philosopher, for knowledge concerning what it is to be virtuous of soul. The contest has been given a judicial twist by the philosopher's accusation that the politician and the soldier were wrong in claiming to know what is best for the souls of young men and how to obtain it. (Indeed, how could they know what is fitting for the city if they do not know what is fitting for the souls of young men; that is, how could they know what is fitting for the whole if they do not know what is fitting for a significant part of that whole?) But by threatening the leaders in this way, the philosopher risks arousing their angry self-defense, a threat

93

that extends both to their willingness to search for truth and to their willingness to accept his leadership in their deliberative community.

As it turns out, everything seems to be fine in the end. The soldier is satisfied that he is no more ignorant than the politician, who is himself satisfied that he can acquire the science or wisdom that he needs by turning to the musically wise and linguistically clever man. And the fathers and the leaders all agree that the philosopher should take the lead in educating their sons. But there are one or two notes of uncertainty. For one thing, nobody but the philosopher is impressed with the fact that none of them seems to know about virtue; how, if he too lacks that knowledge, can he instruct anyone else? And for another, although the fathers consent to take instruction from the philosopher, the leaders do not say that they are willing, and, as we shall see, there is every reason to doubt that they *would* be willing. Nor is it certain that he will himself undertake to teach the boys—so the philosopher indicates; that must depend on the will of the god.

The second half of the dialogue presents a profoundly interesting inquiry concerning the virtue of courage and its nature. The task of this part of the study is to examine that inquiry with care, so as to determine, if possible, what the dialogue has to teach us, both on its surface and in its depths, about manliness and courage.[1] This inquiry, we soon learn, is not for the fainthearted. To inquire with Socrates, you must be willing to submit your soul; be willing to put your beliefs and even your life to the test; be willing to risk everything and to lose everything. Truly you must be willing even to face death in order to gain the victory.

The interpretation offered here of the second half of the *Laches* is very different from what the reader will find in other scholarly literature on the dialogue, concerning which there has emerged something of an orthodox position.[2] That consensus, originating from the studies by Hermann Bonitz more than a century ago, views the inquiry as a progress from a merely behavioral account of the virtue (190e), through an account in terms of temperament (192b), then to an account combining the two elements of knowledge or wisdom and temperament. But it conceives the cognitive element wrongly (193a), and goes on to the final account offered by Nicias at 194e–195a, which understands the cognitive element correctly but now ignores the other necessary aspect of courage, the temperamental element of endurance. The true account, on this view, is indicated by "combining the remaining, uncontested and in that way recognized as valid sentences" (Bonitz), that is, the second plus the fourth definition, or more simply, the correct understanding of the third (see the discussion in section 2.6).

On the interpretation to be developed here, however, the inquiry into courage in the *Laches* examines not four but two basic conceptions of courage, the first a traditional or conventional conception of courage defended by Laches, and the second a progressive or enlightened conception defended by Nicias. On this view, the first three definitions are closely related, each presenting an aspect of the traditional idea of civic courage, according to which manly courage consists in the prudent or law-abiding hardiness of soul and sense of honor that makes a man ready to stand and endure even death in battle against his city's enemies. This political conception of courage is examined in all three of its chief respects in the first part of the inquiry: on the level of the kind of voluntary action in which it is manifested, on the level of the kind of habits of will and emotion on which it depends, and on the level of rational intention and civic responsibility. The results of that examination are not what one would anticipate from looking at the bare words of the dialogue. Socrates does not simply reject the conception of courage that Laches represents and defends. In fact, Socrates will come to the defense of the traditional understanding in the second half of the *Laches,* once it is shown that Laches cannot defend it. Properly guided, traditional manly courage has an important, indeed a necessary, place in the community of men.[3] This is not to say, however, that there are not very real defects in the traditional conception springing from the very nature of manliness, and suggesting that there may never be an end to human conflict, never be "peace on earth, good will among men," a disturbing conclusion for those of us who would like to believe otherwise.[4]

The second part of the inquiry is concerned with a conception of courage very different from that of the first part. This progressive conception of courage as a form of wisdom or science is represented and defended by Nicias. On this view, it is possible for individual men—not many, perhaps, but a few— to transcend the relationship to nature and to other men that puts them in unending conflict, and to attain a higher level of being, a level in which there is harmony and fulfillment without the need for aggression and self-sacrificing endurance. True courage thus consists in knowledge or wisdom, so that one stands above the world of good and bad fortune and never succumbs, through a false understanding of things, to foolish hopes or fears. This, too, is a noble conception of courage, but it is more noble than Nicias comprehends. For the inquiry will prove Nicias to be even less able to defend the conception of courage as a form of wisdom than Laches can defend the ancient conception as noble civic endurance. And the conception of courage that Socrates refutes in the second part of the inquiry is not, on our reading, the conception that Nicias first ventured; it is a more vulgar idea of enlightenment that Nicias finally has in mind, and this idea of manliness and courage is firmly rejected by both Laches and Socrates. The *Laches* leaves open the possibility that a wondrous form of courage exists, but its conclusion suggests that it will never be enough; as long as men do not devote themselves, fully and unconditionally, to the pursuit of wisdom and virtue, there will always be a need for the old, violent kind of courage oriented to victory and honor, and for macho men like Laches, who are unaccustomed to the joys of inquiry and music.

4.2 Introduction to the Inquiry (189d–190e)

Socrates begins the second half of the dialogue by abruptly pulling back from the inquiry he had just persuaded everyone they needed to make, an inquiry about their teachers and those they themselves had taught regarding virtue (189d4–e3). He says only that we should perhaps "examine ourselves" in this respect, and in its place suggests another kind of inquiry, adding that it proceeds somewhat more from the beginning (*archē*). For if we happen to know that which, when "put alongside" or "made present in" another thing (*paragenomenon:* this word can mean at least two quite different things), makes that thing better, and if we are able to put it alongside or make it be present in the other, then it is clear that we know this very thing concerning which we would be counselors as to how someone might "most easily and best" obtain it (189e3–7).[5] Socrates notes that Laches and Nicias perhaps do not yet understand what he is saying, but by this example they may learn it (*mathēsesthe*) more easily: For if we happen to know that sight, when joined to or present in eyes, makes them better, and we are also able to make sight joined to or present in eyes, then surely we must know concerning sight itself "what then it is" (*hoti pot' estin*), concerning which we are consulting how it "most easily and best" might be acquired. But if we did not know what sight or hearing is, we would hardly be counselors or physicians worth mentioning concerning eyes or ears, as to how someone might acquire sight or hearing "most beautifully" (189e7–190b1). Laches, more confident now than Nicias, perhaps, since the test concerns not who our teachers have been but what we know at firsthand about virtue, speaks first, saying that Socrates speaks truly (190b2).

It is an interesting start to the new inquiry and not only because of Socrates' use of *manthanein,* a word, as we have seen, associated with learning for oneself or study, which suggests that Socrates has taken on the role of teacher (see section 3.7; also *Euthydemus* 277d–278c). The first and most striking feature of Socrates' speech, however, is his analogy: Virtue is to the soul as vision is to the eye. If this be true, then virtue is found in some act or function (*ergon*) that is essential to and constitutive of whatever it is to be a human soul (compare *Republic* 352d–354a). In ordinary words, then, the analogy says that we need to understand what man or human life is *for,* what our purpose is, in order really to understand what human virtue or excellence is: anything less than that kind of teleological knowledge will leave us without the right standpoint from which to define human excellence or any of its "parts." Is human life for itself only, mere physical well-being and procreation? Or do we live for something greater, to rule and be victorious in the city's contests and thus to prove ourselves the best, as the gentlemen would have it? Or does one better spend these days on something small, such as inquiry and the pursuit of teachers of virtue and truth, as Socrates tells us? This is a fundamental matter that affects the whole inquiry and needs constantly to be brought back into view. The well-known Platonic doctrine that we cannot know what courage or prudence or any of the human virtues are unless we know what human life is for contrasts sharply with the modern understanding of ethical philosophy, which, in part at least, is founded on the premise that teleological knowledge of that kind is simply unavailable to human beings and that moral or ethical wisdom, such as we have it, is radically fragmented. Obviously, we must be at least sufficiently daring in our own inquiry to consider whether the inquiry by Socrates does not discover a truth in the ancient opinions, a truth not fragmented in that way, but whole and whole-making for those who can embrace and endure it.

In addition to this main point, the analogy raises a number of other suggestions, though it is not obvious what, if anything, we are to do with them. One is that virtue is somehow *natural,* the soul doctor's task not being one of putting something alien into souls that are innately blind but rather one of removing impediments to what is already there. Another is the model of *part and whole:* as the eye with its own good is part of the body, so perhaps the individual soul or man must be understood as part of the larger community, made to serve its needs. Related to this is the thought that virtue might consist in the sight or belief common to all, the *law* that makes courage not only a virtue but a duty.[6]

There are two other minor points to be noted about Socrates' introductory speech. First, there is the addition of hearing to sight toward the end. Might this suggest the distinction between seeing, that is, learning for yourself, and hearing or being persuaded by another? As we know, Laches sets great store both on what he knows for himself, through experience, and on what he hears from those whom he trusts. It will give away no secrets that Laches' ability to "see" what needs to be understood about virtue and human life will prove woefully deficient; the best Socrates can manage to do is to help him learn to "hear" it better. Finally, there is the barely noticeable shift from acquiring in the "easiest and best" way to acquiring sight or hearing in the "most noble or beautiful" manner. A very small point, this dropping of the "easiest" and "best" and replacing it with "finest." Yet is the alteration not entirely appropriate, if in the end what is to be possessed requires courage to achieve it? Are not the best things also the most difficult to obtain? Is not even the good better when it is harder?[7]

Socrates continues, with Laches now as his interlocutor (190b3–e3). He asks, and Laches agrees that they must know what virtue is, for if they didn't know that at all, how could they be counselors as to how to acquire it in the finest manner? Prompted further, Laches is willing to claim that they know what virtue is, and since they do know, can state what it is. But Socrates suggests that they not try to examine the "whole" of virtue, since that would perhaps be too much for them. Rather they should look into some "part" of virtue, which would make the inquiry "easier," and Laches agrees. But since the many opine that *hoplomachia* aims at making the virtue of courage to be in the souls of the young, presumably that is where they should begin. So first they will try to say what *andreia* is, and then later ask how to make it present in young men—at least to the extent that it is dependent on exercises and study, rather than on nature. So what then, Socrates asks Laches, is courage?

Our complete view of this exchange and its place in the dialogue depends on which account of the formal structure of the *Laches* we accept (for the possibilities, see section 2.5). But whichever it is, the substantive results of the discussion are to redefine the methodology of the inquiry and to change its object. Concerning the methodology, Socrates has narrowed the criteria for possessing the art of treating souls. Without objection from Laches, he has ruled that it is no longer sufficient to possess the knack of producing good products. One must know the object of the art, know what it is that one is trying to bring about in the young men, as well as be able to do it (compare *Gorgias* 462b–465e, 500e–501b; *Phaedrus* 260e). The first kind of knowledge Socrates calls *eidenai*, "to grasp the form of the thing," and the test for knowing "what it is" is whether or not one can "give an account" (*didonai logon*) of it. Laches does not appreciate the possible complexity of this demand, seems not to realize that the physician's knowledge of sight may be very different from that of the patient, who could describe his experience of it but might know nothing of its nature. The second result of the discussion preliminary to the inquiry proper is to determine a new object of inquiry, the part of virtue that is identical with courage. Both steps in Socrates' procedure call for some comment.

First of all, his dialectical question, What is it? for an account of virtue or its parts must be distinguished from the kind of search for an account that the sophist Prodicus would make. We cannot here consider in detail the nature of the Socratic question or the kind of inquiry Socrates pursues; that, at any rate, will be discovered as we continue.[8] But we can distinguish the kind of analysis Prodicus would make in seeking to define courage from the kind Socrates carries out. Prodicus would consider various possible examples of courage, how it appears to one man or city and how to another, and he would attempt to become precise about important distinctions between the different kinds of ways "courage" is used, with the aim, in part, of identifying a correct usage that could be agreed upon, such as the distinction that Nicias makes later in the inquiry between unreasoning boldness and foresightful courage (197b). Socrates, too, will consider various different examples of courage in the attempt to fix its proper meaning. But the Socratic search is not for what "we ancient Greeks" mean, or how we use the word. Socrates' search is first of all about what "you," his interlocutor, means by courage, the understanding you attribute to the word in the light of your belief that you in fact have experienced and possess the virtue in question. Thus the Socratic search for a definition typically begins with someone who can make some valid claim to possessing the virtue in question—Laches courage, Charmides moderation, Cephalus justice, Euthyphro piety, Lysis friendship—at least by the conventional standards of Greek society. The problem that Socrates is concerned with, however, is that those standards are not enough. Those standards have become sufficiently questionable that "we" do not know if the old virtues are still our best guides to living a good life. The problem that Socrates is concerned with is the problem of whether or not there is some essence that we can discover that will enlighten us not just concerning what we mean by courage, but concerning what we ought to mean and how we ought to conceive of human life, what it is to live excellently, which presumably will include what it is to live courageously. Not until we know that will we have come to the end of the Socratic inquiry, though of course much less than that will suffice for conceptual analysis such as Prodicus engaged in. But is not the latter at best a preliminary to, rather than a form of, genuine philosophical inquiry?

The other main step taken by Socrates in the introduction to the inquiry is to select the part of virtue they are to consider (190c8–d8). Given that Laches has earlier used *aretē* synonymously with courage (189b5), it is understandable that Socrates would hint that virtue as a whole is too much for them. It is also interesting to note that the opinion of "the many" influences the selection; perhaps "the few" would begin with another part of virtue, to learn what is best for young souls (such as wisdom). But the most important aspect of this decision is that of raising another question, one that will dog the inquiry that follows. Since Socrates has just given Laches and Nicias a model for understanding virtue, that it stands to the soul as vision to the eye, how is that model of the whole of virtue to be understood in relation to its parts, especially courage? Above all, if virtue is divided into parts, can the soul also be divided into parts, and if so, what part of the soul does courage perfect? Plato's ancient and modern readers all know that Socrates teaches in the *Republic* that the soul is divided into parts, and the central part, the spirited element or *thymos*, is the part of the soul in which courage resides and which courage perfects. Will this doctrine, or some influence of it, be found in the *Laches*, and if so, does it contribute to a genuine understanding of courage? Both Laches and Nicias appear to be spirited men, though perhaps in very different ways. As it turns out, the word *thymos* never appears, even once, in our dialogue. But this does not mean, as we shall see, that the *Laches* does not have something to teach us about courage and the spirited part of the soul.

4.3 Laches Gives His Definition and Socrates Responds (190e–191c)

Laches responds quickly to Socrates' question, starting with a manly oath, his first of five, the second of seven, all told, in the dialogue.[9] "By Zeus," he says, "that's not hard. If someone is willing to remain in the ranks and ward off the enemies and not run, you know he is courageous" (190e4–6). Socrates then blames himself for this answer, restates Laches' definition, omitting two key elements and changing a third, and offers three examples that purport to refute it (190e7–191c6). Before considering what Socrates has to say, let us examine the definition itself.

By Laches' definition, the courageous man (1) "is willing;" (2) "to stand in the ranks and ward off the enemy;" (3) "and not run." These three components point to three different aspects of the act of exemplary courage. First of all, the courageous man chooses his action freely, as a matter of honor and duty. His distinctively civic willingness contrasts to the unwillingness of other men who fight only because they are coerced, like the Persians driven by the whip and fear of the eye of the king, or like mercenaries who fight for money and run when their confidence in winning is gone (see Herodotus, *Persian Wars* 7.104, 8.86, 90; *Nicomachean Ethics* 3.8).[10] Second, the courageous man "stands and wards off the enemy," which means that he thrusts himself into a violent public action in which he is fighting for the freedom and welfare of the city. This action cannot be understood without reference to the *taxis*, or battle line order, in which he is fighting together with others: he does not just stand, he holds the position to which he has been ordered by his commander (compare *Apology* 28d, 29b). Nor can it be understood without reference to the other men—the enemies—with whom he is fighting; it is a struggle for dominance.[11] Third, the courageous man "does not run," that is, he does not succumb to the natural fear that each man is prey to when he runs the most terrible of risks, the fear of violent death and the end to his human existence.

Laches' definition represents nothing less than the basic, traditional Greek conception of patriotic or political courage (see *Nicomachean Ethics* 3.8). This fact has not been sufficiently appreciated in the scholarly literature.[12] Thus Laches' definition is found, almost word for word, in Tyrtaeus' ancient Spartan war songs: "This is prowess (*aretē*) . . . when a man standeth firm in the forefront without ceasing, making heart and soul to abide, forgetteth shameful flight altogether and hearteneth by his words him who standeth by" (*Poems*, number 12, lines 13–19).[13] The same conception is adopted by Theognis, who condenses the idea into "standing firm in the forefront" (*Poems* 1. 1003–6).[14] We run the risk of seriously misunderstanding the *Laches*, if we do not appreciate the classic character of this first definition, and the fact that it refers not only to behavior (discussed at 191a–d), but to will or emotional control (discussed at 191d–192b), as well as to intellect or rational motivation (discussed at 193a–d). This is not to say that Laches understands his own conception of manly virtue or courage sufficiently; a significant part of Socrates' task as his teacher in this dialogue will be to bring Laches to a better understanding of what civic courage and duty really involve. It is only to say that we as Plato's readers, if we are to read the text beneath the text, must not be taken in by Laches' (or later, Nicias') failure to know what he is talking about.

At this juncture, we can see what a difficult task Socrates is facing when he begins to examine Laches' definition. On the individual level, it states Laches' real belief about courage, the truth as it conforms to his own experience, the nature of courage insofar as he claims it as his own. How can Socrates possibly take this away from him? Will it not be like trying to convince a U.S. marine that *Semper Fi* is nonsense? And insofar as this definition presents the classic ancient conception of citizen war courage, the Spartan ideal of civic spiritedness, the manly physical courage of the ancient he-man (*anēr*), the quality the Romans called *virtus*, it seems truly irrefutable. How can this idea of courage, hallowed by tradition and the blood of thousands of men who died believing in it, be wrong?[15] But as we have suggested, to prove this wrong perhaps is not Socrates' intention. Possibly he does not intend simply to refute this conception but to probe it, understand it better, discover its strengths and weaknesses. Then he will indeed wish to examine the different aspects of the traditional understanding in relation to voluntary action, habits of the emotions and will, and the operation of practical reason in conduct. In fact, as we shall see, Laches' notion of courage, rightly understood, might prove to be one form of what it means to be courageous. It is, after all, much like the one used by Socrates himself in defending his seemingly obstinate stand at his trial (*Apology* 28e–29b). But now let us return to the dialogue.

Socrates begins gingerly, careful to emphasize that Laches has spoken well and that the "blame" for this answer falls on himself, this latter remark puzzling Laches (190e7–10). Socrates wishes to move Laches from his present position, but if he is not careful Laches will simply dig in and refuse to listen. (Surely Laches has not forgotten the forensic aspect of the inquiry.) Indeed, we can see in the action of the drama from 190e–191d a kind of doxological mime, insofar as it enacts something like what Socrates says the Spartans did at Plataea: when he approaches Laches' position, it is tightly drawn, so he retreats at first, opens it up slowly, then turns upon it and wins the victory. To open Laches' position, Socrates first must show him that warrior courage, even when strictly understood, involves more than Laches has indicated. He does this by means of three examples, the first two being drawn from barbarian warriors, the last from the manly Greek men Laches so admires, the Spartans (191a1–c6). Like Laches' definition, these examples have been largely misunderstood in the scholarly literature on the dialogue.[16] (An excellent commentary on the passage, however, may be found in Montaigne's essay "On Constancy.")[17] On one level, they are what they seem: focused on the behavior that corresponds to Laches' notion of courage, they intend to show Laches that courage also can be expressed in other kinds of action. At a deeper level, they introduce what one may call *the* philosophical theme of the *Laches,* the relationship between courage and intelligence, and hint at another important and related theme, that of the relationship between boldness and endurance in courage. On this deeper level, Socrates' examples prefigure the argument of the entire first half of the inquiry.

Socrates begins inconspicuously to attack Laches' position by simplifying his definition in the manner indicated above, dropping "willing" and "not running" and altering "ward off," so as to say Laches calls courageous the man who "standing in the ranks fights the enemy" (191a1–3). Laches replies that he does say that, and Socrates asserts that he does, too, but what of the other man, who fights the enemy fleeing (*pheugōn*), not standing? (191a5–6) This naturally confuses Laches, since the Greek word *pheugōn* tends to mean impulsive flight, not controlled retreat, and he asks how that could be? Laches may also be remembering Socrates' courage in the retreat from Delium, though Socrates tactfully never mentions that episode here. Instead, he draws Laches' attention first to the manner of fighting of the Scythians, the famous horsemen and nomadic warriors of central Asia who like the Greeks also defeated Darius (see *Persian Wars* 4.97–102, 118–42), and then to the authoritative poet Homer, who praises Aeneas' horses that they "know to pursue and flee very swiftly hither and thither," and who praises Aeneas himself for this knowledge of fear, calling him a "counselor of fright" (191a8–b3).

These examples are interesting. For the Scythians exemplify in Herodotus not just a manner of behavior in battle, but a manner of clever or wise fighting, since they do battle only when they chose, under circumstances conducive to their victory (see *Persian Wars* 4.127). Furthermore, the Scythians are the exemplary representatives in Herodotus of the barbarian manner of freedom and boldness (see 4.126–28, 142; also 62–66). Temperamentally, they have that characteristic boldness, daring, and dash of cavalrymen, as if they had taken into themselves the quick, restless, irritable humors of the horses they tame. This quality of bold quickness to seize an opportunity is missing from Laches' definition, which emphasizes enduring defense rather than daring attack, but boldness is, as the dialogue will make abundantly clear, an essential aspect of war courage, and in fact it was the dominant aspect of Athenian courage (see *Persian Wars* 6.112–13, 9.26–27; Thucydides, *Peloponnesian War* 1.70, 7.21). Socrates already is hinting at something the traditional understanding of courage does not appreciate sufficiently (partly because it is oriented to the courage of the troops, rather than the commander).

The second and central example of the three is even more suggestive. The reference concerning the horses' knowledge is to two passages in the *Iliad*, 5.222–23 and 8.106–7, the reference to Aeneas himself to 8.108. These passages contrast two decisions by Diomedes, in the first of which he defies fear, takes a stand, and defeats Aeneas (thereby winning the horses), in the second of which he obeys the prudent Nestor's advice to retreat before Hector, though his heart is torn at the shame of it.[18] Were Diomedes not predisposed to "take a stand," his willingness to obey military wisdom would be meaningless. Furthermore, the example presents us with the idea of two different kinds of courage, the obedient kind possessed by the horses and the commanding kind possessed by the charioteer, and it suggests the very model of the relationship between the reasoning and the bold and enduring parts of the human soul that Socrates will take up next. For what Aeneas' horses know is how to obey: they respond to the guiding reins of their master rather than to the terrors of the immediate sensory environment. What the charioteer knows is where they should carry him: into battle, to stand boldly and risk his life against the enemy, to win the victory (unless there is no hope of victory and retreat is the only sensible thing to do). Again Socrates appears to have done much more than merely introduce a different kind of courageous behavior; he seems to have suggested a basic pattern for understanding the operation of courage in the human soul, even if the relationship between a man and his emotions proves more complex than that between a charioteer and his horses.[19]

Laches accepts Socrates' first two examples, noting that they present the mode of cavalry fighting, whereas he was talking about hoplite fighting (191b4–7). (We might similarly compare the courage of the fighter pilot to that of the combat infantryman.) But this does not seem to disturb him. Why not? The answer would seem to lie in the historical associations of these different kinds of fighting for the ancient Greek. Sea warfare aside, the armored infantry dominated the ancient battlefield until the great Roman defeat at Adrianople by massed Gothic horsemen. Infantry warfare placed a premium on the collective discipline of the men in the ranks and on the ability of those men to endure the terrible, if relatively brief, violent clash of the opposing spearmen forming the battle lines. By contrast, the cavalry sought to attack opportunely, avoid a prolonged struggle unto death, and win by speed and skill. (In this way it was similar to sea fighting.) The Greeks attributed the latter, individual kind of fighting, to the barbarians, whose boldness they did not deny, but the Greeks thought such courage vastly inferior to the kind of fighting courage needed by the hoplite in the ranks, which did not permit the excuse to run away. (See Brasidas' statement of this traditional opinion in Thucydides, *Peloponnesian War* 4.126–27.) To a man such as Laches, cavalry courage is indeed one form of courage, but it cannot be compared to Greek, civic, hoplite courage—to real courage and manliness. But then Socrates turns and really surprises him by citing the conduct of his beloved Spartans in their greatest victory, in Herodotus' explicit words the greatest victory of all time, their defeat of the Persians at Plataea in the battle that ended the war and preserved Greek freedom (191b8–c5). Did the Lacedaemonians not flee at first from the men with the wicker shields, and only then, when the Persians' ranks were broken, turn around to fight like horsemen and thus win the victory? A stunned Laches can only respond: What you say is true.

This example is the most interesting of all. But again, if we are as unmusical as Laches, we will not see its deeper aspect. For the story of the Greek victory at Plataea, as Herodotus solemnly tells it, is a Keystone Kops calamity, centered on the wonderfully Spartan pigheadedness of one Amompharetus, and on the wonderfully Spartan churlishness of one Pausanias, who was as chickenhearted a hero as any in Greek history. The point made in the story of Amompharetus (*Persian Wars* 9.53–57) is the same as that suggested by the story of Diomedes, namely that there is an implicit conflict between devotion to the manly ideal of standing up to danger and not running from a fight, and the equally important military ideal of obeying one's commander, whatever he commands. As for Pausanias, not only did he show anything but classic Spartan resolve in his willingness to battle the Persians (see 9.46–48), he called out frantically to the Athenians for aid when the Persians attacked, and at any event almost waited too long before leading the Spartans in victorious attack (9.61–62).[20] The courage of a commander who is only willing to stand and fight when he can no longer flee hardly seems a good example to prove Socrates' point![21]

The third example, then, must be something other than merely a counter to Laches' definition. For it does not fit the Spartan conduct at Plataea very well, and Plato surely knew that. However, Socrates' description of the Spartan mode of cavalry fighting does fit quite precisely Herodotus' account of the Lacedaemonian conduct at Thermopylae under Leonidas, where he says the Spartans proved their skill by employing this very technique of battle (*Persian Wars* 7.71). Can we really suppose that Plato confused these two episodes in his mind? Of course not. The point of this example, no less than that of the others, is not only the one Socrates explicitly makes with it. What the examples show more significantly is that despite Socrates' objections to an overly rigid conception of the action of courage as "taking a stand," *this willingness is essential to courage wherever it is found.* The willingness of Leonidas and the Spartans to stand and die at Thermopylae was for the ancient Greeks and is for all time a living symbol of manly courage and freedom and dignity, a victory that cannot be compared, except by the grossest of spirits, with the sordid affair at Plataea (see 7.208–10 especially the closing lines of 210). Indeed, seen this way, Herodotus' whole account of Greek courage in standing up to the almost overwhelming Persian invasion is a testimony to the truth of Laches' definition, the truth of civic courage. But the other aspect of the third example is important too: The Greek victories over the barbarians were not owing merely to their superior civic courage, but to their superior discipline in battle and their superior skill and knowledge (see 8.86 and 9.62–63). For the Greeks, but not for the barbarians (or Spartan dolts like Amompharetus), intelligence entered into and shaped the very form in which they exhibited their courage, just as the willingness with which they went to battle was shaped by the freedom they knew they were fighting for. The Greeks who won at Marathon and Salamis and Thermopylae did not disdain science, for they kept their minds focused not on glory but on victory, nor did they fall short in courage. The two went perfectly together. But what will be the story in our dialogue? Will Laches and Nicias prove to be like those great heroes, or more like Amompharetus and Pausanias?

4.4 Socrates Explains the Kinds of Courage He Has in Mind (191c–e)

Socrates proceeds to sweep away Laches' defenses, though again not without emphasizing that he was himself to blame for Laches' failure to answer well, since he himself did not question well (191c7–8). What he wanted to question Laches about was not simply the courageous (1) in hoplite fighting, but also (2) in cavalry, and (3) in the entire warrior form (*eidos*), and not only those in war but also (4) those courageous in the dangers at sea, and those courageous toward (5) poverty or (6) sickness or (7) even politics, and further not only those courageous toward pains or fears but also those who are terribly clever (*deinoi*) fighting against desires or pleasures, whether by standing and enduring them or by deliberately turning against them to defeat them (191c8–e3). Despite the seemingly vast difference between what Laches and Socrates have in mind when they think of courage, Laches, we are puzzled to note, agrees emphatically: "Very much so, Socrates." Socrates then says that all these are courageous, but (1) some possess it in pleasures, (2) some in pains, (3) some in desires, (4) some in fears, and others are cowardly in these things— and again Laches agrees. So what then is it, which is the same in all of these? But Laches does not yet understand (*manthaneis*) the question (191e4–12).

This part of the dialogue has attracted considerable attention in contemporary scholarly literature, and it is not difficult to see why. For Socrates may seem to be broadening the range of actions to be considered courageous in such a way as to conceive of courage as a universal human virtue, relevant to noncitizens and citizens, slaves and freemen, women and men (compare the discussion in section 3.6 of Socrates' remarks at 186b).[22] This would indeed involve a radical transformation of the concept of manly courage and point the way to a new understanding of virtue and of human nature. We should realize, however, that such a step might not have been regarded as admirable by the ancient reader, for on the one hand such an inquiry would question the order of justice in Athenian society and thus might corrupt the young who heard it. On the other hand, the very idea of a universal human nature might seem mistaken, a failure to acknowledge the innate and essential differences among human beings that correspond to different arenas of activity in a well-ordered society.

In addition to broadening the range of courageous actions, Socrates may also seem to be relocating the zone of conflict of virtue, taking it from the public battlefield and placing it within the privacy of each soul, reenvisioning the enemy not as the opposing soldier but as the passion that from within urges this soul to do what he does not want to do. This would also involve a radical transformation of the traditional Greek conception of courage, if only because the idea of courage as inner self-control is apolitical. To a medieval Christian or modern reader, it might, of course, seem that there was no reason why a slave could not be courageous, but this would have made no more sense to most ancient Greeks than the notion that a virtuous woman might be manly. Furthermore, this conception appears to overextend the range of courage and blur the distinction between it and moderation or self-control.[23] If the Socratic conception of courage is indeed the one presented at 191c–e, it would seem to be very different not only from what the ancient Greeks but even from what many modern readers mean by courage.

On the view being presented here, however, Socrates is *not* introducing a radically new conception of courage. This cannot be taken to mean that he is not pointing out aspects of the traditional understanding that General Laches tends to forget, or that he is not emphasizing a feature of the traditional understanding that Laches has left out of his definition. He does both, yet he is not radically transforming the traditional conception of courage at 191c–e. Critics have made too much of the so-called broadening of the kinds of actions that may be considered courageous and have clearly misunderstood the import of his placing the virtue within the soul. Let us look again at the text.

There are three main points to consider. First, does Socrates radically transform the traditional concept of manly courage by introducing at 191c–e a whole new set of situations involving actions in which courage may be manifested? Second, does Socrates radically transform this concept again at 191d, by reinterpreting courage as emotional self-control? Finally, does Socrates not confuse courage with moderation or self-control at 191e, by suggesting that it is courageous to fight against pleasure and desire no less than to endure or fight pain and fear?

Our answer to the first of these questions is no. The text makes it clear that Socrates thinks courage can also be expressed elsewhere than on the battlefield, but it does not support the conclusion that he thinks of courage as a "universal human virtue."[24] We might wish to think that Socrates was wise enough to know that all humans need to face life and death, need faith and courage, but the *Laches* will not confirm this hope. It only tells us that Socrates seems to believe that in addition to the competitive, masculine, warrior form, courage can also be manifested by standing up to the fear of drowning, or the pain of disease, or the travail of poverty, or political dishonor. And this is by no means a radical extension of the traditional concept, for the ancient Greeks realized no less than we do today that a man needs courage in order to endure such hardships or evil turns of fortune.[25] However, if Socrates were to assert at 191c–e that these situations are as important a test of manly courage as the test of battle—if he were to say that Laches' definition did not point to the premier or essential test and manifestation of courage—then he would be transforming the traditional notion in a way that his fellow citizens would not have approved. But he does not say that, and in fact he can be inferred to suggest otherwise. It is interesting, relative to this question, that the first and only time the Platonic term *eidos* is used in the *Laches* is in reference to the warrior "form" of courage. Might this be a sign that that form represents more fully the essence of courage than the self-respecting endurance that stands up to the dangers at sea, or sickness or poverty or political defeat?[26] Be this as it may, the broadened list of actions that can manifest courage (191c) does not prove that Socrates is radically widening the traditional concept. It only proves that he is pointing out other kinds of actions that can manifest courage—even if they are complementary to its most shining expression—kinds of actions that Laches himself must acknowledge he has not considered.[27]

Thus it becomes all the more important to assess Socrates' second so-called transformation of the traditional notion, his apparent installing of the virtue in the soul. Certainly, if the idea of courage as involving an internal movement of the soul were something entirely new to Socrates—as most commentators on the dialogue seem to think—then Laches would be confronted with a conception of that virtue utterly alien and indeed repellent to him. But nothing like this is true at all. Socrates is still teaching Laches about the conception of courage that the latter believes in. As we have seen, even Tyrtaeus, writing for unmusical Spartans, sings of manly courage not simply as "standing firm in the forefront of the battle line without ceasing" but also as "making heart and soul to abide" (*psychēn kai thymon tlēmona parthemenos*); and the conservative Greek tradition represented here by Laches understood the *gnōmē* underlying courage in action as "resolve" or "fighting spiritedness" (see the discussions in sections 1.6, 3.3, 3.4). Furthermore, the model of courage as involving a struggle and dialogue between soul or mind and heart already had its classic expression in Homer, the foundation of all Greek *paideia* (see especially *Iliad* 9.401–10; *Odyssey* 20.9–24). We shall examine these paradigmatic ancient Greek accounts of the inner workings of courage in the next section. But the point here is that there is nothing new in the idea that courage involves an interior struggle or that it requires a model of the soul in which self-conflict and self-debate occur; it is an essential part of both the old tradition and the old idea. This is not to say that Socrates will not identify again the things that seem to be missing in the traditional model and conception. Nor is it to say that by leading Laches to define courage at 192b in terms of endurance, Socrates does not call attention, in a way that a man such as Laches may tend to forget, to the ultimately solitary nature of human decisions and of the human soul.[28]

Finally, there is the double question of the relation of *andreia* to matters of pleasure and appetite, and of whether Socrates is guilty of widening the concept too far. In fact, if he *is* guilty of the charge, Laches should not agree so emphatically at 191e3 to what Socrates says. But this puzzle has a simple answer, one having to do with the different connotations of *andreia* and the modern conception of courage. For Laches, manliness, though fully expressed only in the actions of war, naturally includes a whole set of other physical and mental habits without which the citizen-soldier would be incapable of fighting bravely and would lack the willingness to do his duty, if only because of physical and emotional exhaustion. This intrinsic relationship between manly courage and endurance is pictured already in the figure of Paris in the *Iliad,* and it is a point made several times in Herodotus (see *Persian Wars* 1.155, 6.11–17, 7.102; compare also *Republic* 556b–d; *Phaedrus* 239c–d; *Symposium* 219d–220b). Hence from the conventional ancient Greek point of view, there is nothing unusual about Laches' emphatic agreement that manliness does involve physical discipline in regard to pleasures and desires. The man who is effeminate, or pleasure- or money-loving, or self-indulgent or lazy, or the like simply cannot be a citizen-warrior; he would not have the will to persevere in the violent work of hoplite warfare.[29]

Even so, we might still think that there is a problem here. Does not Socrates confuse moderation and courage when he speaks of "clever fighters" against pleasure and desire (191d) and when he seems to treat as equals all four kinds of habits of courage (191e)? This is a complex matter, but it is instructive that Socrates does not provide any examples of voluntary actions corresponding to courage in pleasures and desires, as he does the seven kinds of voluntary actions corresponding to courage in pains and fears. Of course the reader might view this as a merely accidental omission on Plato's part, but it seems wiser to continue to apply the "law of logographic necessity" to Plato's writing (see section 2.1). Then this omission, together with what Laches says later about courage and prudence (193a–d), suggests that neither he nor Socrates would want to assert that "cowardice" was expressed in, say, the decision to get drunk, or the decision to while away the afternoon in bed, but rather that moderation or self-control corresponds to these kinds of actions. How, then, is the psychological conception tendered at 191c–e to be understood in relation to these actions? On this view a courage-like quality is to be found in the *movements of the soul* that involve the firm control of passions, the enduring restraint of appetites and their corresponding pains of frustration or fears of loss, no less than the endurance of ordinary pain and restraint of ordinary fear. But courage as a virtue of choice is expressed only in *rational actions* having to do with danger and suffering, not temptation and pleasure.[30] We will need to see, as we continue reading the *Laches,* if this interpretation is not consistent with what follows.

The interpretation that has been given of 191c–e is at any rate consistent with the other puzzling detail generally overlooked, the distinction between the two modes of operation that courage employs, for the "clever fighters" would seem to be not only restraining and enduring their unwilled appetites or fears but also deliberately training them—training themselves—so as to weaken their power and gain the victory in time over unwilled emotional habits. Consider, for example, a woman who "courageously," as we say, overcomes her addiction to smoking. It is only in relation to her will that we say it is courageous for her not to take a proffered cigarette. The rational habit of choice she now has is a habit of self-control in these situations; it is supported by, but not to be confused with, a quality of courage, or better, "fortitude" (the term we will use to describe Laches' second account). On this view, Socrates would be suggesting that a fully adequate understanding of courage not only must pay attention to its expression in action, but also must pay attention to the struggle in the soul, to the role of the will and inner courage in relation to the coming into being of moderation and all acts of self-restraint from temptation. But if this interpretation is correct, he is not confusing the operation of courage and the operation of moderation or self-control, because he realizes that human action, as the expression of rational choice, involves not only the will and the emotions, but also the intellect and action. In choosing not to take that cigarette, the woman in our example is choosing to do the moderate thing; she is choosing to be moderate or self-controlled, not brave. It takes a kind of courage to do it, but it is not an act of courage. Does this blur the distinction between courage and moderation, or not rather get that distinction just right?

4.5 Laches' Account of Courage as "Fortitude of Soul" (191e–192b)

Laches is slow to respond, for he still does not understand what Socrates has in mind. We can appreciate why this might be so. Laches knew what he was talking about at the start: the universally accepted ideal of civic courage and manliness. But Socrates has led him to agree that manliness is present in many ways in the soul, and it is not at all clear how these struggles of the soul are related to what, for Laches, must remain the true test of being a man, the willingness to stand in the battle line.

Socrates helps Laches to discover what he, Socrates, has in mind by giving an example (192a1–b8). It is as if Socrates had asked what quickness is, which exists in running and cithera playing, and speaking and learning, and many other things, and we possess it pretty much in the actions of the hands or legs or mouth and voice or thought. If someone asked Socrates, What is quickness? he would answer that it is the power (*dynamis*) of accomplishing much in a little time, whether in voice or in a race or in all the others. So now Laches should tell Socrates what power it is, the same in pleasure or pain or in all the other things they were saying it exists in, that is called courage? To this Laches responds that in his opinion it is "a certain fortitude of soul" (*karteria tis . . . tēs psychēs*), if he should say what it is by nature (*physikos*) in all of them (192b9–c1). Indeed he should, Socrates replies, if we are to answer what was asked of us. But Socrates will soon go on to prove that the power that Laches here literally calls a kind of "strength" or "hardiness" of the soul is both more and less than what he means by "courage."

Socrates' example of quickness illustrates once more the conviction that there is a text beneath the text in the *Laches*. Superficially, he is merely offering an example to teach Laches how to form the general concept that applies to each of the habits listed at 191e. Just as the abstract quality of quickness is found in speaking or running, although these are not the same and the person quick in one might not be in the other, so it would seem possible that the same person might have the abstract quality of fortitude in pleasures (manly versus effeminate) but not in pains (soft versus tough), or in desires (self-possessed versus self-yielding) but not in fears (easily frightened versus unshakeable). If there is a power by which we come to acquire the virtues in each of these habits of feeling and will, that power would seem to be a kind of "strength of the soul," an inner ability to resist the power of these passions to move the person to action that is contrary to his will, the power to retain the capacity for self-rule and self-motion despite circumstances that flood the mind with blinding emotions. On the surface, the illustration is fine, and Laches seems to have learned his lesson well.

When we examine the example more carefully, we realize that Socrates is ignoring the distinction here between mere quickness or slowness in motion and quickness or slowness in accomplishment, in action (compare *Charmides* 160b).[31] Socrates is able surreptitiously to ignore this distinction by using the word "accomplish" (*diaprattomenēn,* 192b1) and quietly dropping the examples of playing music and learning as opposed to the more physical activities of running and voice. But obviously, quickness and slowness do not stand alone as measures of things to be accomplished, unless it is a footrace (even there one must run in the right direction!); there is virtue in goal-attaining quickness or virtuosity, but not in the impatient quickness that in music and learning or understanding and everything else so often misses the mark. Socrates will soon go on to make a similar point with Laches, arguing that mere endurance or fortitude is not enough; what one wants is intelligent fortitude, directed to the right goal.

A second interesting feature of Socrates' example comes to light when we ask why, of all possible examples, he chose quickness to illustrate his point.[32] The answer seems to be that quickness is associated with boldness and decisiveness, the ability or inclination to seize an opportunity, to wade in and attack, if sometimes rashly, just as slowness may be associated negatively with overcaution or indecisiveness, the inclination always to wait to see things more clearly, before doing anything at all, or positively, with the absence of unthinking, undeliberate rashness. These distinctions suggest the kind of approach to the virtue of courage that we find in Aristotle, when he speaks of it as hitting the "mean" between its opposites (see *Nicomachean Ethics* 2.7, 3.7), that is, between rashness (too quick to move oneself) and cowardice (unresisting to being moved by another). In fact, Socrates may even be hinting here at the complex notion of the mean that Nicolai Hartmann found in Aristotle, the idea that courage lies not only in the mean between mere daring and overcaution, but also in that between obstinacy and lack of will to resist.[33] For if quickness and slowness embody different modes of motion analogous to daring and its absence, then immovability or gravity and nonresistance or lightweightedness seem to be the corresponding analogies to the presence and absence of endurance.[34] At any rate, if courage itself is opposed not only to undue flight but also to undue attack, the full account of courage must include not only the ability to resist movement but also the ability to swiftly bring it about. So again something may be missing from Laches' account of the natural power that underlies courage insofar as it includes the full warrior-*eidos* sense of the term. Courage must consist in something more than mere wise or prudent endurance and the power not to be emotionally dislodged; it must also involve the will to attack boldly and win the victory, and the power to move swiftly toward its object.

Now let us place Laches' account of the inner operation of courage in historical context. We recall that the idea that manly courage involves a struggle and dialogue between heart and soul or mind is found in the Greek tradition from the beginning, in the classic statement of Tyrtaeus, "Making heart and soul abide," in the Spartan, conservative tradition that identified courage with *gnōmē* in the sense of "resolve" or "fighting spiritedness," and in the source, Homer. The classic Homeric passages both involve Odysseus.[35] In the first scene, Diomedes has been wounded by an arrow, and Odysseus is left alone to fight the Trojans. He speaks then to his own "great-hearted spirit" as follows: "Ah me, what will become of me? It will be a great evil if I run, fearing their multitude, yet deadlier if I am caught alone, and Kronos' son drove to flight the rest of the Danaans. Yet still, why does the heart within me debate these things? Since I know it is the cowards who walk out of the fighting, but if one is to win honor in battle, he must by all means stand his ground strongly, whether he be struck or strike down another" (11.404–10).

The model of human choice presented here does not merely contrast reason with passion, but includes all three parts of the soul that are identified by Socrates in *Republic* 4: (1) the desires or passions, which urge him to immediate pursuit or flight; (2) practical reason, which articulates the goods at stake in the situation and attempts to persuade the whole man of what is best for him; and (3) "spirit" or what we might call "ego" or "will," which must be persuaded by his mind to adopt a course of action, suppress contrary emotions, and execute his intention.[36] Note that the example illustrates the distinction between the substantive aspect of manly courage, its determinate orientation to certain objects, and the formal aspect of manliness, the capacity to act in accordance with rational purpose. The mind of a person such as Paris, whose manliness of will has been habitually weakened, counsels him differently from the way the minds of men such as Diomedes and Odysseus counsel them.

The second classic example of manly endurance in Homer is found at *Odyssey* 20.9–21. Odysseus has just been seized with rage at the traitorous conduct of the servant-women in the household: "The spirit (*thymos*) deep in the heart of Odysseus was stirred by this, and much he pondered in the division of mind and spirit, whether to spring on them and kill each one, or instead to let them lie this one more time with the insolent suitors, for the last and latest time; but the heart was growling within him. And as a bitch, facing an unknown man, stands over her callow puppies, and growls and rages to fight, so Odysseus' heart was growling inside him as he looked on those wicked actions. He struck himself on the chest and spoke to his heart and scolded it: 'Bear up, my heart. You have had worse to endure before this on that day when the irresistible Cyclops ate up my strong companions, but you endured it until intelligence got you out of the cave, though you expected to perish.'" Homer goes on to tell us that Odysseus' heart "in great obedience endured and stood it without complaint" but that "the man himself" was twisting and turning with anger and thoughts of revenge (20.23–30).

In this instance, it is Odysseus' spirit that must be restrained from the act of punishment that, moved by anger, it wants to inflict on the servants, and it is also Odysseus' spirit that must endure, or restrain itself from action, guided by his mind. As in the action in the *Iliad*, the spirit or heart must assent to the persuasive voice of reason, but whereas the action in the *Iliad* involves his heart enduring its fear and his mind recognizing the cowardice of flight and the principle of honor he should act upon (the "whip"), in the *Odyssey* the action involves his heart restraining its anger and his mind "bridling" it by reminding it of a previous experience in which, guided by intelligence, it too was saved. Thus the heart or spirit would appear to be moved by perceived self-interest, but self-interest in the broader sense of the term, a sense that includes preservation of loved ones and of pride, the self that is essentially social or political as well as physical. It is the task of reason to make the heart and the whole man aware of this broader self-interest so that he will constrain his impulsive passion and act in accordance with his will. The human freedom of the will, that a later age made a bare metaphysical property, is for Plato essentially related not only to man's rational nature or power of mind, but also to his social or political nature, to the attachments of the spirited ego to the things we care for as our own, particularly our loved ones and our standing in the human community.

The two passages cited above are *the* paradigmatic secular examples of the operation of the soul in controlling the passions of *thymos* in the ancient Greek tradition.[37] We must understand the second account of courage in the *Laches* in relation to them. Just as the citizen-warrior in Homer and Tyrtaeus and Herodotus was the common ancient Greek model of the virtue whereby the community preserved its freedom against external enslavement, so Homer's "much-enduring" Odysseus was the common Greek model of the man with "strength of soul"—the man who preserved his freedom of will against wayward passions of fear and anger, the man who by the end of his pilgrim sea journey never lets his emotion, be it anger or fear, hunger or lust, or pride or even love deflect him from what his intelligence says is best: his home, his wife, his kingdom. What underlies and preserves Odysseus' resourceful mind's power to guide him well is his "much-enduring" spirit or heart, the power within him that must assent to the guide of reason and with that assent empower Odysseus, the whole man, to act. It is this underlying, empowering ability and resolve to hear the voice of reason or honor and to turn against his own enemy emotions and thereby restrengthen his will and moral self-certainty— this "Odyssean" characteristic—that Laches, however dimly, has in mind when he speaks of strength of soul as what is natural in the acquired habits of manly self-control. This is not to say that an Odysseus, exhausted by many dangers or overwhelmed by many temptations, cannot momentarily lose his fortitude and thereby his courage; he too can fall into panic, throw down his arms, and run (see *Iliad* 8.92–98). But the man of courageous principle and strength of soul soon recovers. The unenduring man who lacks strength of soul, by contrast, cannot preserve his intention of mind, but he all too typically abandons his will and thereby further weakens his power to act decisively in the world, his freedom. A man with *karteria tēs psychēs* will be strong-willed and enduring in adversity or pain, brave in danger, and self-possessed in his pleasures; but the person without it will be weak-willed or unenduring or cowardly or readily self-indulgent. Lacking inner constancy, he or she also will be prey to hypocrisy and self-deception. A person with no strength of soul would not even be recognizably human: its mind completely severed from the power of bodily self-motion, it would simply respond to immediate sensory stimuli by flight or pursuit, whatever the mind sought to direct. The thorough-going akratic would lack utterly the power of human action as we understand it, would be a pure Cartesian thinking thing. It could understand nothing of duty or purpose or self.[38]

It is now evident that Laches, together with Socrates, has arrived at two important insights in their inquiry on the nature of courage. First, he has identified the most obvious aspect of the traditional Greek understanding of courage, the idea of the kind of voluntary action in which it is manifested, courage in the battle line. Second, he has identified the less obvious aspect of that traditional understanding, the concept of the underlying power of the heart or will or spirited ego. In the form of "strength of soul" this enables the manly man to "make heart and soul abide" and do what he, the whole man and especially the citizen, knows is right. With Socrates' help, Laches has brought under scrutiny not only the visible or phenomenal aspect of the traditional civic idea of manly courage, but also the invisible or noumenal aspect, the ancient Greek model of self-mastery and freedom of the will. (This model of the soul and its freedom should also be examined, but such an inquiry is beyond Laches' capacity.) In bringing this hidden aspect of the traditional ideal into focus, Laches, guided by Socrates, has pointed to the human power that, *together with mind,* distinguishes us from the beasts. He has thus pointed to the very power of doing what it is one wills to do, as a matter of conscious desire or principle. (This is not merely doing what one desires; this power comes into view when one recognizes the possibility of doing out of desire and impulse what one does not will to desire and do.)

Despite this achievement, Laches' understanding of the operation of courage and of human freedom is profoundly incomplete. For one thing, he does not seem to understand that fortitude does not stand alone; that it exists only in relation to the guiding intelligence that must determine the goods to be achieved in action and that sometimes must persuade the whole man that those indeed *are* the goods he truly desires. Furthermore, Laches seems not to realize that the natural human power of fortitude must be distinguished from the acquired habit or trait of character formed by training and self-training, in which this natural power attains its proper form by means of its attachment to the proper objects. (Laches is still confusing, as he did at 184b, the acquired trait of manliness, courage and strength of will, with the innate capacity for it.) But this is to ignore the decisive impact of moral education on the formation of will and character. Nor does Laches seem to realize that this same natural power whereby a man holds his passions in check has a passion most properly its own, the passion of moral anger, the passion driving a man to attack those whom he thinks intend to take what belongs to him or prevent him from getting what he needs. (Laches will display such anger later on, in reacting to Nicias.) Finally, and most important, Laches may have identified what it is in the soul that makes a man able to endure adversity, but he has *not* identified what makes him put himself in danger in the first place, what makes him daring or bold. He has understood why it is that Odysseus does not run from the Trojan army or prematurely release his pent-up anger, but he has not understood what brought Odysseus to the walls of Troy to begin with, or what led him into the Cyclops' den, together with all that followed. Laches understands better what it is that makes a man stand and fight for his loved ones than what it is that makes one eager to initiate, explore, and attack, what it is that real men need. Laches' conception of courage takes the orders for granted; he does not question how they arise, what makes them worthwhile, or why he should obey. But can one call him truly free, if he remains so bound by the chains of steadfast opinion?

4.6 Socrates and Laches Redefine Courage as Prudent Fortitude (192c–d)

The picture of manly courage that has begun to emerge looks something like this: Courage is manifested first of all by the loyal citizen-soldier on the battlefield, holding his place in the ranks and facing the enemy and not running, and thereby preserving freedom for his city and family. But this is not the only kind of voluntary action in which courage can be expressed; it also can be expressed in peacetime, in the dangers of the sea, or in relation to sickness or poverty or political disgrace. Such courageous acts, like acts of war, presuppose the powers of fortitude to control and train the emotions so that the man acts on the basis of his reason, not on the basis of his fears or desires or the immediate pull of pleasure or pain, which distorts the judgment. How we are trained and how we train ourselves in these matters of strength of will, including the appetites for pleasure and money and the aversion to effort or pain, is directly related to our capacity for freedom and courage in the full sense of the word, the manly courage that is expressed in war and politics, or in enduring the unavoidable misfortune and suffering that befalls us as private individuals. Thus manly courage must be understood not only in relation to the actions in which it is manifested, but also in relation to the habits of feeling and will underlying it and making it possible, and to the part of the soul, traditionally called the "heart" or "spirit," by which a man endures evil in pursuit of his good. But as Socrates will now show, this is not yet the whole story, even with regard to the traditional Greek account of manliness and courage. It is also necessary to examine the ideal of courage on the level of rational choice and civic responsibility, to understand it in relation to the good or goal for the sake of which the courageous man endures sufferings or even risks his own life, to understand what courage is for. Focusing simply on action, we can lose sight of the powers of the soul that enable a man to do what he wills. Focusing simply on the will, we can lose sight of the rational object of his will—what he seeks and ought to seek to bring about in the world by his action. Unless we know what courage is for, we may waste it, foolishly, on unworthy objects. Where would be the virtue in that?

Socrates begins his examination of Laches' second attempt at a definition with gentle irony, noting first that all endurance cannot seem to Laches to be courage, for he is pretty much certain that Laches holds courage to be among the nobler things. To this Laches responds vehemently, "among the noblest" (*tōn kallistōn*), as if to say: It is the noblest thing! (192c2–7) Socrates next asks if endurance (or fortitude), together with prudence, is not noble and good, and Laches agrees. But if it occurs together with folly, is it not harmful (*blabera*) and injurious (*kakourgos*)? Yes. When asked if he would say that something harmful and injurious is noble, Laches replies: "Not with justice, Socrates." Socrates draws the conclusion that Laches will not agree that such fortitude is courage, since it is not noble, but courage is noble, and Laches says he "speaks truly."[39] But then, Socrates says, prudent fortitude (*phronimos karteria*) would be courage, on Laches' account. To this Laches gives only the halfhearted answer, "So it seems" (192c8–d12).

Before examining Socrates' argument we should once again note the importance of translating precisely the Greek words involved in this passage. As was stated in the preface, an imprecise translation can cripple the student's effort to understand a Socratic dialogue. Thus here and later in the *Laches,* to translate *phronimos* as "wise," rather than "prudent," leaves the Greekless reader to conclude that Socrates does not distinguish between the two, that is, between the intellectual virtue more obviously relevant to the life of the mind, as opposed to the intellectual virtue more obviously relevant to the political or military leader. But this distinction will prove essential to the inquiry, though it becomes clear that this is so only in the discussion with Nicias. It is also important to understand the connotations of the Greek words *blaberos* and *kakourgos,* used by Socrates at 192d. The first simply means "harmful," but with the connotation "harmful to oneself." (Its opposite is *ōphelimos,* the "beneficial" or "helpful," i.e., again especially to oneself or one's own; this word is used by Nicias at 181e1.) *Kakourgos,* on the other hand, means "injurious," with the connotation "injurious (or harmful) to another." We shall find out shortly why this is important. Finally, it is also important that "justice" be used to translate the Greek word *dikaion* at 192d6, rather than "right," which is easily confused in this kind of context with "correct" or "true."[40] Now let us look at the argument.

What is most characteristic in the passage at 192b–d is that Laches allows Socrates to blur over several distinctions that might have been made or that a more intellectually daring interlocutor might have compelled him to make. By narrowing the possibilities to just two—prudent versus foolish fortitude—and by linking prudent fortitude to what is both noble and good, and foolish fortitude to what is harmful and injurious, Socrates can force Laches to the conclusion that he only half-heartedly accepts at 192d. But of course there are other alternatives. Just to name two, Socrates could have asked Laches about simpleminded or innocent fortitude, on the one hand, or about clever fortitude, on the other (compare *Republic* 348b–349a). The simpleminded fortitude would be self-sacrificing or enduring and benefit or at least not harm another; it might well appear to Laches to be noble, even if by the criterion of individual benefit or harm it would not be good. The clever or calculating fortitude, on the other hand, would be steadfast and enduring for the sake of what was beneficial (or not harmful) to oneself, but not for the sake of what was merely helpful or not injurious to others. In fact, the clever fortitude might well *have* to be injurious to others, as it would inevitably be in war. But this kind of nonprudent but not imprudent fortitude would not be noble, or at least one could not with any justice call it noble. We recall, however, that a man such as Nicias, who seemed to identify the noble with individual victory or advantage, might think it noble (see section 3.3). (The question implicitly raised here about the unity of virtue is a much discussed topic in contemporary philosophical ethics, though such discussions neglect an aspect of the problem very important to Plato.)[41]

Seen in this light, we realize the significance of Laches' use of *dikaion* at 192d6, for it is justice that links the noble and shameful (that which is viewed as superior and as inferior) to the good and the evil (compare *Gorgias* 461b, 482c–484c; *Protagoras* 359e). Someone shamelessly unconcerned with justice, with the law and the common good, may well conclude that Machiavellian or Calliclean fortitude of soul together with Machiavellian or Calliclean cleverness is virtue, because it enables the man who possesses it to realize his purposes in the world and be victorious over all his enemies and attain the kind of princely power that befits his nature. Such a man would have nothing but contempt for the ordinary man's "softness of soul" (*malachia tēs psychēs*), even if he were a conventionally brave and obedient citizen, that is to say, for his lack of genuine prudence and timid unwillingness to pursue his own good unhampered by foolish scruples (see *Gorgias* 491b). This is courage not in the traditional sense of the term, bound by morality and directed to the common good, but courage in the raw, whereby the strong or tyrannical man is able, showing neither fear nor effeminacy, to assert himself and save himself and attain the dominion he desires (see *Gorgias* 482e–484c, 491e–492c; compare *Republic* 343a–344c, 572c–573b, 574b–575a).[42] But Laches does not even think of this possibility: Laches is—we have seen this from the beginning (180b)—a patriot and a man devoted to the city and to the city's welfare. So long as the inquiry is conducted with Laches, it will be impossible to discover whether courage might not conflict with justice: Laches lacks understanding of the kind of intellectual daring or boldness and of what may seem private or merely one's own good, that would make such an inquiry acceptable to him. So long, then, as the inquiry is with Laches, it must continue to refer to a courage that is a part of that virtue that is in conformity with justice, that is proscribed by law that all citizens must obey. And so long as the inquiry is with Laches, courage will be controlled by shame and willing to sacrifice itself for the common good.

What is perhaps the source of Laches' reluctance to agree here to Socrates' redefinition of courage, and what will soon prove to be at least part of the reason that this new definition fails, is the thought that courage must be prudent if it is to be noble. For *phronēsis,* while it has no Machiavellian connotation in Greek, or even so markedly the sense of avoiding evil (rather than attaining good) that prudence connotes in English, does connote a virtue that attains what is good for oneself and not only for the other. Then the courageous man will never harm himself merely for the sake of others. This might be thought to mean that he will not sacrifice his private good for the public good. But Laches would never agree to such a thing, obviously quite the contrary: He would call it "noble" (not "simpleminded" much less "foolish") to risk death or suffer pain or loss for his country, even though he might be forced by a clever sophist in a courtroom to admit that he should not, properly speaking, call it "prudent." And yet Socrates is not interested in revealing at this point precisely this potential contradiction between what Laches calls noble and what Laches calls good, nor will he be the one who does it (but see 197b–c). Socrates is interested in another, equally fundamental and problematic contradiction that seems to threaten the coherence of the traditional conception of courage, the potential contradiction between the kind of self-regarding prudence that the enduring patriotic soldier has concerning his own honor, and the kind of prudence and fortitude that is connected with victory for the city. Laches would never dare think it noble to do anything contrary to the law; but he might—indeed he will!—do what is contrary to his city's welfare. And what urges or drives him to do so is somehow entangled at its very roots with what makes him brave.

4.7 Socrates Refutes Laches' Understanding of Courage (192e–193d)

Socrates now asks Laches: In what is courage prudent? In all things, "the great and the small" (*ta megala kai ta smikra*)? To examine this question, Socrates suggests a number of examples. The first presents a man who endures in investing for the sake of financial gain (192e1–4). Laches rejects the idea that this man is courageous, we may suppose on the grounds that the object of the enduring is too small, too unworthy to be regarded as noble.[43] But what about the physician, who, when his sick son begs for something that will be bad for him, does not bend but enduringly refuses? Laches again says that this is "not in any way" (*oud' hopōstion*) an example of courage (192e6–193a2). Socrates next asks concerning a man who is willing to fight, based on a prudent calculation whereby he knows that others will come to his aid, and he will outnumber the enemy and has besides a stronger position—is this man more courageous than the man in the opposing army who is willing to stand and endure? Laches says it is the opposing man (193a3–b1). This answer, of course, takes the inquiry in a new direction, for Socrates then suggests that the courage of the second man is more foolish than that of the first, and Laches agrees. It follows that the man with the knowledge of horsemanship who endures in a cavalry fight will be less courageous than his counterpart who endures without that knowledge (such knowledge enabling one to escape danger more easily)—as will the man who endures with a skill in slinging or archery or the like—and those willing to dive into a well without being clever at it, or some other such work, are more courageous those who are clever in these things (193b2–c5). Laches responds haplessly, "Yes, for what else can one say, Socrates?"[44] Socrates then completes his refutation (193c7–e10). He concludes that such as these are more foolish in running risks and enduring than those who do it with skill (*meta technēs*), to which Laches can only reply, "So it appears." But before it appeared to them that foolish boldness and endurance are shameful and harmful? "Yes." But courage, it was agreed, was something noble. "It was agreed." Whereas now we say that this *shameful* thing—foolish endurance—is courage. "So it seems." Does Laches then opine that they speak well? Laches forthrightly answers no, and Socrates goes on to draw his conclusions about the *aporia* they have fallen into.

We may divide our commentary on this part of the dialogue into three parts. The first will be concerned with the initial examples, in which Socrates and Laches wonder whether courage is shown "at all" (*hopōstioun*) in the choice and action. The second part will be taken up with the latter examples, in which Socrates asks which of the paired kinds of action shows "more or less" courage. The third part of the commentary will be concerned with the new words

Socrates introduces at the end of the discussion, "the shameful" (to *aischron*, 193d1, 6) and "the bold" (*tolma*, 193d1).

The first examples address two different aspects of the question about the greatness or smallness of the object of courage, aspects having to do with the object that is to be achieved and with the suffering to be endured. At first it seems that Laches is simply inconsistent. Just before, he had agreed that a man can show courage in relation to poverty and sickness, but now he says that the investor cannot show courage in taking a chance in order to make a big profit, and that the doctor cannot show courage in refusing to give in to the patient's pleas for the sake of his recovery. But if wealth or health as goods sought for by the courageous man are too small to count as proper objects of courage, then why should poverty or sickness count as sufficiently great evils to be endured? A *consistent* Laches might answer that the good preserved by the courageous man sunk into poverty or disease is his own sense of honor and dignity, but the good sought by the investor or even the physician is not sufficiently noble for his action to count as courageous, despite the risk involved (which in Socrates' examples, at any rate, is small). There is a difference between running grave risks in magnanimous or great public actions and patiently not surrendering to misfortune, but it is not this difference that marks the one and not the other as courageous. Not only big risks for the sake of big things, such as for the sake of victory over Sparta in the Peloponnese, but also big sufferings for the sake of honor and manliness itself, may count for Laches as courageous. A risk for what is ignoble cannot be courageous and may well be foolish. Nor can too little a pain or danger call forth courage. But the enduring of evils corresponding to goods that it would not be noble to pursue can be courageous, so long as the suffering is sufficiently great, for what is preserved in these cases is reason or honor, which is always something "great."[45]

The second example gains in depth when we see its irony. Here the focus might seem to be more on the greatness of the evil endured. Since the physician need not endure the physical evil himself, Laches with manly insensitivity thinks it is but a small thing to put up with, like the complaining of the troops when the march is long or the rations meagre. Yet surely it makes a difference when the patient is in the doctor's own household. Then the cries and the desires are one's own, and it is much harder enduringly to refuse them. Furthermore, when we reflect on what it is that makes the physician refuse to hearken to them, we realize that the patient's well-being does not depend only on his *technical* knowledge remaining firm, or only on his *legal and moral* knowledge that it is his responsibility as a physician to administer the proper medicine, no matter what his patients want. Rather his *love* of his son and concern for his welfare are also essential: a concern that might even make him ready to endure the son's hatred, if by enduring it the father helps the boy return to health.

It is with this lesson in mind that we should once more consider the third example, the man on the hill, and the reference Socrates is making through it to Laches' failure at Mantinea (see section 1.4). For Laches was the man who did not endure on the hill, though he knew as a general that it was imprudent not to wait for the expected Elean aid and preserve his advantage of position. Unlike the physician who was righteous, prudent, and courageous enough to endure his own son's screams for food and water, Laches was not sufficiently righteous or prudent or courageous enough to endure his troops' cries that they be ordered to attack immediately, or their muttering that not to attack would be cowardly and treasonable. Why did Laches succumb to the foolish cries of his "patients," and permit them to kill both him and themselves by attacking the manly Spartans in the plain? We can now begin to answer this question. The answer does not have to do with Laches' lack of technical skill; there is no reason to suppose that he was so stupid as not to know what was the militarily prudent or wise thing to do. The answer must rather have to do with his softness of will. Laches was physically tough and brave, but his better judgment could be dislodged by his fear of disgrace. This was not only a failure of will and emotion, it was a failure of rational choice and public responsibility, a complex failure that, as we shall see, reveals fault lines within the whole Greek tradition that Laches represents. Laches was the doctor who obeyed his patients when they objected to the medicine. He had not sufficiently learned that even to rule your own household, you must love your own not as an equal, but as the father, responsible for defending the whole against its enemies, caring more about what is good for one's own than about currying favor with them.

The second group of Socrates' examples concern what is "more courageous" (*andreioteron*, 193a8) and what is "more foolish" (*aphronestera*, 193b2). These examples confirm the impression that Laches' construes prudence as something merely technical. He sees it as a calculating power and skill that makes the same situation less dangerous for him than it would be for another man, one who did not have his skill and experience. This point is brought out nicely by the terminology that Socrates uses in his examples, all the way from "calculating prudently" (*phronimōs logizomenon*) at 193a4 to "prudence" (*phronēseōs*) at 193a7 and then descending to "science" (*epistēmēs*) at 193b5, to "art" (*technēs*) at 193b10, to mere "cleverness" (*deinoi*) at 193c3. Socrates summarizes the kind of knowledge that the prudent man has as "skill" (*technē*) at 193c10. But this understanding is radically incomplete. It fails to recognize that prudence in every field has its source or principle in the unwavering apprehending and organizing of the technical deliberations and action by the goal (*telos*) that governs within that field, the goal, for instance, of victory in the art of strategy, the goal of health in the art of medicine. The most technically able and knowledgeable general can fail his country owing to his lack of prudence and fortitude, because his mind is too easily dislodged from the cause of victory by his desire for pleasure or his fear of disgrace; but this would not be only a failure of his art. The most competent physician can fail his patient because he is swayed by undue pity or because he is tempted by money, and this again would be a failure not only of his art, but of his prudence and justice as well. The greatest of generals and skilled men in every field, by contrast, *never* lose sight of the goal, but are constantly and in every way intent upon it. By conceiving prudence in a merely technical sense, Laches has forgotten the ordering role of the principle that, even in the bloody art of war, links courage and reason and justice in the virtue of the commander. It is no surprise to us that he also forgot this principle at Mantinea.

This is not all that Socrates discovers in the last part of his inquiry with Laches; indeed, it is not even his most important discovery. What he also discovers is an inherent conflict in the traditional Greek ideal of honor and virtue, a conflict going to the heart of the ancient Greek ways of thinking about courage and manliness. This conflict is formally expressed in the dialogue as the difference between measuring the virtue of the act of courage by the greatness of the risk or suffering that the courageous man is willing to endure, and measuring it by the standard of rational intention and civic responsibility— by prudence. For it would seem, as Laches says, that the man willing to run the greater risk and endure greater evils must be more courageous than the man who runs the smaller risk and endures lesser evils. Is this not why we hold the courage that willingly risks or suffers death to be the greatest courage, because death is the greatest evil?[46] Do we not regard the man willing to brave death as admirable, whatever goal, almost, that his heart is set on, because he shows the willingness to stake his life on something greater than mere survival?[47] Laches' incapacity to distinguish prudence from art leaves him unable even to articulate this problem. Since for Laches the prudently brave man by definition runs a smaller risk or endures a lesser evil than the imprudently brave man, it seems obvious that the latter will be braver. But then the folly of the man who risks defeat or death for an ignoble or unworthy goal is on a par with the folly of the man who does the same for a noble or worthy goal but lacks the expertness to ensure or make likely his success. Then Laches has no way to make magnanimity—the will to achieve noble goals or actions— an essential part of courage, no way to order courage to the ends of reason and justice. Indeed, Laches is then utterly at a loss to contradict his men, for he cannot measure the lesser nobility that impels them to prove their honor and superiority in attack against the greater nobility of the victory he is duty-bound to lead them to. In the end sheer foolish daring or enduring must seem courageous, but even Laches knows that this is not right (193d). He needs to be liberated from the opinions that bind him, if only to be freed for the responsibilities with which he has been entrusted. Laches needs a man who will teach him what he must know about prudence and the role it has to play in setting courage to the proper task.

Laches' perplexity about "blind" as against "prudent" courage is an *aporia* at the heart of the Greek tradition of manliness and courage. For on the one hand, it is essential to that tradition that courage be subordinated to the common good, and on the battlefield this means to the will of the commander. (Laches understands this part of courage well; he knows how to endure and obey.) On the other hand, it is also essential to that tradition that a man lives and dies for his honor—that he do nothing to sully his honor and that he strive, in all ways, to magnify its brilliance among men. (Laches does not understand the part concerning boldness.) The Spartan comedy displaying this conflict of principles was seen at Plataea in the person of Amompharetus.[48] The Athenian tragedy displaying the conflict was seen at Mantinea, in the troops and in the commanders, including Laches. At the heart of this conflict are two principles, equally important to the ancient Greek tradition of honor and virtue: courage and military obedience. For the Greek citizen-soldier, perhaps for all warriors, courage is an end in itself, its display the mark of superiority or virtue that he seeks; even the appearance of cowardice is unacceptable because it makes him seem "less of a man."[49] But if courage (and its display) is an end in itself, it is a virtue potentially in conflict with the equally necessary and important principle of obedience and command. Now if reason is to rule in battle, and if the action that seems courageous is nevertheless foolish, or if the seemingly cowardly is wise, it is absolutely vital that the men who are commanded actually carry out the order that in their soldiers' hearts they must hate to do, such as hold off a bold attack or beat a prudent withdrawal. Only then will victory be won and the freedom of the city be preserved. But what should they do when discipline and law and reason tell them to listen and obey, but courage and freedom and honor tell them to do otherwise?[50] So long as courage is rooted in manly pride, must there not always be a conflict between these two principles in the soldier's heart? Perhaps the wise commander will know this and will persuade his men that the cause of victory is after all the goal they all are fighting for. But he could only know that he must do this if his was a ruler's kind of courage, the kind in which the will to victory and responsibility of command was more important than how he appeared in the eyes of others. And precisely this is what Laches did not possess. Laches' love for his men and his concern for how the Athenians would see him blinded his judgment at Mantinea, making him "forget" his duty to command on the basis of calculating prudence, for the sake of the common victory. Laches could not stand alone against his men because his courage was not rooted in duty and daring and love; nor could he lead them to victory because he lacked the power of persuasion rooted in prudence.

The dilemma that Socrates uncovers here points to an enduring philosophical problem. For Plato and his Socrates, the inquiry concerning courage must begin with men such as Laches—men of action who are willing to die for their honor. But such men typically are not motivated by abstract moral principles, nor do they live examined lives. The Socratic attitude that disdains public approval is all but incomprehensible to them (see *Apology* 28b–29b). Men of Laches' type are essentially other-oriented, despite their self-reliance. But this means it is highly misleading to regard the principles motivating their actions as somehow on a par with the principles motivating a Socrates.

The problem posed by the kind of courage that Laches represents—the problem of the relationship between philosophy and autonomy and moral courage and physical courage—is, in fact, largely ignored in contemporary ethical philosophy, which may be one reason why there has been comparatively little interest in this part of the dialogue. But however questionable it is that such courage is truly virtuous, the civic courage of men such as Laches would seem essential to the well-being of their cities, and the theoretical problem posed by the trait of character they display would seem essential to the philosophical inquiry that seeks to know "what courage really is."[51]

It is in relation to the conflict between the principles of fighting courage and obedient duty that we have to understand Socrates' words at 193d, where he says that not only foolish endurance, but also foolish "daring" (*tolma*) is "shameful" (*aischra*) as well as harmful. This is the first time in the dialogue that Socrates has spoken of what is shameful, though he did say earlier that foolish endurance was harmful and evil and therefore not noble. Now as we have seen, a man such as Laches might still think that a less-than-wise enduring or daring was courageous, and if not noble, at least not shameful. But here Socrates pins the label that Laches fears most on the very aspect of courage he best understands. Here Socrates' refutation of Laches goes to his innermost being, not his words alone but what he thinks life is for. Here Socrates begins to teach Laches that whatever is foolish is shameful. Somehow Socrates must help Laches out of his quandary, bring him to the point where he can see clearly principles other than courage and honor to guide him in battle, principles that would enable him to fulfill better the responsibility of command. But to do this, Socrates may need to call on whatever there is in Laches of a quality that, as we have seen, Laches himself understands but poorly, the quality mentioned here for only the second time in the dialogue, boldness (*tolma,* 193d1). Of course it was folly at Mantinea, and this is part of the lesson Socrates intends here also. The goal must be worthwhile, and the risk must never be made larger than is necessary. Boldness for its own sake is no less a folly, and may be a greater one, than endurance for its own sake. But there is in boldness something that seems in the deeper text of our dialogue to be more closely associated with the intelligence needed to command than mere enduring obedience. Boldness is active, hungry; it does not simply respond defensively but involves the will to search out opportunities and attack in the interests of victory. Boldness is an Athenian trait, a restlessness to conquer new worlds and not be content with the given. Boldness is above all a quality that allows a man to challenge the conventional order, to question the established rules and the universally accepted opinions, to stand alone or as one of the few, proudly apart from the many. *"Navigare necesse est, vivere non necesse!"*[52] Neither endurance nor prudence is enough: boldness is needed, too. Indeed, it may be that one cannot attain real prudence without it.

4.8 Laches' Aporia *and the Laughter of Courage Herself (193d–194b)*

With Laches' admission at 193d10 that he and Socrates are not speaking beautifully, the first stage of the inquiry comes to an end. Together with Laches, Socrates has examined the traditional ancient Greek ideal of manly courage and found it wanting. At the level of voluntary action, the traditional view tends to overlook the kinds of action other than hoplite fighting that can manifest courage, including the kind of bold attack undertaken by cavalry soldiers and the manly endurance of evils that cannot be avoided. At the level of the will and the feelings, the traditional view tends to be self-forgetful, ignoring both its own model of the operation of the mind and spirit and whole man in the formation of choice and the distinction between the natural human power underlying the habits of fortitude or lassitude and those habits themselves as acquired through deliberate social training and self-training. And at the level of responsibility or justice and rational principle, Socrates uncovers for Laches a contradiction at the heart of the ancient tradition concerning manly courage, a contradiction between the principle of honor and the display of courage as an end in itself, on the one hand, and the principle of obedience to the commander (whose wisdom may dictate inaction or even retreat), on the other. This criticism is especially relevant to the kind of courage needed by a commander, a courage that must be bolder and more prudent than the kind needed by the line soldier. Laches, however, does not seem a very promising candidate to examine this latter, more sophisticated kind of courage.

Now when we turn to the passage at 193d11–e7, we do not find Socrates saying anything about Laches' failure to defend his conception of courage, but rather that he and Laches are presumably not "harmoniously tuned" in the classic Dorian mode to which Laches had earlier referred (188d; see the discussion in section 3.8). For while someone might say that in their actions they shared in manly courage, he could not say it of their speeches; Laches agrees that this is "very true" and that it is in no way noble or fine. Of course, the dialogue has again reached a delicate point, as it had at 191c. If Socrates had turned on Laches and said, "You, Laches, are not in harmony," the spirit of the inquiry would have reverted back to the mode of a trial, and Laches might not have been willing to go on. But Socrates says nothing like this. Rather than saying "you," he says "we"; he shares Laches' predicament; they are a team. Nor does Laches fall into charge and countercharge: he has been taken up into the spirit of inquiry and is now genuinely perplexed. We can understand why. He had thought *andreia* was manly patriotic courage and the noblest of virtues, but now he has been taught that there is a conflict between the principle of courage itself and the fact that courage must be reined in by prudence; courageousness by itself is not noble. This is shocking to him. He has been struck at the center of his being and is at a loss how to continue.

Laches seems a model of genuine Socratic *aporia* because he has been refuted in his own real beliefs about what is central to the good life, both his rational and volitional center, his innermost ideal of excellence. Socrates has called that principled belief of his about what is worthwhile or noble and good into question, though he has not—and this is vital—threatened Laches' claim to being noble and good, namely his claim to manly courage. It appears that partly for this reason Laches is not angry with Socrates but rather at himself, as he will say next (194a8–b1). Thus he seems to fit the pattern of the genuine elenchus characterized at *Sophist* 230c, where it is said of those who are made to contradict themselves: "Those who see this grow angry with themselves and gentle towards others, and this is the way in which they are freed from their high and obstinate opinions about themselves." Socrates has in effect split Laches who before was one into two: the man he was before, who thought he knew what courage is, and the new man to whom the inquiry has given birth, the man who has discovered that the first man did not possess what he claimed to possess. This new Laches is the long-forgotten youthful part of Laches who wants to know. He is the still small part of Laches whom we recognize as a distant weak cousin to the powerful, unrelenting fellow whom

Socrates has living with him (see *Hippias Major* 304d–e; see also section 3.8). He also is a Laches bolder than we have seen hitherto. This new boldness has its root in the natural love of victory that Socrates has released in Laches by calling into question his trust in common opinion; by loosening, to some extent at any rate, the bonds of *aidōs* that held that common certainty in place. Will this new Laches now grow stronger, as the inquiry continues, or will he fall asleep again, shouted down by the old Laches, who in his haste to protect what is his own cannot endure the thought that his gold may be dross? Or is this new Laches prepared to fight for his own survival, even if it means that he must kill the old Laches who is not ready to share his house with anyone, much less with a critical sort of fellow who wants him to give away what he fought so long and hard to get? Or can these two somehow be friends?

With Laches having acknowledged the *aporia* they are in, Socrates goes on (193e8–194a5), asking him if he will not obey or hearken to the part of their speech that bids them be abiding and endure, particularly in the search, lest they be laughed at by Courage Herself for not seeking for her courageously, if perhaps "endurance herself often is courage." This last phrase, *"autē hē karterēsis estin andreia"* may also be translated: "this very endurance [i.e., the endurance needed in inquiry] is courage." Laches then declares that he is not ready to quit, because a certain "love of victory" (*philonikia*) has taken hold of him, and he is truly vexed. For he is of the opinion that he has in mind (*noein*) what courage is, but he does not know how it fled away from him, such that he cannot now get hold of it in words. Then Socrates, for the first time in the dialogue, addresses Laches as "friend," and encourages him in the search, saying that the good hunter must pursue and not quit, and Laches agrees (194a6–b7). But Socrates does not attempt to pick up the trail with Laches, asking instead if he is willing to invite Nicias to join in the hunt, as he may be "more resourceful" (*euporōteros,* 194b9) than they are—thus teaching by example that greater resources need not offend courage. Laches' last words in the part of the inquiry that he shares with Socrates alone are, "I am willing; why not?" (194c1). It won't be long, however, before Laches questions the fitness of his old ally Nicias to share in Socrates' and his own community.

Let us begin our reflection on this remarkable exchange by noting that a whole new kind of action—philosophical inquiry—has been added to the list of situations in which courage can be manifested. This was not included, of course, in Socrates' list at 191c, and it is unlikely that the old Laches would have accepted it. But now Laches knows that the true understanding of courage must also make room for courage in the speaking that is cognitive doing, for the kind of rational seeking or knowing that is itself enduring and bold. Laches himself has now experienced the dizzying, blinding pain of *aporia,* and he may realize that this new experience calls for a kind of courage different from the *andreia* he had known, yet that somehow both are courage. Laches had stepped confidently onto the mat, but when he was thrown he had the truthful courage to admit it, to hold open his mind, if only for a moment, to the shameful admission that he "didn't know what he was talking about." If we return to the account in the *Sophist* again, we find that this experience has two different but related aspects. One is the experience of epistemic shame, of the discovery that one has been something of a fraud, that one is less than one thought. It is the power of the Socratic elenchus to test the student's willingness not to run but to stand up on behalf of one's will to truth and face this affront to honor; this makes it a uniquely valuable instrument for teaching virtue in the form of moderation.[53] The other is epistemic fear, the discovery that the more or less well-defined world one was living in was something of an illusion, that one simply is not well-grounded in the way one thought one was. It is also the power of the Socratic elenchus to test the student's willingness to endure this shock to his certainty, which suggests it as a test for teaching courage.

In its most powerful form, the cognitive endurance that Socrates and Laches have discovered would seem to involve holding one's mind open to the fearful vertigo of the Unknown, refusing to allow our will to safety and comfort to return the mind again into the steady grooves of common opinion. Instead of returning or remaining in that well-lit place, the aporetically struck student feels called out—into darkness. Somehow this world of darkness promises a more beautiful vision than what he knew before, but one can hardly overstate the difficulty of moving into epistemic uncertainty, the skeptical abyss of the mind. The calculative thinking of the commander who seeks to foresee his enemy's plans is not itself dangerous, does not itself require that he endure in what is fearful to the human soul; but the thinking into which Socrates has led Laches does. (Of course the commander must endure in preventing the fear of defeat and the uncertainty of battle from dislodging his judgment, but the thinking itself is not fearful.) If it is true that the Socratic elenchus is directed to men's real beliefs about what life is for, then it takes no small effort of will and courage really to think all that into question—for what the student is then fighting his way into is the blazing thought that his whole manner of life, no less than that of his father and his father's father, may have been a fraud. Thus the opposition between courage and cowardice may seem to be more fundamental than that between knowledge and belief, for the latter does not come to be without the former.[54] Far easier is it to think that the one who suggests such a thing should be punished, never heard in public. Far easier is it to force the mind back down into the familiar grooves, and then try to forget that life without philosophy is a coward's way to live.[55]

The other remarkable thing about the exchange is Socrates' wonderful image of "Manly Courage Herself," laughing at him and at Laches for not holding her tight. Here in a so-called early dialogue is a Form, personified in a particularly vivid and active role! Courage Herself has come like a goddess on the scene at the moment of *aporia* concerning the traditional conception of courage, at the moment where the suspicion emerges that they do not know what they are talking about, at the moment where they realize they do not possess her, at least not in words. She has come on the scene, moreover, not as a beautiful but lifeless figure, but as a mocking, erotic creature who challenges these manly men to catch her. It is an amazing image. Whatever can it mean?

It means this much at least: The image is a charming pedagogical hook to pull Laches into further inquiry. We recall that Laches' greatest fear is his fear of contempt from his fellow men, the malicious laughter that takes away a man's honor, the judgmental ridicule that every man who does not possess "wondrous" virtue is prey to. But with the image of Laughing Courage, Socrates has found the perfect poetic correlative to the new kind of fear and the new kind of shame that he and Laches have experienced. Courage Herself is to replace the city and the eyes of his hoplite comrades as the new mirror of Laches' self-knowledge. Shame and fear before her, at not bravely enduring in seeking, is to replace his old shame and fear before them, at not bravely enduring in fighting. By this means Laches may come to stand to fear and shame in a new way, oriented not by his will to seem good in the eyes of his fellows, but by his will to know what he is talking about, to grasp truth as it really is, and to stand alone. If the defect at the core of the courage that Laches has known hitherto is that it is rooted in honor no less than in what is good for the city, perhaps the courage that Socrates has now introduced him to—the courage that is ashamed and afraid of ignorance, and boldly desirous of knowledge—will help Laches acquire the kind of courage he needs to prudently lead and not foolishly be led by his men and their muttering eyes. Perhaps this new, and if you will, feminine, lovely courage will enable Laches to be courageous in a way that the old, manly, violent kind would not. Perhaps the courage that is born with the love of truth is not only higher and nobler than the courage born with the love of honor, perhaps it is the only way to gain the victory.

Laches has proven more responsive to Socratic dialectic than we first thought he would be (section 3.8). Despite his unmusical nature, he has submitted himself to the power of the elenchus and has been brought to an *aporia*, at least to its first step. He has not yet been brought to the kind of puzzlement Nicias spoke of, where the interlocutor sees that all of his ways have been called into question and that he "must become more forethoughtful of his life ever after." For as we learn at 194b1–4, Laches has discovered only that he "can't say" what apparently he still believes he knows or has in mind. This is not the same, by any means, as learning that one "doesn't know"; it is not yet the turning of the soul toward the light; it is at best the turning of the soul away from the shadows. But Laches has been made to experience once again, as he had not perhaps for many years, that power greater than his own will, still there in him: the power of nature whereby "all men desire to know." Characteristically, he experiences this love in the form of *philonikia,* an aggressive spiritedness determined to win, to say exactly what the courage is that he has in mind. Again, this makes one uneasy: Has Laches not realized that the courage he possesses and has in mind may not be the beautiful Courage Herself that Socrates now holds up before him? Might the love of victory impelling him still be too much the martial love, which, loyal to its own, takes pleasure in battle and defeating the enemy, and not enough the lover's love, which lets go of everything it has to find its joy in union? But let us not judge Laches too hastily. Let us rather follow Socrates and think of him as a friend in our community of inquiry. Laches has proven himself an honest seeker and has declared his willingness, indeed his ardor, to continue in the fight for truth. Even now he is generously willing to let his former rival take the place of honor as they continue the search. Perhaps his *philonikia* will become *philosophia,* if he will be brave and inquire to the end.

In the meantime, as Socrates bluntly suggests (194b8–9), the dialogue needs someone "more resourceful" than the unmusical Laches. Such a one is ready at hand, in the person of a man well attuned to words and learned wisdom, the man whose very name in Greek means "victory." With this man the dialogue will commence upon a whole new way of thinking.

5

The Inquiry with Nicias

5.1 Nicias Joins the Inquiry and Gives His Account of Courage
(194c–195b)

SOCRATES BEGINS THE SECOND HALF of the inquiry into *andreia* by turning to the problem-solving Nicias, inviting him to join his friends who are "storm-tossed" in the perils of thought and in need of rescue. Nicias should tell Socrates and Laches what he thinks courage is, thus releasing them from the problem-knot their minds are tied in and giving his own thoughts the stability of speech (194c2–6). Nicias is only too willing, having thought while they were speaking of something fine that he had once heard Socrates himself say, namely, that a man is good in that in which he is wise and bad in that in which he is ignorant. To this Socrates responds with his only oath of the dialogue, "Truly by God you speak, Nicias!" The general concludes that if the courageous man is good, he must be wise, and Socrates asks Laches if he hears Nicias (194c7–d6). Laches replies that he does, without understanding what Nicias is saying. (This announces again the theme of "hearing" and "understanding," which plays an important role throughout the inquiry; see section 4.2). Socrates replies that the man seems to be saying that manly courage is a kind of wisdom (*sophian tina*). Laches responds contemptuously, "Wisdom, my eye! What kind?"[1] Then Socrates shows Laches how to question Nicias, asking if it is perhaps the kind of wisdom taught by a music master such as Damon (e.g., flute playing), and, if not, what kind of knowledge it is and of what. Laches, pleased to see Nicias being pressured and still not addressing him, says that Nicias should tell them straight out what he thinks (194d7–e10). Nicias then defines courage as follows: "The knowledge of what is to be dreaded and dared" (*tēn tōn deinōn kai tharraleōn epistēmēn*), whether in war or in anything else (194e11–195a1). Laches tells Socrates' this answer is absurd, because obviously wisdom is separate (*chōris*) from courage. To Socrates' explanation that Nicias denies that, Laches swears another oath, saying that Nicias is talking mere nonsense! Socrates replies that they should then instruct Nicias, not abuse him. Nicias interrupts to observe that Laches wants Socrates to prove that he, Nicias, is talking nonsense, because Laches was proved just now to be doing so. This all-too-perceptive insult finally prompts Laches to address Nicias himself, and Laches declares that he will now try to prove that Nicias *is* talking nonsense (195a2–b3). Thus ends Nicias stormy induction into the community of inquiry. Thanks to Laches, the mood of the conversation has clearly reverted back to the mode of a contest, but he will find Nicias too slippery a speaker for the likes of him to throw.

Obviously, Nicias has brought something new into the inquiry, a view of courage that appears not to have been acquired through experience but from his teachers. Whereas Laches began by describing what he had seen of courage, Nicias begins with what he has heard. We should therefore be inclined to mistrust what he has to say—except that it might have come from Socrates! This is certainly a surprising development, but just as certainly any interpretation of the *Laches* must attempt to explain the close association drawn here between Socrates and Nicias, especially since several times in the forthcoming discussion Socrates explicitly disassociates himself from Nicias (196c–d, 197d, 198b–c, 199a). If the definition does stem from Socrates, might it somehow contain the secret truth about courage? Or might Plato be criticizing his own teacher's view on courage, as one critic has suggested? But if it is not from Socrates, as he himself indicates (197d), why is it almost identical with the account of courage that Socrates seems to defend at *Protagoras* 358a–360d, and why does the discussion of it at 195b–196a appear so like the discussions of courage and honor we find in the *Apology* (28b–29b) and in the *Gorgias* (511c–513c)? If we are to steer a course safely through these perilous waters, it will be crucial to determine exactly what *Nicias* means by his words. We have already been alerted to the fact that these are words he has heard, but then perhaps he has not understood them, and his account of them will prove, under examination, to be superficial. *Then* if the definition is refuted, it will not be the Socratic understanding of courage that is shown to be inadequate, but some other.

While Nicias' relation to Socrates is problematic, his relation to the tradition of sophistry or wisdom has been well established in the dialogue, both through his connection with Damon (reemphasized at 197d) and by the content of his speech on *hoplomachia*, particularly the claims he made about the relation between military science and courage (182a–d). At first glance, it would seem to have been this tradition that he has drawn upon in formulating his definition.

As we saw in reviewing the historical background to the *Laches,* Athenian military thought conceived of courage as the confidence or daring born of military skill and experience (section 1.6). This is no less true of Spartan courage on land than of Athenian courage on the seas, according to the Athenian admiral Phormio, because all men are naturally frightened of and flee from whatever is unknown and potentially dangerous to them, until they gain the confidence that is born of repeated success or mastery (Thucydides, *Peloponnesian War* 2.88–89). Thus it is not *gnōmē* in the Spartan sense of resolve or will, but *gnōmē* in the Athenian sense of intelligence or skill, that is the essence of courage.[2] The skilled and confident commander would know what is really "terrible" or endangering (the arrival of an experienced enemy general, the destruction of a supply depot, fear and muttering in the men, his line of retreat cut off) and must be avoided, and what is really inspiring or encouraging (the advantage of surprise, superior numbers, superior science, timely reinforcements) and is the occasion for attack. Armored in this way by skill and foresight, he would be confident that he knew what he was doing, that he had command over the battlefield. He would know that his daring was not rash but prudent, his enduring not obstinate but wise. He would be assured of victory.

The fact that Nicias represents the distinctively "Athenian" notion of courage means, as we have come to realize, that Laches' reaction to him has to be understood not only as a reaction or antagonism between the two men, but also as a representation of the "Spartan" or traditionalist criticism of the Athenian-Periclean views and of the sophistic movement in general. Nicias not only stands for something new and unfamiliar and therefore disturbing to a crusty old soldier such as Laches, he stands for something that challenges the relevance of patriotic courage as Laches understands it, something that in Laches' opinion will convince the young men who listen to him that they are brave when they are not. The fact that Nicias is also head of the government makes it all the more galling and wrong (197d). Now Socrates would of course have to expect this reaction, but he seems to want to keep Laches in the inquiry, even to encourage him to question Nicias on his own. Somehow, Nicias has something important to teach Laches, namely, something about the relation of intelligence and boldness to courage, or perhaps about the importance to prudence and courage not only of the public good, but also of one's own private good. We have already seen in this surprisingly hostile exchange, however, reason to make us doubt that Socrates will succeed in his efforts. Laches seems intent not on examining Nicias' views to see if they might be true, but on refuting them out of hand, to prove Nicias no wiser than he himself had proven to be. This does not mean, however, that Laches' role in the inquiry, or even Socrates' efforts to keep him involved, will be uninteresting to us. On the contrary, the very limits that mark Laches' ability to understand Nicias, both intellectual and volitional, will be crucial to our understanding of the dialogue.

In addition to the problem that has just arisen concerning the relation of Nicias' views to the Socratic conception of courage—which would appear to be very different from the sophistic or technical conception of courage—there is also the puzzle of the relation between the progressive Nicias, who is identified with Athenian science and love of honor in his speech at 181d–182d, and the conservative, pious Nicias, who was devoted to divination and let the moon's eclipse fatally delay his army's escape from Syracuse (the incident referred to at 198e–199a; see section 1.3). While we cannot at present fully address this question, it is important for us to develop somewhat more fully an aspect of the matter considered only briefly in our earlier discussion: the question of the relationship between Athenian science and the sophistic movement, on the one hand, and ancient piety, specifically the ancient Greek attitude toward prophecy or seercraft, on the other, is vital to the understanding of the inquiry with Nicias and of the ancient view that courage is a form of wisdom. These remarks will serve initially only to make all the more puzzling the seemingly contradictory roles in our dialogue of Nicias as a man associated both with the Sophistic Enlightenment and with the most backward kind of piety.

First, one is reminded of another point made earlier, that there are fundamental differences of belief and concern between the ancient world in which the Platonic dialogues are set and the modern world we know (see section 1.1). Among the most fundamental of these are the very different experiences and relationships we have with nature from those of men in ancient times. We heirs of science, Greek and modern, are more or less secure in our relationships to nature: we know its basic laws, we have a clear picture of our immediate stellar system, and we are familiar with the geography and geology and climate of the whole earth; we have even come to understand and conquer so many diseases that we view those we cannot control as aberrations from the norm. Nature has been desacralized, depersonalized, tamed. None of this was true in ancient times. In particular, sublunar and celestial events (lightning, thunder, eclipses of the sun and moon) reawakened ancient terrors—terror of uncertainty, of nature filled with malevolence and danger. This is the nature we encounter today only in science fiction horror films, but even there we do not encounter horrifying, threatening, disorderly nature as the ancients did, for the disorderly events of the heavens were to them signs and works of the angry gods. Thus fear of nature and fear of the divine went hand in hand.[3]

What all this has to do with Nicias and the Sophistic Enlightenment begins to be clear when we compare the story of Nicias' and the Athenian army's reaction to the eclipse of the moon over Syracuse with the story Plutarch tells of Pericles' reaction to an eclipse of the sun during a sea attack that he was commanding. On that occasion, too, the men became frightened at this sign of cosmic disorder, but Pericles calmly raised his cloak in front of his face and said, "Thus blocks the moon the sun," thereby teaching that knowledge of the natural causes of things banishes fear and superstitious terror (*Lives*, "Pericles" 35; compare also "Pericles" 6 and "Nicias" 23). Pericles was able to do this because he had studied with Anaxagoras and had acquired not only the scientific information that Anaxagoras had to teach him, but more importantly the scientific attitude of mind, which sees the natural cosmos as a stable, autonomous order, not as a sensory or pragmatic field in which gods or spirits work their black and white magic and must be appeased.[4] For us, science is first of all a human thing, a field of inquiry or a way of knowing commanded by man as a rational being; we do not see it in its most basic power, as immediately liberating us to rationality from an empathetic relation to nature and thereby reshaping the world of experience. But to the men of Plato's time, science and philosophy were paths of liberation from ignorance and superstition, paths of enlightenment that won courage for men in their relationship to nature.[5] This is a chief element in the historical background to the idea that courage is a form of science or wisdom, for the alternative of scientific confidence as against superstitious fear was still very much alive in the fifth century B.C., as both Pericles' and Nicias' actions proved. The pragmatic common sense of men who had not learned from the sophists about the true order of nature, of men who were not armed with the intellectual weapon provided by the scientific attitude, was at risk of falling back into the old terror when those men encountered things in the heavens they could not explain.

One final point. The ancient Greek view of science did not carry with it implications of determinism in human affairs. Whereas the natural philosopher could predict celestial events and the skilled general or politician might be thought to foresee what his opponents would do, Anaxagorean science and, later, Aristotelian science do not imply that human freedom is an illusion or that all events are predetermined. On the other hand, there is an analogy to this concept in the ancient notion of fate. Seers such as Tiresias and Cassandra foresee *perfectly* "what is to be"—unlike a Pericles or an Alcibiades—but the terrible thing about a Cassandra's foresight is that no one believes her, or that if they do believe her, the actions they take to avoid the outcome prove futile. Now much as an unenlightened, superstitious view of nature undermines courage in the man lacking a scientific education, so belief in fate must undermine courage as well, for if things are fated, what is there to do? At best, perhaps, one can appeal to the gods, whose will might alter the things that are to be. But there is no use in relying on your own actions, your skill and courage and foresight, for they are too weak, too dim. Notice that here, again, the ancient Greek religious and scientific points of view appear diametrically opposed, and recall the discussion of the Promethean image of Rational Man that arose in fifth-century Athens (section 1.6). Courage, on this view, is rooted above all in *intellectual* manliness, in the self-assertion of human rationality against the bondage of conventional political or religious (i.e., superstitious) custom. Human reason is thus tied essentially to courage, because human reason must, for the sake of progress and freedom and further enlightenment, boldly violate the past, violate its sacred nature and destroy its unquestioned authority, in the process of exposing it for examination. But human reason in this sense is also allied with human freedom and opposed to the religious concept of fate. One who stands fully upright will not bow before lightning or eclipses of the moon but will know them for what they are: mere natural phenomena that someday may be snared by human art; and he will also not be fooled into thinking that his fate is sealed by the signs a seer might read; he will know it is his responsibility not to foresee but bravely to master Fortuna.[6] So it seems it will be only the intellectually liberated man—a man, perhaps, like Nicias—who will be freed for the fully human, rational courage. Such a man will know that his fate lies in his own hands, his destiny is his own to make or ruin.

And yet Sophocles, in the great choral ode in the *Antigone,* perhaps the supreme song of Man in his Pride, proclaims that clever, all-resourceful Man cannot escape from Death. Not even Nicias with all his sophistic resources, it would seem, can master this fundamental evil, this fundamental fear. Even if there is a state of enlightenment or mastery in which we are beyond the ordinary fears and uncertainty of the human condition, it would appear that we can never overleap this fear, this uncertainty. Or can we? Is there not perhaps a kind of knowledge that will liberate us from all the ancient terrors, even the terror of violent death? Obviously if there is, it must be a state of certainty that will make us sure against all fears, brave against all dangers. A man like Nicias would want very much to know about such a teaching and acquire it for himself. Wouldn't we all?

5.2 Nicias Defends His Account against Laches (195b–196a), Who Fails to Understand Him (196a–c)

Laches sets out to refute Nicias by proving that although doctors and farmers and in general all craftsmen know what is to be dreaded and dared in their own craft, this does not make them courageous (195b2–c2). Presumably what makes something dreaded to the doctor or farmer is his knowledge that he is facing something evil that he cannot counteract by his art, such as a fatal disease or a killing frost, but Laches does not make this point explicit. Socrates then asks Nicias if Laches has not made a good point, but Nicias replies that doctors may know what is healthy and what is sickly, but it is not within the doctor's purview to know if health is to be dreaded rather than sickness (195c3–8). The man with the art of courage, by implication, does know this. Nicias then asks Laches if he does not think that for many it is better *not* to get up from an illness; or does Laches say it is always better to live and not often superior for many to die? Laches agrees, and then Nicias continues, asking if he thinks that the same things are dreaded by those for whom it is profitable to die as by those for whom it is profitable to live, and Laches now agrees that they are different.[7] Nicias does not attribute the knowledge of this to doctors or other craftsman, but to the courageous man (195c8–d9). Socrates then asks Laches if he comprehends Nicias' meaning and Laches says that he does; it is the seers or diviners whom Nicias is talking about, for who else can know for which of us it is better to live than to die? Confident now that he has Nicias cornered, Laches turns on him, asking sharply if he claims to be a seer, or if he is neither a seer nor a courageous man.[8] But Nicias slips away again and denies that it belongs to the diviner to know these things—for the diviner can know only the signs of what is to be, for instance whether a man is to meet with death or disease or loss of property or victory or defeat in war or some other contest; but what is better (*ameinon*) for him among these things to suffer or not to suffer, that is no more for a diviner to judge than anyone else (195d10–196a3).

At this point Laches throws up his hands and, turning again to Socrates, says that he fails to understand Nicias, for Nicias admits that neither a seer nor a doctor nor anybody else is the courageous man, unless perhaps he means "some god" (*theon tina,* 196a6). So Nicias is unwilling to admit, nobly, that he is talking nonsense, but keeps twisting around, hiding his own perplexity. He and Socrates could have done the same thing had they wanted not to appear to be contradicting themselves, and there would be some reason for this in a law court. But why should anyone seek vainly to put on cosmetics or "adorn" himself with empty words in this kind of gathering (196a4–b7)? Socrates, however, says that they should inquire further regarding what Nicias has in mind, for he may not be talking simply for show. Then if Nicias is saying something, they will accede to it, and if not, instruct (*didaxomen*) him. To these conciliatory words Laches replies that Socrates is welcome to inquire, but as for himself, he has perhaps inquired enough. Socrates concludes this section of the dialogue by saying that the inquiry he makes will be "in common" on behalf of himself and Laches (196c1–9).

Certainly, nothing thus far has prepared us for the explanation that Nicias now gives of his definition, and not surprisingly Laches fails to understand him. Hitherto, Nicias has been a spokesman for the distinctively Athenian, scientific view of courage, but here he has introduced an entirely new issue. How does knowing whether it is better for a sick man to live or to die compare to the kind of courage that is shown on the battlefield? This appears to be a wholly new kind of knowledge, one having nothing to do with the ability to distinguish real as opposed to apparent dangers and opportunities, or with the mastery of adversity or advantages. And what is the meaning of the contrast between the knowledge of the seer and the man with this science, who is able to judge whether it is better to suffer or not to suffer the things he lists at 195e? Is Nicias suggesting seriously that the man with this art can calmly suffer these things such as defeat or death, rather than victory, because he somehow "knows" that it is better for him to do so? Recall the idea of courage mooted at the end of the last section, the idea of a condition of enlightenment and self-mastery in which one has passed beyond all the terrors of life, even that of painful death. It may be some such state of supremely self-sufficient, self-certain courage that Nicias has in mind here. But is there anything to it?

Let us begin to answer these questions by considering Nicias' example of the man who knows that it is better to die than to go on living with his sickness. This is the first explicit mention of death in the inquiry. Laches' original definition had referred implicitly to the noble, public death that might be suffered on the battlefield, but it is here in the *Laches* that we are faced for the first time with the terrible words "to die" and "death." Moreover, the kind of death discussed here is in no way associated with a deed that might live on in the city's memory. It is a painful, private, isolated death, distinctively that of an individual. Laches agrees that for many it is better to die than to live; but this acknowledgment does not detract from the uncanny nature of death, when one thinks of it not as something suffered by everybody but as one's very own. This very notion—that courage is shown above all in knowing and even in choosing one's own death—raises the question that Nicias does not answer. For if courage somehow consists in the knowledge that there is something worse than the one seemingly absolute evil that ends all opportunity for the pleasures and joys of life, what is that thing? What is it that somehow transcends life itself as a good, such that it is better to die than to do or suffer that thing? What is it that, in Nicias' account, the courageous man fears as something *more* fearful than his own death? We know what Laches might think: freedom and honor transcend mere life (*zōē*), because without them the dignified life (*bios*) of the citizen is impossible; therefore slavery and disgrace are more to be feared than death. But Nicias does not adopt the proud ancient republican point of view; he seems rather to be affirming that some private good is superior to life, or some private evil is worse than death. But again, what could that possibly be? Is not one's own death quite simply the greatest of all evils, which the rational man, not caught up in dreams of glory, dreads more than anything else and views as the one thing at all costs to be avoided? Isn't it?[9]

Nicias' further explanation of his definition is also puzzling. We can understand why Laches might think that Nicias has the seers or diviners in mind, for surely one of the most difficult things about important decisions is the uncertainty that attends them. Would it not be so much easier if we only knew all the consequences of our intended actions? Would it not be obvious what we ought to do, because we could "see" what good and evil things would come about in the unknown future? In this sense, the seer might well be considered the one who alone could act with complete confidence, while other mortals must struggle against the anxiety over what is to be. But this of course is not what Nicias says he has in mind. The diviner may know "what is to be"—that is, if one is to suffer death or disease or loss of property, or victory or defeat—but he does not know "whether it is better" for someone to suffer these things. To be sure, Nicias is contrasting here the *moral* or *evaluative* knowledge of the courageous man to the merely *predictive* knowledge of the seer, a point that has been noted and amply discussed in the scholarly literature.[10] But let us also notice some further points about Nicias' explanation of his definition that have not been sufficiently considered, and these will reveal more fully for us the complexity and ambiguity of his remarks here.

First, Nicias speaks not of the courageous man's knowledge of what he is "to do or not do," he speaks only of what he is to "suffer or not suffer" (*pathein ē mē pathein,* 196a2). The knowledge that belongs to the art of courage seems curiously passive; the dialogue again is presenting an account of courage that does not seem to make room for the quality of boldness or daring. Second, the courageous man apparently does not possess his knowledge merely in the abstract, for it belongs to him to decide in the concrete situation "what is better." This presupposes that his ability to judge is not distorted by his fears and suggests that his knowledge is, in fact, realized in action. This brings us to a third point, for we also perceive that Nicias' list of foreseen evils corresponds to the list Socrates gave at 191c, provided we show a correspondence between dangers at sea and death, and, similarly, courage in war and politics to Nicias' last category of victory and defeat in war and other contests. Whereas in this case it is suggested that courage consists in (1) the knowledge of whether it is better to suffer or not to suffer such things, in relation to the first list it was suggested that courage consisted in (2) the ability and will to endure those things and the passions they evoked. Once these two accounts are made to correspond in this way, we are reminded of Bonitz's thesis, for perhaps here would be evidence for Plato's thinking that the idea of courage somehow involves both (1) the *knowledge* of "what is better" or what one ought to suffer or ought not to, and (2) the *ability and will* to do so (see section 2.6). Presumably without the knowledge of what one ought or ought not to suffer—without the right guiding principles of practical reason—the man will choose the wrong ends, betraying courage through cowardly flight from the harm or danger he ought to know to risk or suffer (or perhaps betraying it the other way, rashly to risk evils in exchange for goods he ought to know he should not pursue). But without the ability to control his passions and act on his knowledge or judgment—without the powers of fortitude—he also will go astray. We shall return to the question of the Bonitz thesis later in our discussion of the dialogue. Suffice it to say that the *Laches* has not yet shown that the idea of a science of courage will stand the test of diligent examination.

This too is noteworthy: We can relate the goods and evils that Nicias lists at 195e–196a to separate human arts—for example, health and sickness to medicine, life and death to the skill of the ship's pilot, victory and defeat to military or legal or political strategy, wealth and poverty to economics (which includes farming). Thus the kind of knowledge Nicias here associates with courage is not only different from the knowledge of the good that guides each of these arts as its principle, but it would also seem to be a ruling art in relation to them, a second-order knowledge of what is better than any of their particular ends. Is courage then the political wisdom that the sophists teach under the title of virtue (see *Protagoras* 321d)? Or is it perhaps the art of statesmanship that Socrates himself envisages in the *Charmides* (171a–175a), *Gorgias* (517a–518c), and *Republic?* While neither conclusion is warranted yet, it does seem clear that the Nician science of courage at least implies a far more comprehensive knowledge than such a man as Laches would associate with *andreia*.

Finally, there is the shocking fact that Nicias adds military defeat to the things the courageous man might choose to suffer. This confirms the suspicion that he is adopting a private rather than a public point of view. No patriot could ever choose defeat for his city over victory, but ancient Greek history is filled with individuals who did so, and the historical Nicias is notorious for the many times he chose something less than victory, abandoning battlefields, military office, political contests, and even plans of military action out of fear of personal harm.[11] Still, this may not be what his words here mean, for just as the earlier example suggested that courage implies or consists in the principle that there is some unstated evil that somehow transcends dying, so the present list now may suggest that courage implies or even consists in the principle that there is some unstated good somehow transcending victory, somehow transcending the very good that confirms superiority or virtue and wins undying fame or honor. To determine Nicias' meaning, we must answer two additional questions: First, what could this good be that Nicias is now referring to? And second, do his present words not contradict the impression he left with his earlier speech, when he asserted that victory in war and other contests was the highest good, the greatest victor the man of greatest virtue?

By way of addressing these questions, let us begin by examining Laches' final response, particularly the remark that Nicias must have "some god" in mind. Why would Laches think that Nicias conceives of the courageous man as some kind of god? It seems reasonable to suppose that Laches is considering the list of evils Nicias has given and the apparent equanimity with which Nicias believes the courageous man can face them—death, disease, poverty, victory, or defeat. Surely what Nicias is really saying is that the courageous man is some kind of superhuman, *invulnerable* being, someone secure against any evil, like a god forever young and at ease because he cannot be harmed. But for Laches this is absurd. Obviously it is just as much a precondition of real courage that we *can* be harmed and that the things Nicias lists truly *are* terrible for us, as it is that we deliberate and choose in the midst of uncertainty. Obviously Nicias is confusing courage with divinity, whereas the very condition of manly courage is that men are not divine, not somehow immune to pain and shame and death. So this would seem to be the reason he accuses Nicias of twisting and turning like a man in a courtroom, trying only to win, rather than facing the matter nobly and admitting his perplexity.

But Laches *has* identified here the very context in which victory in the true sense implies a willingness to forego victory in the ordinary sense of the word (see section 4.8). For in the process of philosophical inquiry, if the *Laches* is our witness, there *is* a good that transcends victory—the good represented so marvelously by Socrates as Courage Herself, the Logos, the Truth they seek. Again the action of the dialogue has suggested something that the speeches do not. Nicias evidently suggested that the courageous state of mind implies both a principle that defines the *limits* beyond which the truly courageous man will not go, even when his own life and safety are in jeopardy—the coward by contrast recognizes no such limits—and a principle that defines the *goal* to which the truly courageous man is oriented as he lives his life and chooses what he is willing to suffer or not—the fool by contrast thinks one of the goods Nicias lists to be primary, or, conversely, he thinks none of these things matter at all.[12] But beyond suggesting that there is "something" that transcends the evil of death and "something" that transcends the goods of life and health and wealth and victory, Nicias did not say precisely what they might be. Now, however, Laches may be seen to have suggested *for the reader* a candidate for the orienting good of a perfectly rational and virtuous courage—the good of the intellect, truth. This suggestion of course conforms very nicely to what we know of Socrates' public views on human happiness or true "profitability," where he makes it clear that in his view one can suffer no evil that is worse than injustice and ignorance, and one can uphold no good that is better than virtue and truth (see especially *Apology* 29b–30b; *Crito* 47c–49d; *Gorgias* 470e; *Republic* 347e, 354a). Indeed, in the *Gorgias* Socrates explicitly praises the pilot who knows that it is better to die than to live with a soul filled with the sickness of ignorance and vice (see 512a–e).[13] But we have no way of knowing if this is how *Nicias* would interpret his definition. For Nicias might mean nothing more by his first principle than that it is better to die than to live a painful, lingering life of illness, or by his second that it is better to surrender victory than to risk trial and execution; Nicias may mean only that the distinctive mark of the courageous man is to foresee and choose what will cause him less pain or more pleasure in the long run without being blinded by immediate impressions. This would be a view of the "science of courage" that he might well have learned not from the moralist Socrates, but from a hedonistic sophist like Damon or Prodicus, or from the father of sophistry, Protagoras.[14] And of course we have no way of knowing if for Nicias these are merely words or if he would support them with deeds as well.

These latest reflections have brought us back to our dilemma about Nicias' role in the dialogue. For if he is the spokesman for the Socratic conception of courage, then why does Socrates go on to criticize and eventually refute him? But if Nicias is not the spokesman for the Socratic conception, why does what he says conform so neatly to what Socrates himself has said, both in other dialogues and in the earlier discussion with Laches in this one? The answer would appear to be that while Nicias' *words* may present us with a view of courage that corresponds to the view that Socrates defends in other dialogues, we cannot know if this is his *meaning* until Nicias has been examined more thoroughly than Laches is capable of doing. For it still is possible that Nicias "doesn't know what he is talking about." The slippery Nicias may simply have remembered an account of courage that he heard Socrates or some other wise man profess or examine, and he may successfully defend that account here against Laches, but he may also turn out to understand it much less adequately if he is put to the test by someone more resourceful and enduring. Socrates is not prepared at 196c to agree or deny that Nicias is "saying something." He will be prepared definitely to assign the source of Nicias' opinion only at the end of the next section. Only then will he be ready unequivocally to refute Nicias' definition on his own and Laches' common behalf. But it will not be the mere words that he refutes then—it will be the meaning that *Nicias* attributes to those words.

For his part, Laches has revealed himself to be both remarkably limited in his understanding and remarkably unenduring in the inquiry. His inability to understand Nicias' example seems especially odd, since we may well think that he would have no trouble admitting a kind of knowledge of principles that the brave man would rather die than violate. But Laches' discussion with Nicias has revealed him as a pure man of action, that is, as someone incapable of articulating his moral principles or beliefs or values and subjecting them to critical examination. For Laches there are principles moving him to action, such as defending the city or fighting for his honor against Nicias, and there are matters of knowledge, including the sciences of war such as horsemanship or bowmanship, but there is no "knowledge" of matters of principle. These are simply at work in his life, like customs or habits or laws so familiar that we never remove ourselves from their effects upon us to see them as they are. Regarding Nicias' second example, here we can appreciate more easily Laches' bewilderment, for surely he would be utterly perplexed by the radically unconventional suggestion that the courageous man would sometimes rather suffer defeat than victory. Laches' thought, by contrast, moves purely within the horizon of common opinion, in which all the evils Nicias mentions are simply undesirable, and only a traitor or a coward (or an invulnerable and hence transpolitical god) would think it better to suffer defeat than victory. But Laches will soon see the implications of Nicias' way of wisdom for his own more conventional stance in the world, and he will not like what he sees. As for his endurance, it is certainly disappointing that the man who just before had declared his *philonikia* in the fight for truth is now so ready to give up. But this should not be surprising, either, if we recall what he said earlier about his attitude toward speeches (188c–189c; see section 3.8). Since Nicias has now, in Laches' eyes, been shown to be a blowhard, not a real man, Laches is no longer interested in whatever Nicias might have to say. But even if Laches will not now bring himself to inquire with Nicias—and he will, in fact, inquire just a little bit more on his own account—Socrates does not intend to excuse him entirely from the investigation. If Laches cannot "see" or learn for himself, perhaps he can at least "hear" and take instruction from what occurs after Socrates takes over the inquiry on their joint behalf.

5.3 Socrates Examines Nicias on the Nature of Courage (196c–197c), and Laches Angrily Withdraws from the Inquiry (197c–e)

Socrates now begins to question Nicias, first emphasizing that he and Laches now "have the argument in common" (*koinoumetha . . . ton logon*), then establishing the point that courage, as Nicias understands it, is not something every man would know, whether a doctor or a seer, or even, as a Greek proverb said, something "every pig would know," and thus a pig could not be courageous (196c10–d11). But then it is clear that Nicias would not even trust the fabled Crommyonian sow, a fierce wild boar killed by the hero Theseus, to have been courageous. Socrates adds that he does not mean this comment only playfully, but it is necessary for Nicias either to deny courage to any wild beast or else to admit that a lion or leopard or boar knows things that few human beings know. Someone who supposes courage to be what he does must say that lion and deer and bull and monkey are by nature alike in respect of courage (196e1–9). At this point Laches interjects, exclaiming, "By the Gods!" that Socrates speaks well. Laches then takes up the inquiry again, exhorting Nicias: Answer us truly, whether you say those beasts, which we all agree are courageous, are wiser than we are, or whether you dare, in opposition to everyone else, to call them not courageous. But Nicias does dare and replies that he does not call beasts, or anything else, that from thoughtlessness have no fear of the dreadful "courageous"; he calls them "fearless" and "foolish." Or does Laches believe he calls all children courageous, who through thoughtlessness have no fear? He believes rather that the fearless and the courageous are not the same; few have a share in courage and forethought (*promēthias*, 197b3), while many men, women, children, and beasts have a share in rashness, boldness, and fearlessness with lack of forethought. So what Laches and the many call courageous, he calls "rash" (*thrasea*), but he speaks of the prudent things (*ta phronima*) as "courageous" (197a1–c1).[15]

At this point Laches simply explodes: "Behold, Socrates, how well, so he thinks, he adorns himself with words! And how he tries to deprive those whom everyone agrees have manly courage of this honor!" Ashen, Nicias quickly retreats, saying that he was not referring to Laches, for he says Laches is wise, and Lamachus, too, if the two are courageous, and so too are many other Athenians. But Laches is not so easily mollified, and noticing Nicias's hedge (the "if"), he angrily, but now better self-controlled, replies that he will not say what he could, lest Nicias call him a true son of his deme, Aexonea, whose people were noted for their abusive tongues (197c2–9). (Laches may be playing a loose pun here on the ordinary meaning of *eirōneia*, "sarcasm.") Socrates encourages this self-control, noting that Laches seems not to have perceived that Nicias has acquired his wisdom (*tēn sophian*) from their comrade Damon, who keeps company with Prodicus, who of all the sophists most beautifully distinguishes such terms. But Laches, still angry, replies sarcastically that it is certainly more proper for a sophist to adorn himself with such words than a man whom the City (*hē polis*) thinks worthy to head it! Still trying to calm Laches, Socrates addresses him with the honorific title, "O blessed one," saying that he supposes it is proper for the man in the greatest office to share in the greatest prudence (*megistēs phronēseōs*). But it seems to Socrates that Nicias is worthy of further examination regarding what in the world Nicias looks to when he assigns this name "courage." Laches' curt response to this is that Socrates can examine him all he likes! Socrates is not willing to "release" Laches from his community in the argument: Laches must put his mind to it and coexamine what is said. And Laches, recognizing Socrates' authority, agrees to do so (197d1–e9). From now on, however, Laches will pose no more questions to Nicias. His role as learner will be that of an auditor.

Obviously, this section marks an important dramatic change in the dialogue. The conflict between Laches and Nicias, which has been growing in intensity, has boiled over into open hostility. Laches is no longer on speaking terms with Nicias for reasons that are at the heart of Laches' pride. Furthermore, this anger has withdrawn Laches from the inquiry, at least as an active participant. Socrates' efforts to keep him involved have not entirely failed, but it is now clear that Laches' eagerness to win, his *philonikia,* will not sustain him in *philosophia.* If Socrates is to teach Laches, even after the manner of morally upholding persuasion, he will have to find a way to remove some of the anger that now threatens to blind Laches to whatever is said. Socrates already has found the way to do this, by identifying Laches with himself, as members of a common team. Laches' anger will be tamed by this sharing in Socrates' words as the inquiry continues, and at crucial points Socrates will reaffirm Laches' place at his side. In addition to these changes in Laches' role, Socrates has indicated a significant change in the nature of the examination of Nicias' definition, by locating the *source* of Nicias' thinking on the meaning of courage and by suggesting his own increased doubts about whatever Nicias then means by courage. For it is now clear that the question we posed in the last section concerning the origin of Nicias' ideas has been answered: Socrates is not that source. Thus it will not be a Socratic but rather a *sophistic* theory of courage that will be examined and refuted in the remaining portion of the inquiry. But why has Socrates come to this conclusion about Nicias' views, and how does his question about the courage of wild animals relate to the rest of the inquiry?

First a note on the Crommyonian sow. Socrates' choice of this myth is itself interesting, not only because of the reference to the fabled first king of Athens who won his crown by going down into the labyrinth and killing the minotaur— the story that forms the mythological mime of the *Phaedo*, where Socrates will kill the Fear of Death—but also because of the nature of the beast and Theseus' reasons for killing it.[16] We learn from Plutarch that whereas Theseus fought men only when he was forced to by their injustice, he went out of his way to fight this beast, holding it a noble thing to subdue such a creature willingly and thus tame the earth (*Lives*, "Theseus" 9). Taken as an image of the soul, the Crommyonian sow represents mythologically the uncontrolled appetites or uncontrolled temper that the hero sets out to subdue in himself. Rather than indicating Socrates' agreement with the thought that a wild beast is properly called courageous, the myth thus understood forms a mythological mime: Bestial anger must be tamed, as part of the path of the hero on his way to virtue and victory.

Be this as it may, Socrates' argument seems clear enough: If courage simply takes the form of knowledge and does not draw on any other than the intellectual powers of the soul, then whatever it is that animals have that makes some of them predators (lions or leopards) and others prey (deer) or that makes some ferociously resist attack (wild boar) and others simply flee (monkeys), they must all have an equal share in courage, that is, none at all.[17] Somehow this argument exposes the fundamental difference of opinion that holds be-tween Laches and Nicias, and somehow Socrates, although he surely cannot agree with the view Laches expresses, is nevertheless on Laches' side in this argument. How can it be? Let us look at the responses of Laches and Nicias, and then at the bit of drama that follows.

To understand these two responses, we should note before all else the personal pronouns they use: whereas Laches speaks only of "we," Nicias speaks of "I."[18] Laches, by contrasting daring (*tolmas*, 197a4) to what "all of us" think and say, sets up the opposition that we found so important in discussing Laches' own apparent failings in the kind of courage needed by a leader (see section 4.7). It is only the man who can break with the "we" and think as an "I" who is able to establish some basis from which to judge things, other than what everyone thinks or wants, but this the honor- and opinion-bound Laches cannot do. Nicias, on the other hand, can set himself apart as an I or as one of the proud few against the many, thanks to his sophistic teachers, and the thing that distinguishes him, he says, is not the mere daring to oppose the views of the many, but foresight and the prudent acts that come of it. So, whereas Laches is identified here with the many, or with the city in the mode of common opinion and common values, Nicias is identified with a group separating itself from the mere opinion of the city and its values. These men set themselves off as individuals "wise" in their thoughts and actions, unlike the irrational many, who are as unthinking as wild animals. We will return to this point shortly, but first let us consider the views of Laches.

Nicias has learned one thing from his teachers that Laches has *not* learned, namely that human reason makes a difference in speaking and thinking clearly about courage. Whereas Nicias is right in his unwillingness to assign the same quality of courage to rational and irrational beings, Laches, merely following common speech habits, will call the lion or wild boar "courageous," just as Homer sings of men turning on their enemies "like a great bearded lion" (*Iliad* 17.108–12) or standing their ground like a "wild mountain boar" (13.470–75).[19] Now we might wonder why Laches falls so easily into this habit. After all, he is certainly capable of distinguishing manly courage from whatever you want to call it that lions or women or children may have, since on his own definition, that is, the first, none of them can be courageous. But we also noticed earlier in his speech (184b; see section 3.4) and in his second account of courage, the one prompted by Socrates (192b; see section 4.5), that Laches is prone to conflate the natural and that which takes the form of habit or custom. Herein, then, is the solution: Laches views what belongs to *ethos,* the acquired ways of life in the *polis,* as if it were a matter of *physis.* He apparently cannot distinguish "the civic," the moral-political beliefs and habits acquired through informal familial and civic instruction by praise and blame (the kind of thing Protagoras talks about in his famous speech on teaching virtue) from "the natural," that is, what springs up as it were automatically and without deliberation or art.[20] But this failure is revealing; by it Laches is shown to be a man who acts unthinkingly, merely following habits of mind that seem ingrained in him. His courage is that of a man who has never examined what the city has taught him as being honorable and disgraceful. Laches is the natural man, the political man who forgets about nature because he identifies himself so completely with convention.

Nicias, on the other hand, both distinguishes himself from the city and conventional opinion and identifies the specific difference that makes man human and not animal—the difference of rationality, symbolized in the Athenian Enlightenment by the figure of Prometheus (see section 1.6). But just as Laches is prone to blur the difference between the kind of courage that he stands for and the kind of courage or natural fighting or predatory instinct that is much stronger in some animals than in others, so Nicias is prone to blur this difference too, even if he is able, as Laches is not, to separate prudently rational daring from mere impulse.[21] Thus Nicias says that what Laches and most people call courageous he does not, and this apparently refers to every sort of courage lacking his kind of prudent foresight. Specifically, Nicias would appear, by his previous argument if not as clearly by his fearful words in response to Laches' attack, to do the very thing that Laches accuses him of: He denies that what Laches (a model of civic endurance) and Lamachus (a model of civic boldness; see section 1.4) have is really courage. Whereas Laches seems to conflate the human and the bestial (though he separates out the divine as something clearly above the human), Nicias sharply distinguishes the godlike Promethean wise men like himself from the merely human, who whether grown citizen-warriors (e.g., Laches) or women (e.g., Xanthippe) or mere children (e.g., the young Aristides and Thucydides) are all little more than animal-like in their virtue. Laches' conceptual failure here is obvious and all too revealing; he does not consider how reason makes a difference; he fails again to link prudence and courage, to bring the two together. Laches bespeaks a virtue merely human, and as a result is at a loss to distinguish it from what is natural. But Nicias' conceptual failure here is also, if less obviously, great and revealing; he does not consider how human society and the bonds of love, pride, and ordinary civic self-consciousness and freedom make a difference. Nicias bespeaks a virtue that *seems* higher than the merely human, but he fails to appreciate the human, the conventional, denigrating it to the level of the merely natural. Indeed, Nicias reveals the corruption at the heart of sophistry, the corruption that Aristophanes attacked and Socrates fought so hard to overcome: the corruption of dividing human things simply into the rational and the irrational or the scientific and the appetitive, of failing to see the distinctively social and political heart and will at the center of human things and thereby also failing to understand human nature, including—especially—one's own.[22] And this failure is not merely intellectual in character since it arrogates to itself a wisdom that it does not possess.[23]

Laches, then, is the enraged voice of the city and its justice, when he indignantly accuses Nicias of trying to steal from him the very property he treasures most: his *timē*, his honor, his civic courage (197c2–4). For if no one who lacks sophistic foresight or science or wisdom is courageous, then all the unreflective freedom fighters of history, Greek and otherwise, had no more manly courage than the least child or animal. Not his words—he is practically reduced to sputtering, he is so angry—but his deeds prove that Laches is only too willing to kill to keep what he believes is rightfully his, and this too is the voice of the city: that most basic spirit of manly justice, which will not surrender its (conventionally) rightful privileges, either to external or internal enemies, without a fight.[24] Laches shows us the very real danger that the city poses to all inquiry, because when he must decide—when his innermost opinion of what is right and good and of his own virtue is at stake—Laches' mind is not open, and will not be opened, to think into the uncertain. Laches would let truth die a thousand deaths before he would give up his claim to manly honor and courage, before he would surrender his own self; indeed, Laches would kill a thousand so-called wise men before he would let them take his life of manly honor away. "Semper Fi, do or die"—that is the stuff he's made of. And there will be no *polis,* no liberty without him, so long as men are men and liberty and empire are worth killing and dying for.[25] But Nicias, drawn by the Siren song of a false wisdom, has forgotten that he most of all, as the head of the democratic government, depends on unsophisticated men such as Laches and Lamachus and "many others" for their support, until Laches' anger so rudely has reminded him of it, and he now moves as quickly as possible to repair the damage. By his *words* at 195b–197b, Nicias would appear to have won the contest that he has fought with Laches since they first proved themselves rivals in advising the youths. But by his *deed* at 197b–c, Nicias shows the weak stuff he's made of, dropping his shield and running like a deer when the leonine Laches turns on him, though even in his running Nicias cannot resist the "if" that betrays his real opinion. The doxological mime reveals the rash emptiness of his words.

It is now clear that whatever Nicias might have learned, or rather heard, of Socrates' opinions about courage, it is no longer such views, but those of Damon and Prodicus, that are now on trial. We also suspect that Nicias has begun to betray a misunderstanding of the conception of courage he had himself introduced at 195b–196b, a courage radically different from the technical kind Nicias had been identified with earlier. In the Socratic-like kind of courage Nicias nimbly if somewhat vaguely defended in 195b–196b, the guiding foresight may have consisted not in the science of danger and opportunity but in a radically different stance of the rational soul toward good and evil and what the man knows of them. There is no reason to think, on that view, that the courageous person believes he will not suffer something evil, only that he thinks what he suffers by so doing will be "better" than the alternative (on Socratic foresight/forethought, see *Laches* 185b; also *Protagoras* 313a–314b, 361b; *Gorgias* 501b). But now we notice that Nicias seems to suggest that the wisely courageous man will do only what is prudent, which normally would mean what will cause him no harm. This view of courage might well be opposed to the one that was considered before, but it is still consistent with the sophistic teaching that courage is shown in actions that may appear daring to others but are not really dangerous to the man of skill and foresight. There is thus a strong hint at 197b–c that Nicias is reverting to his old, Athenian notion of courage, one all-too-distinctive feature of which is that it does not cover the situation in which one cannot avoid suffering, but must endure it as a matter of what is right.[26] In the end we may need courage most of all when things are not in our control, regardless of how intelligent and foresighted we are, as when we must suffer a death that can no longer be avoided—when one must step forward boldly and pay for the life of truth.

As for Socrates, he, at any rate, has confirmed for himself both the source of Nicias' opinion and the further direction of the argument and his efforts to teach Laches through the inquiry. They must go on together, Socrates and Laches as one team, to examine fully Nicias' sophistic opinions and to determine whether Nicias does indeed participate in the "greatest prudence," as would be proper for the head of the government. Here is another instance where it is all-important for the Greekless reader of the dialogue to have a precise English translation in hand, lest the distinctions that Socrates is drawing become confused. Socrates himself quite pointedly distinguishes the *wisdom* (*sophia*) that Nicias has acquired from his sophistic teachers from the *prudence* (*phronēsis*) that Socrates says is proper to the head of government; Nicias has the one (which of course is a fraud; see *Apology* 21b–23a), but does he have the other? The action of the dialogue has already suggested that he does not, and his speeches will confirm this. Socrates, on the other hand, will display, in his last attempt to teach Laches, one source of prudence that, if the man had adhered to it at Mantinea, might have saved Laches from death and the city from defeat. In this way, Socrates will ground his own acceptance of Lachean-Lacedaimonian civic courage in a source that secures it as a prudent form of endurance, even if it does not make it intelligent and bold. This does not mean, however, that Socratic courage lives in easy harmony with the kind that Laches stands for. While "prudent" and "enduring" may go well together, there is more to Socrates than prudence alone, even if he is not wise.

5.4 Socrates Defines His and Laches' Principles for Thinking about Courage (197e–199a)

Socrates introduces the second part of the inquiry with Nicias by telling him to start again "from the beginning" (*ex archēs*, 197e10–198a1). This suggests that the discussion to follow may be seen as comprising a third part of the inquiry as a whole, the first part having been dominated by the examination of civic courage and the relation between Socrates and Laches, the second by presentation of the implicit conflict between "Lachean" civic consciousness and the sophistic "Promethean" wisdom represented by Nicias, and the last

part by the conflict between Socratic political philosophy and Nician pseudowisdom. This portion of the inquiry will, like the second, be divided into
three segments. (Both the inquiry with Laches and the inquiry with Nicias
taken as a whole are divided into seven parts, corresponding to the sections
in chapters 4 and 5.) In the first segment (197e10–199a5) Socrates establishes
the three principles that will ground both his proof in the second segment
(199a6–d3) that Nicias' definition must be revised to "the knowledge of good
and evil" and his proof in the third segment (199d4–e12) that courage so
understood must be identified with the whole of virtue. But with the latter
proof it is clear that Nicias' attempt to define courage has failed, just as Laches'
had. Nicias' response to his *aporia* is very different from that of Laches,
however, and as a result of what he and Laches say then (199e13–200c2) it
is obvious that the inquiry has come to an end. The dialogue closes with the
return of the fathers Lysimachus and Melesias to the conversation and the
unlikely prospect of Socrates teaching them all the next day (200c2–201c5).
Let us turn again to the text.

Socrates' first remarks to Nicias are to remind the latter that from the
beginning the two have examined courage as if it were a part of virtue, there
being other parts as well which, taken all together, are called virtue; Nicias
agrees. Then Socrates asks whether Nicias says that these parts are the same
as what he says: courage, moderation, justice, and some others. The list
conspicuously excludes both piety and prudence, but Nicias does not point
this out. In these, then, Socrates concludes, they agree (197e10–198b1).

Now, however, they should examine what is to be dreaded and dared,
whether Nicias believes one thing, and we—Socrates and Laches—believe
something else. Socrates is to tell Nicias what they believe, and if he does not
agree, he should instruct them. For they believe the things causing fear are
terrible (*deina*) while those that do not are confidence-inspiring (*tharralea*),
and they believe that fear is caused not by past or present evils, but by expected
evils. For fear is the "expectation of future evil" (*prosdokian mellontos kakou*,
198b9). Socrates then turns to Laches for the first of only two instances in
198a–199e to confirm that this is also his opinion. So there you hear our view,
Socrates says, that the future evils are terrible, and the future things that are
not evil or are good inspire confidence. Do you speak of them that way? I do,
Nicias replies. And it is to the knowledge of these things that you give the
name "courage"? Exactly, Nicias answers. This completes the discussion of
Socrates' second point (198b2–c8).

Finally, Socrates moves to the third question to be examined to see if
"you"—Nicias—agree with "us." It seems to Socrates—and he gestures here
to Laches—that in regard to the things of which there is knowledge, it is not

something different, to know about what has come into being, how it has come into being; nor is it something different, to know about the things coming into being, how they are coming into being; nor is it different, to know about what has not yet come into being, how most beautifully it might or will come into being; rather it is all the same knowledge. Thus concerning the healthful, it is nothing other than medicine—it being one—that for all times oversees the things that are coming into being and the things that have come into being and the things that will come into being, as to how they come into being. And concerning the things growing from the earth, farming stands in the same way. And in matters of war, Socrates is sure that "you"—referring here to both Nicias and Laches—would bear witness that the art of generalship has foresight in the finest, most beautiful manner (*kallista promētheitai*) concerning what is to be and in other respects, and it thinks it is fitting to rule, not serve, the seer's art, since it has a finer knowledge of the things relating to war, both what is happening and what is to be. Socrates concludes dramatically, "And the law (*ho nomos*) orders thusly, that the seer shall not rule over the general, but the general over the seer," and then for the second time Socrates turns to Laches and asks if "we" shall assert these things. Laches confirms that "we" shall. Then Socrates turns to Nicias and asks him if "you," Nicias, assert with them, that the same knowledge perceives concerning the same things, whether future or present or past, and Nicias replies, "I do, for that is my opinion, Socrates" (198c9–199a9).

This completes the first stage in Socrates' refutation of Nicias' definition. Each of the three steps defines one important aspect of the understanding of manly courage that Socrates believes he and Laches hold in common, but that he has reason to doubt Nicias shares with them. Obviously, the culmination of the introductory sequence occurs at 199a1–3, when Socrates points out the rightful relation between the general and the seer, as ordered by "the law."[27] This remark also clearly alludes to Nicias' disastrous decision at Syracuse harbor to let the seer rule over him—an allusion, as noted earlier, that is being made in a surprisingly *ad hoc* manner (see section 1.3). We must examine each step in Socrates' preparatory argument to understand the refutation that follows and the allusion to the historical Nicias' calamitous behavior, as well as why it is made here.

To begin, then, it is instructive that Socrates makes it clear they are not going to examine a concept of courage that might be something other than a "part" of virtue; they will not examine a concept of courage possibly separate from virtue, or one that could be the whole of virtue. This reminds us of the curious fashion in which Socrates began the inquiry with Laches at 190c–d, where he took his guidance from the many (section 4.2). But it also reminds us of the complex discussion with Laches at 192b–d in which Socrates established that if courage is fortitude it must be prudent as well (section 4.6), and of Nicias' speech at 181d–182d, in which we saw that Nicias' account of virtue did not seem to be tied to justice or moderation (section 3.8). Looking back to those earlier discussions, we can see that insofar as courage is considered a part of virtue, whose whole includes moderation and justice as well, the conception of courage being presupposed has a decidedly political or public character. As we saw in the discussion with Laches, if courage is a part of virtue, it is allied with justice through notions of what is shameful and what is honorable, not opposed to it, as sophists such as Thrasymachus and Callicles argue, taking their start from what they say is by nature. But it is not then distinct from the other virtues, as sophists such as Protagoras argue, taking their start from common sense and a hedonistic conception of the good. If courage is a part of virtue, as Socrates and Laches suppose, then virtue must itself somehow form a whole; and the most obvious candidate for the unifying principle is *prudence,* specifically the prudence embodied in the law of a free community of men ruling themselves and both by duty and by choice willing to fight to protect their liberty and property.[28] Looking forward, however, to the conclusion of the inquiry with Nicias, we also are forced to recognize that if there is a courage that is not a part but the *whole* of virtue, this courage might not conform to justice or moderation or any of the other communal, prudent virtues. The greatest prudence, of course, being political, must enact justice and conform to law, and if courage is ruled by prudence, so will that courage conform. But wisdom may not be political or law-abiding, and if courage is a form of wisdom, it may be that courage as wisdom is opposed to justice, moderation, piety, and the greatest prudence, and not allied with them at all.[29] Thus Socrates' first principle links him emphatically to Laches and to the city's notions of justice and the good, and it prepares the way for refuting Nicias' definition, insofar as that definition somehow arrogates to courage a comprehensive wisdom or mastery possibly in conflict with civic virtue.

It is, however, Socrates' second, central principle that lays the basis for the decisive argument in his refutation of Nicias. The crucial notion that he and Laches share, it seems, is that of fear, and the crucial point about their notion, as he and Laches agree to define it, is that fear is a kind of opinion, a "foreopinion" of an evil that is not yet, but is to be. It is this principle that connects Socrates' and Laches' earlier discussion of courage and the passions (in which fear did not always have a unique role) and the present discussion of courage and knowledge. For in this new account, fear would appear to be a kind of knowledge, namely the knowledge of the terrible, as well as being a passion and impulse to movement. The idea, of course, is that fear is not mere intellectual or theoretical foresight of future events, but that it is gripping, that it seizes heart and mind and orders the body to flight.[30] If, though, we define fear as "the foreopinion of future evils," and if we further assert with Socrates and Laches that future evils are terrible, then it would follow on Nicias' account that the knowledge of the terrible and the knowledge of future evils that take the form of fear will be the same. The chief point to fix in mind here is made at 198c: Socrates and Laches together hold that the foresight of future evils is to see them as terrible, and so to be fearful, and the foresight of future things that are not evil or that are good is to see them as not terrible and so to feel safe or hopeful or boldly self-confident; Nicias agrees to this. What Socrates and Laches do *not* say but Nicias insists on is that courage is *identical* with the knowledge of these things; it is the foresight that takes the impassioned form of fear or confidence. It is this latter identification—which Socrates indicates by omission that he and Laches do not share in—that will prove to be the basis of Socrates' next argument. Unlike both Socrates and Laches, Nicias makes no room in his understanding of "the science of the terrible and the confidence-inspiring" for the courage that "overcomes" or "overrules" the fear of future evils by enduring it for the sake of future goods—for instance, the courage that endures the terrible fear of death for the sake of the city's freedom and victory. Unlike Socrates and Laches, Nicias does not allow for a contrast or conflict between the knowledge (*epistēmē*) by which the coura- geous man knows what to do and the opinion (*doxa*) by which he is afraid. We shall explain this point more fully in discussing the next segment of Socrates' argument. Obviously it will be crucial to consider how Nicias' admissions here about fear and confidence are related to what he said at 195b–196b about courage as the knowledge of "what is better," and to his disconcerting statement to Laches at 197b that courage is a kind of bold foresight that attains prudent things—disconcerting because it might revert to his earlier, technical account of courage according to which the courageous man would not willingly suffer evils for the sake of what is better.

Then there is Socrates' third and final point, the most complex of the three, and his strange additional remarks about the art of strategy and the relationship ordered by the law between the general and the seer. As for the idea of every science or art knowing things past, present, and future, we note that Socrates does not distinguish here those merely contingent particulars that the farmer or doctor in his wisdom may remember or perceive or foresee from what might be thought to be necessary general rules of agricultural or medical science. Instead, he groups both of these objects of knowledge under the past, present, and future things the farmer or doctor knows. This is one reason why it is appropriate for him to imply that the artist's knowledge is of "things that come to be" or of processes, rather than "things that are" or beings.[31] It must also be the reason why he does not consider the possibility that the artist might possess the general knowledge, but not apply it in the particular case; the artist as Socrates and Laches conceive of him knows the universal or general *in* the particular, knows that this air portends a killing frost or else a merely dangerous one; his is a practical, not a theoretical, kind of knowledge. This point is also underscored by the fact that Socrates reintroduces the role of technical mastery or of action on the part of the knower, a feature of the craft proficiency that dropped out of Nicias' account at 195b–196b of the knowledge belonging to the courageous man (see section 5.2). But Socrates stresses that the knower he has in mind knows not only how things have become and how they are becoming and how they will become, but how they most beautifully *might* become (*hopē an kallista genoito,* 198d4), an optative expressive of the conditional nature of their becoming—conditional on the actions that are to be taken by the artist, who knows how they contingently might, not necessarily will, most beautifully come to be through the action of his art. We cannot appreciate the full significance of this new point until we compare what Socrates has to say here (with Nicias agreeing) about the nature of the knowledge of past, present, and future things with what he says next. We *can,* however, appreciate one important aspect of it, by considering how it applies to what Socrates says about the knowledge of generalship and the example he gives by allusion to Nicias' future actions at Syracuse.

For Nicias doubly betrays himself at 198e–199a, when he implicitly agrees that the general foresees most beautifully the things of war! The second part of this double betrayal consists in the implicit contradiction between what he says here about the knowledge of the general and what he had said at 195b–196b while defending the seemingly Socratic notion of courage that he mooted there. For it cannot be the general, according to Nicias, but rather it must be the man of wise courage, who best knows what is good and evil in war; it is only the latter who can judge if what is to be is *truly* good or evil, truly safe or fearful. It would be only on the sophistic-Promethean model of the science of courage—the model he had adhered to at 181d–182d—that Nicias would say that the general knows these things best, but that is the clear implication of what he says here again. Under the pressure of Socratic questioning, Nicias has "forgotten" the distinction he developed at 195c–196a and now fails to distinguish the knowledge of good and evil in war from the artful foresight of what will and will not occur. Thus he has reverted to the technical conception of courage, just as we suspected that he might have in reflecting on his comments at 197b. We shall discuss the significance of this reversion in the next section, since it is only at 199c–e where the full implications of Nicias' self-betrayal become evident. The first part of Nicias' self-betrayal in the passage at 198e, however, comports directly with what Socrates says that he and Laches agree on concerning the law, and we must look at that now. (1) Why do Socrates and Laches say that it is not the seer (who Nicias had said at 195e foresees the future things) but the general who foresees best the things of war (and by implication the doctor the things of health and sickness, and so forth)? (2) What does it mean that the law agrees with this and orders the two arts to be related as superior to inferior? (3) Further, what is the connection of the point here with the "historical" allusion to Nicias' actions at Syracuse, and how, if at all, is this point related to the ongoing education that Socrates is directing at Laches?

Regarding the first question, the answer to which unlocks the whole argument, the key would seem to be Socrates' interesting comment, emphasized above, that the practicing artist, the action-scientist of contingent things, not only knows theoretically what has been, is now, and will be, but knows what "most beautifully might be." For the knowledge that the artist possesses is at work only when directed to a future good not simply coming to be, independently of his knowledge, but as the *product* of his art. We then realize that what differentiates the general's art from that of the seer is that the general's command of "what is to be," unlike the seer's vision, is guided by the principle that he is to achieve victory and that his skill-informed action is to be instrumental in that victory. Thus the general, not the seer, must never forget that his knowledge and action are *responsible* for the future. And so we can answer the second question by saying that surely this is why the law orders the general to command the seer, not the reverse, because the law and the city presuppose what the seer does not: that human knowledge and character, rather than fate, freely determine what is to be. Whereas the comings to be of the past and immediate present cannot be altered, future human actions are essentially open, undetermined. Thus the very passage that might suggest that the knowledge of things past, present, and future is all the same, by Socrates' little addition and by this example reveals a radical difference between human future and past: past things cannot be changed, but those of the future, by the implication of Athenian law, are more subject to human art and *freedom* than to divine rule.[32] It is the duty of the commander to focus his mind and will on victory, not on trying to determine what is to be, precisely because "what will be" is contingent on his skill and determination in the battle or campaign.

This brings us to the final question. We now can see that it is correct for Socrates to allude to Nicias' later actions here, for it is on precisely this point that both Nicias' present and later conceptions of the knowledge belonging to courage would appear to fail. Nicias somehow believes in a science or wisdom that can perfectly master the future and make it wholly predictable and safe, whereas the law and the city believe that the future is largely open, something to be shaped through art and freedom according to the varied abilities of men. Nicias believes that it is possible through this science always to choose what is better and never to have to endure things terrible or evil. This belief in a perfectly prudent kind of boldness, a perfect "science" of courage, will be tested and found seriously wanting in Sicily. For there he will discover that human science cannot master fortune so easily, above all in those actions in which science is pitted against science, man against man. There the kind of certainty and control of the future that he seeks will prove unavailable; the man who once relied on the resources of Promethean foresight to ensure success will fall back upon resources of character he does not have, so that he finally turns to the seers, who after all might know the things that "are to be." Nicias' belief in science or wisdom or foresight is in reality little more than a desperate cover for his inability to face his own freedom and responsibility.[33]

Laches, on the other hand, might now learn from Socrates the very lesson that he most needs to learn: the principle that would keep him from imprudent boldness and foolish, honor-bound courage (see section 4.7). For Socrates has revealed that even command responsibility is governed by the fundamental principle of military action, the idea of obedience to the law. The general who recognizes his responsibility to rule over the seers should also be able to recognize that same responsibility to rule over his muttering men, recognize his responsibility to take the prudent path to victory, not the foolishly courageous path that might lead to defeat, though his own honor might appear at risk. And yet Laches will not remember at Mantinea the lesson that Socrates has taught him here today. The conflict between manly honor and prudence in the form of obedience to the law is too deeply rooted in the ancient Greek tradition and in the psychology of manliness and civic courage. Laches might have thought his way out of it, had he endured in the inquiry, but he will not. (We shall consider later why not.) The passive knowledge that Laches "hears" from Socrates will not save him on the day when he has to choose whether it is better to risk defeat for the city or dishonor for himself. His passive "knowledge," though better in content, will prove no more stable or well grounded than the kind that Nicias heard from his teachers. Laches will have the right opinion, but lacking the arguments that bind such truth to the man who holds them, it will "fly away" under the pressure of the moment (see *Meno* 97d–98a).

5.5 Socrates Refutes Nicias' Definition and Changes It to the "Knowledge of All Goods and Evils" (199a–d)

The stage now has been set for refuting Nicias' definition. This is accomplished in two steps, the argument from 199a6–d3, in which Socrates shows that by his own admissions Nicias must agree to a significant revision of the account of courage that he has given, and then the second step from 199d4–e12, in which Socrates presents Nicias with an interpretation of the new account and shows that this is equivalent to the whole of virtue and is therefore not a part of virtue as they had originally stipulated. Laches' and Nicias' response at 199e13–200c6 to this second *aporia* ends the inquiry.

The concluding argument taken as a whole from 198a1 to 199e12 has attracted more attention than any other part of the dialogue in the contemporary scholarly literature, both on account of its obvious significance for interpreting the *Laches* itself, and on account of its place relative to the question of the parts and whole of virtue (see section 4.2).[34] In relation to the argument itself, disagreement among the critics has largely centered on the two issues of whether or not Socrates accepts Nicias' definition and whether or not he accepts the premise invoked at 199e6–7, that courage is a part rather than the whole of virtue. Debate over the first issue turns on whether Socrates argues fallaciously at 199a6–d3, where he tries to show that Nicias' definition must be amended. Most scholars say that Socrates argues soundly yet rejects the conclusion that courage is the whole of virtue, and therefore Socrates and Plato—or at least Plato—reject the definition. This is the overt conclusion of the dialogue, and it is the position consistent with Bonitz's thesis. This view implies that the virtues differ from one another in definition. A few say that Socrates argues fallaciously and accepts the definition (which they hold is genuinely Socratic); therefore the definition is somehow meant to express the Socratic-Platonic truth about courage. This position might appear to be supported by the discussion of courage at *Protagoras* 358a–360d.[35] On one interpretation of that reading, Socrates holds that courage is one form of knowledge, different in definition from the other virtues, which are also defined as distinct forms of knowledge. While they are different in definition, they are inseparable in existence. This is the so-called Interentailing Hypothesis of the Unity of Virtue.[36] A second issue is whether Socrates agrees with the conclusion of the argument at 199e3–4, that indeed courage is equivalent to the knowledge of good and evil, and this in turn is identical with the whole of virtue, so that the original premise of the argument, that courage is a part of virtue, must be discarded. Most scholars agree that Socrates does not accept this conclusion, yet a few hold that Socrates (or Plato) asserts the unity of virtue in the so-called early dialogues in the sense of the full substantial sameness of the virtues, all being equal to the knowledge of good and evil.[37] On this view, virtue has no "parts" but is necessarily, whenever present, present as one reality (which does not prevent it from manifesting itself in different kinds of actions that appear brave or temperate or right). This in its turn is the so-called Identity Hypothesis of the Unity of Virtue. It would seem to be the view expressed at *Phaedo* 68c–69c, where all the virtues are seen to be equivalent to philosophical prudence or wisdom.

The interpretation presented here does not conform to any of those just now outlined. In our interpretation the definition being examined does not bear the Socratic meaning suggested at 195b–196a; rather it bears the Promethean, sophistic meaning that was Nicias' original conception of courage at 181d–182d, which he seemed to revert to at 197b-c and which he clearly reverts to at 198e–199a, where he implicitly agrees that the technically skilled man would have the best knowledge of good and evil in the domain of war. On our interpretation, Socrates' argument is sound, insofar as it is directed against the understanding of courage that Nicias has fallen back upon. Whether the argument would be sound or fallacious if directed against the Socratic ideal of courage is a moot point, if only because the *Laches* provides no certain guidance as to the way to interpret that meaning, or any hint, even, whether Socrates (or Plato) accepts it. As for the premise that courage is a part of virtue, our interpretation again finds the *Laches* inconclusive. For while it is manifestly clear, both in word and deed, that Socrates, for the purposes of his inquiry with Laches, accepts that premise, it is by no means obvious that he accepts it unconditionally. If there is a kind of courage rooted in wisdom or something like wisdom, it may well be identical with the knowledge of good and evil and with virtue as a whole. There may be a form of virtue somehow transcending the ordinary ways of thinking about good and evil in human actions and souls. It may even be that the *Laches* is meant to point toward this transcendent, wondrous state of being and knowing, though it does not provide us with a clear message regarding this, and therefore probably should not be used to support any grand claims about the Socratic-Platonic doctrine of virtue. As suggested in chapter 2, the *Laches,* even in its depths, seems to support the aporetic surface. With this orientation in mind, let us return to the text.

Socrates begins the first stage of the refutation of Nicias' definition ironically, buttering him up with the honorific title, "O best of men," and leading him to agree that (1) "Courage is the knowledge of what is to be dreaded and dared" (199a10–b2). Nicias also agrees that (2) "Things to be dreaded and things to be dared have been admitted to be future evils and future goods"

(198b3–5). Socrates then asks concerning the third premise that he and Laches shared, and Nicias agrees that (3) "The same knowledge is concerned with the same things, both of things future and of things in all conditions" (199b6–8). This phrase, "in all conditions" (*pantōs echotōn*), is new. In the contexts where Socrates has hitherto spoken of past, present, and future things, he has not hesitated to list them all patiently. But he will use the same phrase again at 199c1 and 199c7 to summarize everything that this knowledge is concerned with. Then, given (1) and (2) and the general rule established by (3), Socrates concludes that (4) "Courage is not only knowledge of what is to be dreaded and dared, for it perceives or understands not only concerning future goods and evils but also those that are coming into being in the present and that have come into being in the past and that are in all conditions, just like the other knowledges" (199b9–c1). Realizing that he has been trapped, Nicias can but feebly reply to this: "So at least it seems" (199c2). Socrates concludes his refutation or modification of Nicias' definition by pointing out that (5) the answer that Nicias gave "us" (still speaking for the Socrates-Laches team) was part of courage—"about a third" (*schedon ti triton*). Yet we had asked what courage is as a whole. Thus it seems, "according to your argument," that (6) courage is not only "knowledge of what is to be dreaded and dared," but "practically a knowledge concerning all goods and evils and in all conditions." So, then, "by your argument" (*ho sos logos*) that is what courage would be. Is it then to be restipulated in this way? What does Nicias say? His answer is characteristic of him throughout the dialogue: "That is my opinion, Socrates" (199c3–d3). (Nicias uses the expression, "in my opinion," *dokei moi*, no less than seven times in the inquiry, beginning at 194c7 and including his chief admissions at 196d11, 198c1, 199a9, 199d3, and 199e2. Despite the promise of his opening words, he does not ascend beyond *doxa* to the level of *dianoia*. See the discussion in section 2.7; also section 3.7.)

Plato gives the reader two important clues to help him discover the philosophical insights underlying Socrates' argument at 199a–d. The first is Socrates' curious observation that Nicias has defined for them a *part* of courage, about a third.[38] Why "about" a third? If the knowledge that is courage is divided into past, present, and future, then Nicias has given them precisely one-third, not "about" one-third. Plato is, after all, not one to be vague about the mathematical. But we have already seen that this division is not only inadequate, it is downright misleading regarding the nature of the knowledge of the future relevant to courage. As Socrates implied in his discussion at 198d–e, the craftsman knows not only "what will be," that is, what will occur as a function of natural processes, he also knows in a very different sense "what most beautifully might be," what might occur if his art is successful in imposing its knowledge on a sometimes very recalcitrant material and if his physical or social passions or his corrupted will do not deflect his mind from its proper focus on the goal of his art. Nicias' conception of the "science of the terrible and safe or opportune" does not allow for this optative object, for "what might be." It allows only for what *will* be, because it presupposes the kind of Promethean science, the mastery of the future, that allows the man of wise courage simply to pick what is better for himself out of the possible futures he foresees. But because on this account there is no gap between the knowledge and the deed—neither one caused by the material nor one caused by the internal failures of the artist—the knowledge of the future cannot be distinguished essentially from the knowledge of what is presently occurring or what has occurred. Because the practical and free has been conceived as the theoretical and necessary, it is precisely the same knowledge that must be at work in relation to the past, present, and future, with only the incidental facts being different. The argument as applied to *Nicias'* understanding of the definition is therefore sound. He does, indeed, conceive of courage as a science of all goods and evils in which the distinctive ontological status of the future goods and evils to be realized through human action is *not* clearly recognized. Nicias has, as it were, a strangely "mathematical" conception of courage, a conception that removes it from the world of real danger, fear, and uncertainty and envisages its possessor as a more godlike being than ordinary mortals. He believes in science but not in freedom. But this vision of courage is not the apprehension of the Idea. Nicias' conception of courage is in fact not even so much on the level of *doxa,* much less *dianoia* or *nous,* as it is on the level of *eikasia,* fantasy. It is a sophistic dream.[39]

The second clue that Plato may have left his reader is the curious phrase "in all conditions," quoted in our summary of the text.[40] At 199b6–7 Socrates speaks of "knowledge of the same things, whether of things future or of things in all conditions," where the words seem only to cover the other conditions, those namely of present and past. But then immediately following, at 199b11–c1, he speaks of courage as perceiving or understanding not only future goods and evils, but those "coming into being and that have come into being and are in all conditions," and here the phrase is used either to summarize or possibly to indicate another kind of being—other than something that became in the past, is now becoming, or will become in the future. Finally, at 199c6–7, he concludes that on Nicias' account courage would be "pretty much" the knowledge of "all goods and evils and in all conditions," and here again this phrase may hint at a kind of knowledge of good and evil involving not just goods and evils that "come into being" but ones that simply "are"—that are of a different ontological status from the goods and evils that the would-be Nician science of courage and the arts in general have as their objects.

For Nicias has not turned out to have an understanding of what is good and evil that is radically different from that of other men, though he may be less civic-minded than a Laches. Basically, it seems that his conception of courage is oriented to the same conventional goods and evils that other men are oriented to, the various kinds of things that come to be—survival and death, health and illness, wealth and poverty, victory and defeat, pleasure and pain. These are the objects of his science, the goods and evils he seeks to obtain or avoid, always taking the prudently better, that is to say the greater good or the lesser evil. There is no evidence that Nicias' knowledge of what is better is oriented by the apperception of those invisible, intelligible objects that Socrates so often speaks of, the Ideas, or by the Socratic concern expressed even in the *Laches* for securing the good and preventing the harm of the soul (185a–187b, 201a–b; compare *Apology* 29d–30b; *Crito* 49d; *Phaedo* 64a–c; *Gorgias* 469b, 481b–c; *Republic* 334b–335d). But there is sufficient evidence for us to conclude that Nicias' knowledge of what is better and worse is *not* enlightened by the radical shift in perspective that the Socratic view entails (see also *Gorgias* 472a). On the other hand, if there are the kinds of overwhelmingly brilliant objects that Socrates mentions, perhaps the knowledge of these would somehow so transform the soul of the knower that in their light he would choose to suffer death or other natural evils as being not relatively but *absolutely* better than to do injustice or remain in a state of epistemic and moral delusion.[41] Then the "knowledge of what is to be dreaded and dared" might indeed be nothing other than the knowledge of what is truly good and truly evil for the soul in its worldly journey toward eternity. Then he might indeed be moved, inspired by his contact with that timeless reality, to disdain the petty temporal obstacles to a courageous stand in life. But again, so far as the *Laches* has to teach us, this idealistic vision, moral hope, or whatever we call it is no more than a philosophical dream. Admitted, it has not been refuted as has Nicias' dream of a Promethean science, but it also has not even been clearly articulated, much less examined and justified. The *Laches* hints at it, hints at something transcendent, something in the light of which even the vital concerns of the city may seem only relatively great, may even display it in its action, but it does not take us to that place in speech. We are left to wonder, with Socrates, if it does indeed exist.

To complete our discussion of Nicias' definition of courage, let us compare it with the view suggested by the "team" of Socrates and Laches. The subject of the virtue on Nicias' view is simply man *qua* knower, *qua* intellect. This was no doubt the cause of Laches' initial dismay, for whereas wisdom might be thought of as a quality of the mind alone, it is obvious to Laches that courage is a quality of the whole man or of the will. But on Nicias' account of courage, there is no special place made for the soul or the will or the passions. (Or for the enemy and *his* will and mind and passions!) Even where Nicias speaks of courage as prudent boldness (197b), he makes no effort to account for the relation between the underlying natural or instinctive force and the guiding foresight; it is as though man were simply a beast of appetite led by intelligence, not a being some of whose emotions were themselves directed upon distinctively human objects and whose will or spirit was bent primarily upon defending his own and assuring self-rule and liberty. Because the subject of courage for Nicias is the intellect, not the will, it is natural for him to think of courage as oriented to what the man will suffer or avoid, not what he will do or refrain from doing. But this is also to distort radically the operation of courage.

For Socrates and Laches, courage involves both the knowledge of principles of action that the agent rationally chooses to act upon and the pull of contrary passions that the agent willingly endures, his knowledge or rational will (the "I") thus *ruling* over them in an entirely different manner from the way the passions rule over the body of the merely frightened man.[42] The Nician account does not envisage such a duality and conflict in the soul; courage simply takes the form of knowledge of the terrible and of the safe or opportune. The soul itself is not revealed as the locus or subject of debate and decision. How, then, does the "knowledge" of the courageous man differ from the mere "opinion" of the fearful or confident man? (This question is raised implicitly at 198c.) Nicias' answer would seem to be that the courageous man possesses the science to foresee not only apparent but also real safety or opportunity and dangers or evils; thus his fears and feelings of safety or confidence are rational, whereas the merely confident or frightened man's passions are not. This is also why the courageous man, on Nicias' account, never need take a stand against his passions, because they are rational and not irrational passions. Whereas the merely confident man has mere opinion regarding his future, which may undeceive him, the courageously confident man has knowledge and will not be undeceived. The courageous man never has to suffer any real defeats or overcome any irrational fears. His courage operates in the mind and in the world at once. He is the man for whom the conclusion simply is the action; he is the perfect two-dimensional man.

Not only is this man of Promethean courage not required to overcome the sometimes contrary passions rooted in human vulnerability, he need not overcome the very feature of knowledge that makes decision so difficult in the more complicated arts, the fundamental fact of uncertainty. This is the greatest irony of all, since there is hardly a field of endeavor in which uncertainty plays a greater role than war. The field commander constantly finds things contrary to his expectations, constantly is met with a barrage of conflicting intelligence, constantly is forced to decide what is important and what is not, knowing that he may be wrong. This is all the more true since the art of war depends largely on deceiving the enemy, defeating him through fraud and confusion and then surprise (as Nicias himself learned in Sicily; see *Peloponnesian War* 7.73–74). As a result, the commander's determinations are continually assailed by fresh experience; and if he is lacking in the commander's analogue to hoplite endurance, intellectual resolution, he will relapse into hesitation and uncertainty and finally paralysis (as was increasingly true of Nicias in Sicily, *Peloponnesian War* 6.63, 7.48–49; see also his unmanly reliance on hope in the gods in his speech at 7.77). The illusion is to think that there will always be sufficient knowledge, sufficiently clear motivations, to act with confident science, whereas in the greatest crisis this is precisely what will not obtain. When such clarity is missing, when the whole army is moving in the frightening fog and friction of war and everyone threatens to fall into doubt and delay, the commander must *not* falter, and all that will support him then and drive his army on to victory is his resolve, born of the conviction that boldness is good policy and wavering is death.[43] To fail to recognize this aspect of the "art" of war is to confuse the blackboard with the battlefield and to forget that powerful, devious man on the other side, who is trying so hard to kill you.

Finally, the object of courage is also very different on Nicias' approach as opposed to that of Socrates and Laches. For Nicias, it is simply the event that the man will suffer or not suffer, what he perceives as desirable or undesirable, really safe or really harmful. As noted above, this object is not essentially different from the kind of object aimed at by the practical arts or sciences, such as the art of strategy. (This is why Nicias is confused so easily at 198e.) In each case, the object is the result the artist or agent wishes to see occur in the world. Like the pilot who knows that he can ride out the storm and therefore is rationally unafraid, the man with Nician courage knows that he is better off suffering this small defeat for the sake of the victory that will come later, or taking his medicine for the sake of health, or investing his money for the later profit, or even dying a euthanastic death rather than lingering on in agony for months.[44] Foreseeing and calculating rationally what it will profit him to suffer and avoid among his alternatives, he always chooses "what is better," that is, what will bring him more good and less evil. Calm in his rational self-certainty, Nicias' courageously wise man steers his path safely through the world to the end, the master artist of fortune.

We must contrast this to the Socratic-Lachean account. Here the object of courage is radically different from the alternative, not merely "better" but *incommensurably* better, since the courageous act is intended to realize a principle of duty and prudence, something noble and good, but the fear of death or other harm pulls the agent toward an action that is shameful and evildoing, such as dropping his shield and running and thereby exposing his comrade on the battle line. Furthermore, there is another dimension to the Socratic-Lachean object of the courageous act that is in no way suggested by Nicias. This is the fact that the soul also has itself as its object, its own formation and self-enactment, its own being in the sense not of its biological life, *zōē*, but in the sense of its moral and political life, *bios*. On the Socratic-Lachean, but not on the Nician, account, the soul not only chooses "what is to come into being," which events to suffer in the world, he chooses among the possible alternatives "what *he* most beautifully might be." It is in this way, with his knowledge of principles ruling through his will over his wayward passions, that a man is himself a responsible principle (*archē*) in the world (compare *Nicomachean Ethics* 6.2). And it is in this way that there is a realm of distinctively human being and action, of freedom and history, as opposed to the mere becoming or events of the rest of nature.

5.6 Socrates Explains the "Knowledge of Good and Evil" and Completes His Refutation of Nicias' Understanding of Courage (199d–e)

Socrates now completes the argument. He is once again ironic, addressing Nicias as "O divine one" and then asking if the man with such a knowledge would lack virtue in any respect, since he would know about all good things— how in all ways they come into being, will come into being, and have come into being—and about evil things likewise (199d4–7). This is virtually the first time since the beginning of the colloquy with Nicias that the discussion has referred explicitly to the practical aspect of the courageous craftsman's knowledge rather than to the theoretical, his foresight (excluding Socrates' allusion to "what might be" at 198d4). Only now do the full powers of the man with this superhuman virtue come into view—including, it seems, the power to bring about all manner of evils as well as goods. But this craftsman of good and evil is no man of Machiavellian or Calliclean "virtue." For Socrates immediately goes on to explain what he has in mind, asking Nicias if he would agree that such a one would not be lacking in moderation or justice or piety, since it would belong to him alone, as regards both the gods and human beings, to "take due precaution" (*exeulabeisthai*) as to the things that are and are not terrible and to provide himself with the good things, by means of his knowing how to "associate with them rightly" (*orthōs prosomilein*). (The verb *prosomileō* can also be translated as "hold intercourse" with or "converse with," for example, with the gods through prayers and supplications.) Nicias answers that in his opinion Socrates seems to be saying something. But then, Socrates says, addressing Nicias by his name, what he is saying would not be a portion of virtue, but all of it (199d7–e4). Finally realizing how thoroughly outfoxed he has been, Nicias makes his first of four grudging, minimal responses (199e4–12): "So it seems." Socrates reminds him that they had said courage is only one of the portions of virtue. "Yes, we did." But what is now being said does not appear so. "It doesn't seem to." Emphasizing the personal character of the argument, Socrates again addresses Nicias by name and concludes decisively: "Thus we have not discovered, O Nicias, what courage is." Once more, Nicias can but glumly nod: "It appears not." He is unconvinced, or at any rate he is not shocked and angry with himself in the same way that Laches was. We will learn in a moment why not, when we examine his and Laches' responses to this new *aporia*. First we should scrutinize Socrates' very surprising account of the knowledge of good and evil and try to assess its place in the dialogue.

For surprising it certainly is to find Socrates, of all people, describing the knowledge of good and evil in the way he does here. It is not so much that he reintroduces the practical or productive aspect of the virtuous man's knowledge—having followed the deeper strains of the argument, we were prepared for that; it is the introduction of *piety* to the discussion that is most surprising. As we have already noted, piety was not named as one of the parts of virtue that Socrates and Laches together considered at 198a7–9, though moderation and justice were named. But not only is piety conspicuously added to the list here, it is obviously given a prominent place, and indeed Socrates' whole description of virtue from 199d4–e1 seems largely conceived in terms of self-regarding, prudent piety. The words *exeulabeisthai* and *prosomilein* and the notion of self-provision through being in good standing with men and gods call vividly to mind our image of the historical Nicias, who appealed daily to the diviners for advice and sought in every way to remain in good standing with everyone, taking no risks so as to insure that he would always acquire and keep the good things of worldly fortune that he cherished (see section 1.3). Indeed, this development is triply surprising, for (1) not only does Socrates, who just before had alluded to Nicias' disastrous piety at Syracuse, now seem to think so well of it as to picture all of virtue in its terms; but (2) this is the same Socrates, who, as we know, was no true believer in conventional piety; and moreover (3) Plato has once again brought the pious, fearful man of history onto the stage of the dialogue that more than any other is devoted to manly courage and self-reliance. Here, at the very end, Plato identifies that infamous coward of Greek history with the man who earlier had stood for sophistic science. But why does that very different Nicias suddenly reappear and replace the other? And why does Plato make Socrates now seem to want to praise piety, which just previously he had indirectly condemned? Is this really how Socrates conceives virtue? Of course not! So why does he say it? To answer these questions we must consider the overall dramatic meaning of the dialogue, in particular its teaching on the relationship between piety and manliness or courage, a topic that, as we have seen, is especially important for understanding the Greek tradition of thought on courage (see sections 1.6; 5.1).

Let us begin with the question concerning the reidentification of the Nicias of our drama and the Nicias of history. We have seen that Plato's Nicias is strikingly different from Thucydides' Nicias in this respect: Nicias throughout most of the *Laches* is a progressive general who is closely associated with both the doctrines and the leading figures in the sophistic movement, but the Nicias of the *Peloponnesian War* is the "Spartan in Athenian dress," a self-regarding, legalistic, pietistic traditionalist. Why are the two images united again, both at 198e–199a and now here at 199d, when the Nicias of our dialogue had all along borne little resemblance to the historical figure? While this question does not admit of any certain answer, it is appropriate to the literary form of the Platonic dialogue to interpret this reidentification as an ethological-historical and thematic mime: The collapse of the proudly self-confident, "scientific" Nicias of the dialogue, his reversion to the seers and to an abjectly pious view of virtue, imitates what also befell the man of history. For even Thucydides' Nicias is praised, if moderately, for his military skill, and he is associated, at least to some extent, with the Athenian belief in foresight as the key to success in war (see section 1.3). But that fearful Nicias of the *Peloponnesian War,* lacking the moral and intellectual qualities necessary for the kind of risky, bold campaign the Athenians attempted in Sicily—a campaign he had neither planned nor even wanted—broke under the weight of its responsibility and reverted to desperate, unmanly hope and piety. And so does the Nicias of our dialogue, still trying to hold onto something like his position, fall from the virtue that is or has seemed to be a form of wisdom, only to grasp at something like the piety that the man of history also saw in the end as being the totality of virtue.

If this should be the best way to understand the developments of 199d in relation to the figure of Nicias in the dialogue, how are we to understand this passage in relation to the figure of Socrates? Is he now suddenly voicing praise of piety as "all of virtue," whereas shortly before he seemed to condemn the piety of the historical Nicias? To keep from being swamped by confusion here, we must bear in mind what the Nicias of the dialogue has been saying about virtue, namely, that it takes the form of (sophistic) wisdom, and to understand Socrates' seeming praise of piety at 199d in relation to this alternative. In fact, Socrates' account here of "the knowledge of good and evil" presents Nicias with the conservative political alternative to the manly, sophistic creed that all of virtue is rooted in wisdom and that the wisely daring or enlightened man is the one who possesses the supreme knowledge in question. Rather than that man, Socrates is here suggesting, the man with "all of virtue" is the cautious, law-abiding citizen, the man who follows circumspectly the rules of interacting with men and gods and thereby secures for himself the goods of this life; he does not expose himself to the evils that come from indignation or even jealousy (compare *Euthyphro* 15e–16a). This man, of course, corresponds to the Nicias whom we know from the writings of Thucydides, Plutarch, and Aristophanes—the man who in Thucydides' curious judgment least deserved his fate at the hands of the gods since he had always conducted his affairs with a scrupulous eye to conventional virtue. But we need not take Socrates here to be endorsing the conduct of that Nicias, or implicitly praising superstitious piety. For Socrates has already indicated the limits that the law sets to piety, limits not allowing it to arrogate more than what is proper to its command; and he has implicitly condemned the historical Nicias' actions in precisely this regard.[45]

In point of fact, Socrates is not suggesting piety at 199d as a candidate for virtue entire, he is suggesting *justice* for that role, in its twofold character of doing what is fitting toward both gods and men, piety toward the gods being part of what is commanded by the laws of the city (compare *Euthyphro* 12c10–d2; *Gorgias* 507a–b; also *Republic* 331b, 392a).[46] He is describing the justice that renders what it owes to men and gods in the pietistic, prudential terms the historical Nicias would most readily accept. In regard to the drama of the dialogue, this makes it perfectly appropriate that Nicias should agree that Socrates is saying something there, in so describing the man of virtue. But it is not piety or prudence, it is the law and classic civic justice—which includes within its purview of duty civic courage, civic moderation, and civic piety— that Socrates is commending as what must replace sophistic wisdom as the "knowledge of good and evil" needed by men such as Nicias (and Laches too), as what for men of such unphilosophical natures is the image closest to real virtue and real knowledge. This proposal is also perfectly in accord with what he has been teaching Laches: that not even manly courage, and certainly not sophistic science, but justice and the law is what the good man must look to as his guide for righteous conduct both in war and peace. It is the one principle that might gather not only Laches and Socrates, but even Nicias and Lysimachus, into the same community, so long as those laws permit philosophy, and so long as philosophy does not threaten to destroy those laws.

This brings us to our last question, that concerning the teaching of the *Laches* on the relation between piety and courage. We have seen part of that teaching explained through the negative example of Nicias: The law teaches that piety must be subordinate to art and human reason as regards the question of human action and self-reliance, at least in that domain of action where the welfare of the city is at stake, as in the realm of war. This realm—indeed by implication the entire order of things subject to the arts and human action—belongs to the things that might or might not be; through its affirmation of the perspective of the law and the city, the *Laches* upholds indirectly the belief in human freedom and the virtue of manly courage and responsibility as what is needed to confront danger and evil, within and without. This precludes turning in unmanly fashion to the gods for deliverance from the twists of fortune, because either they do not control these things or they cannot be manipulated by human contrivance (contrast Nicias in Thucydides' *Peloponnesian War,* 7.77).[47] Thus for Socrates and Laches, courage would appear to call for the coordinate virtue of patience, for the manly acceptance of "what will be" or of chance—not in the childish form of pietistic endurance, but in the vigorous manly form that accepts the responsibility of reason and action, but also knows its limits.[48] As Socrates says in the *Gorgias,* the wise pilot simply does what he thinks is best and "lets go" of the desperate will to control, beyond reason, what he will suffer (512e). This, then, is one aspect of the teaching of the *Laches* on the relation between piety and courage. The other is less clear, but our study would be seriously lacking if we did not address it also.

For it may also be part of the teaching of the *Laches* that the essential uncertainty of the future, combined with the knowledge of death, is one of the most fundamental taproots of human life; and the desire to control that future and prevent that death, whether through self-exalting mastery of nature and human things or through self-denigrating pietistic propitiation of divine powers, is one of the fundamental modes of expression of the primal fear. Now the city, by its instruction in honor and manly self-reliance and art and patriotic adherence to the law, is a citadel against either form of despair; but the city may not offer enough solace to anyone like Nicias, who is sufficiently intellectually ambitious to seek wisdom and sufficiently directed to his private good to want a security that will protect him against all harm. Might this perhaps have been what drew him to Socrates in the first place? Was he attracted by word of an extraordinary teaching—that there is something more to live than life itself, that there might be a life beyond life in which the "soul," somehow still the man, though without his body, is delivered? This aspect of the *Laches* is undeveloped, and at the end the reader is left to wonder about the Nicias who for a moment at 195b–196a thought it possible to know that it is "better" to die than to go on living in sickness, the Nicias who conceives of even death as something that the courageously wise man might choose to suffer as the better thing for him.[49] Is it just the curiously all-too-human hopeful intellectual failure that allows him to think of his own death as something he could survive and profit from, the all-too-human incapacity to imagine one's own substantial nothingness, our happy conventional ability to know that "man" is mortal and not complete the syllogism? Does Nicias therefore simply fail to conceive the uncanny, liminal, aporetic nature of his own death? Does he think it is another relatively good or evil worldly thing? This would certainly be consistent with the sophistic hedonistic teaching, according to which a euthanastic death is rationally chosen, rather than a merely lingering life—a teaching that is perfectly rational, to be sure, but fails utterly to grasp the unique significance of death for the individual human life, for the soul and for human courage, and fails utterly to address the very real needs of the man who suddenly is undeceived and awakens from his dream to find himself unprepared at the gate or at the all-absorbing seawall of Death. *Ultimately, the anxiety about future things is rooted in the anxiety about eternity, about this mortal coil that I must one day shuffle off. It requires more than sophistic wisdom and the mastery of worldly things to gaze upon the shimmering pool of my own and all of my loved one's deaths and see death as the fate of us all, and then to somehow, through that vision, reconceive one's life as a whole, an act to be played as it "most beautifully might be," a mystery to examine. It requires something of boldness and intellect and the will to endure in this wonderful, terrible truth—it requires courage.* We have no reason to think, from the evidence the *Laches* has given us, that Nicias had that kind of courage. He may have heard the words; he may have been attracted to the song; but he never sailed those waters; he never dove into that well. And so he never acquired, or even but dimly imagined, the kind of daring and magnanimity and perseverance and patience that Socrates had—the kind of courage that affirms this dream of life within the light of an eternal order.[50]

5.7 Nicias' Aporia, and Laches' and His Responses to It (199e–200c)

We began our study of the inquiry with Nicias by examining the relation that existed in ancient Athens between education in Anaxagorean natural science and courage, and by considering the contrast between the kind of liberated scientific attitude toward the cosmos that such an education could engender and the kind of fearful, superstitious piety that was in times of stress the common alternative for ancient man. Insofar as Nicias is represented in the *Laches* as a type of the Sophistic Enlightenment, we would expect him to have shared in the liberating *paideia* and come to its noble vision of heavenly occurrences, if not to the nobler vision that Plato attained. But now, as we have seen, the Promethean Nicias of the first half of the dialogue and of the definition of courage as a form of wisdom or science has relapsed into a figure who looks much more like the superstitious, timid man of history, a man who conceives of all virtue as something like prudent piety. How can this have happened? In the last segment of the inquiry, really the immediate aftermath of Nicias' part in it, we learn why. We have examined the failure of his *logos;* now we will consider his failure as a student. Nicias' response to his *aporia* tells us all we need to know about the quality of his intellectual formation with the sophists and about what we can expect from him in any further study with Socrates.

As soon as Nicias' glumly mutters, "It appears not" to Socrates' decisive conclusion that they have failed to discover what courage is, Laches steps forward and declares sarcastically that he had been so sure that Nicias would discover it, since Nicias was so contemptuous of him when he was refuted. Indeed, Laches had the greatest hope that, with the so-called wisdom (*sophia*) Nicias had acquired from Damon, Nicias would discover it (199e13–200a3). Laches is so pleased that this windbag has been punctured that he falls out of character, speaking for once duplicitously himself!

Trapped and exposed, Nicias lashes back in anger for the first time in the dialogue (200a4–c1). Laches, he sneers, does not think it matters that he himself was just revealed to know nothing of courage; all that matters to him is for Nicias, too, to be shown to know nothing, and not that "You with me" know nothing of those things that any man who thinks he is something should have knowledge of. In Nicias' opinion, then, "You" (Laches) do a truly human thing (*hōs alēthōs anthrōpeion pragma ergazesthai*): you don't look to yourself, but to others. So much for Laches and his attitude toward the truth. "I," however, Nicias goes on to add, think I have spoken suitably on these things, and if something hasn't been said adequately, well then, I'll just correct it later with both Damon and others. Nicias ends his little tirade by climbing again on the high horse and throwing down his last bitter remark, that when he has settled these things, he will instruct (*didaxō*) Laches, for Laches is very much in need of learning (*mathein*). Note that Nicias uses the words "instruct" and "learn" so as not to allow for the important distinction between being instructed and learning for oneself; apparently he did not attend Prodicus' lecture on education (on the distinction see section 3.7). Now confident in his triumph, Laches is satisfied with the cut that Nicias is *of course* a man of wisdom; still he advises Lysimachus and Melesias to turn to Socrates, no less, for the boys' education (200c2–6). With this speech the inquiry ends and the last phase of the dialogue begins, in which the characters revert to the discussion of the boys' and their own future education.

It cannot but strike every reader how differently Nicias reacts to his *aporia* and elenchus from the way Laches did to his (see section 4.8). But it is also striking how differently Laches has responded from the way Socrates did— the other parallel. Whereas Socrates shared in Laches' *aporia,* showing that he, too, was responsible for the truth that had eluded them, and doing everything in his power to keep the conversation from descending to the level of a legal squabble, Laches does just the opposite, rising up from his side of the courtroom to declare, *J'accuse!* There are important reasons having to do with the overall meaning of the dialogue why Laches acts this way, and we will examine these in the last part of our study. But focusing for now on Laches' reaction, we cannot doubt that Nicias is correct. Laches has lost sight of the quest that he had surprisingly discovered with Socrates, the quest to discover "what courage is"—and this means he has lost sight of the beautiful Courage Herself that Socrates conjured up for him as the proper mirror to his new self-consciousness. Laches no longer feels the shame of not knowing what "every man who thinks he is something" should know (as Nicias puts it), the new kind of shame he had felt at 193e–194b, the epistemic shame that momentarily freed him from his ever-present sense of shame before the eyes of the others and turned him inward, back to himself. (Nicias' phrase suggests that most every man has sufficient pride to lay claim to the knowledge of virtue, and conversely anyone who lacks such knowledge should consider himself a "nobody" until he gets it. Compare Socrates' remarks at 201a–b.) Laches' *philonikia,* which then was aimed at his inability to say what he thought he knew about courage, has shifted back to the more familiar human kind of target. Rather than the victory he sought to gain over truth, he now merely seeks to gain victory over Nicias. He has ceased to listen to that "new man" who realized that not knowing is the sickness one has to cure in order to make life worthwhile; the old Laches is back in charge, as Nicias says, "doing the human thing." This is the Laches who will look to the way he appears in the eyes of others again at Mantinea.

Where did Socrates fail? Why has Laches ceased to be concerned with the quest for truth and again become consumed with contentious rivalry?[51] The simplest answer would seem to be that Laches chooses to care more about that rivalry and his standing in the city's contests for honor and rule than he does about the new rivalry that Socrates has shown him (see *Gorgias* 526e).[52]

Unlike Socrates, Laches is not willing to give up the virtue—what makes him think he is "something"—he does not possess for the sake of what he dares hope to discover. He cares not for the greater reality of the soul but the lesser reality of the world. He is unteachable for the very reason we all along feared. Convinced that whatever anyone says, he still "knows what he knows," Laches, civic manliness incarnate, ends the dialogue so fittingly named in his honor as self-certain in his way of life as ever. He is free, but brutish; manly, but obstinate; well bred, but ignorant. His limits are the limits of the *Laches*: he does not reach up for the heavens; he has never left the Cave.

But what of Nicias, who at any rate is sufficiently perceptive to see these flaws in Laches and sufficiently well educated to formulate them in such a striking manner? Will he embark upon the dangerous sea that Socrates has challenged him to sail? His response to the *aporia* shows that he will not, and also why not. Whereas Laches is a kind of Ajax, too dull and manly to turn away from the human contest toward the curiously dangerous music of wisdom, Nicias is a kind of Thersites. Like the weak-willed man, Laches has taken a stand in truth and can be brought to self-contradiction. But his intellectual will is too weak to do anything about it, and he soon falls back into his old ways. Nicias, on the other hand, is like the hardened sinner. He is so blinded by ambition and fear that he fails to see that he, too, does the human thing, even in matters of learning. Laches speaks from his own experience of life, his own truth, and thus he can "suffer" the elenchus and be brought along the path of philosophical inquiry to the brink of his own peculiar aporetic well. That he turns his gaze away and does not dive in marks the narrow limits of his philosophical potential. But Nicias does not get this far; indeed, he seems never to have really begun.

We noted earlier that Nicias did not seem as promising a candidate for the elenchus as would another, more passionate and intelligent man (section 3.7). But now it is clear that Nicias is utterly incapable of learning from Socrates. He still thinks, after all this conversation, that he knows what he is talking about! Unlike Laches, he has not allowed himself to be refuted; indeed, it now seems that his most important opinions were never on the line. Why would this be so? Consider again the discussion of what makes someone a candidate for the elenchus (section 3.8).[53] It was argued that the student must possess real beliefs, thoughts founded not merely on hearsay but on his own experience and concerns in the world. The hypocrite cannot be a candidate for the elenchus, not because he will not act on what he says, but because he will not identify himself with what he says. As Aristotle observes, he uses words like an actor in a play, rather than like a man standing in the truth as he knows it (see *Nicomachean Ethics* 7.3). Thus where someone else would realize his self-contradiction and feel the shame of ignorance, the hypocrite will not. His words not being "his own," he does not defend them as caringly as does the man for whom they represent his real beliefs and who he is. But by the end of his speech at 200c, we know that Nicias' opinions do not represent his truth. How then does he stand to them? This question brings us to the matter of his education with Damon and the other sophists.

For as much so-called knowledge as Nicias has acquired from his sophistic teachers, they have not taught him even at the level of analytic or scientific thought (*dianoia*), much less at the level of synoptic dialectical inquiry and the life of the mind (*epistēmē, nous*). Instead, they have taught him only at the level of memory or opinion (*doxa*), having given him lessons only of the kind that made Socrates suspect all unexamined words (see sections 2.1, 2.2). A Pericles learned more than that from Anaxagoras: he learned a way of thinking about the world that made him bolder in his vision of life and enhanced his already great natural powers (see section 5.1; *Phaedrus* 269e–270a). But Nicias has learned nothing, because he did not bring to his studies the will to question for himself, to think for himself, to understand for himself. He still assumes that learning is a matter of getting instruction, not in the old-fashioned way of gentlemen who are educating their sons but in the new way of the sophists, which provides one with all the knacks of Promethean mastery. This is what the sophists have taught him: that they, and whoever listens to them, are the "best and the brightest." But what they have not taught him is to challenge his mind, to take courage for truth against his opinions, against his concerns. Instead, they have filled him with their lectures, taken his money, and left him caring no more for genuine virtue and truth and prudence than he did to begin with, and having no more insight into what is real knowledge and what is not. Indeed, Nicias now is more than ever convinced that knowledge or learning is a matter of possessing the right words, the correct Prodicean formula, the conceptual distinction that will impress the many and exhibit his godlike wisdom. He has not begun to think of science as a distinctive kind of orientation to the world and to life—an orientation different from the one of everyday opinion and everyday concern. He has been impressed by the high status of learning, but he has not been impressed by the good of learning itself, by knowledge, by truth. Nicias is partly himself to blame for this, but his teachers are, as well, for the sophists, as teachers, are like living men who turn themselves into books: they say what they say, imprinting with the authority of truth their opinions on their students' memories, but never compelling those students to submit themselves to the learning process, to deepen themselves in the painful struggle for truth, to recognize through their own experience the difference between delusion and discovery, to wonder at the things of nature and moral convention and mind. As a result, the students are left in no better condition intellectually than they were to begin with, and they are in a worse moral state because they are now conceited with a wisdom they do not have and, worst of all, a confidence that they can always get more where that came from. But genuine teaching and genuine learning require that the student submit himself to the learning process, which is precisely what the sophists do not require, any more than they provide their students with genuinely prudent instruction. Nicias is an all-too-typical product.

It goes without saying that in the case of the historical Nicias, his intellectual bankruptcy became manifest in the Syracuse harbor, when the heir to Pericles proved no more enlightened or even sound-minded than the most superstitious fishwife. But the intellectual bankruptcy of the Nicias of our dialogue becomes fully manifest only at 200b6–c1, where at the end of his sorry tirade he reveals what his studies really mean to him, in his little fantasy about gaining some new wisdom to trump Laches and put him back down where he belongs. For this, we realize, is what Nicias has always wanted from his knowledge: to feed his self-image of superiority, to vaunt above the "merely human" on the godlike towers that the sophists build. Nicias cares nothing of truth for itself; he cares only for victory in the city's contests. He is utterly corrupt intellectually, and his so-called "teachers" have not revealed to him the baseness of his ways.[54] Nor even can Socrates, for Nicias has made himself immune to Socrates' elenctic medicine. Laches could at least be taken up for a moment in the dramatic form of Socratic inquiry, be brought to a glimmer of insight; but Nicias did not enter the inquiry in anything like the proper spirit, never knew its transforming power, never felt the "sting" of truth. For all his fine talk at 188a–b about not fleeing from Socrates' words and being forced through conversation with him into "greater forethought for one's life ever after," we now know that Laches is right. It is all talk, no will, no love, no action. In fact, it is only the shadow of talk. Where there is no one inside to listen, how can you call it speech?[55]

6

The Conclusion of the Dialogue

6.1 Socrates and the Ongoing Quest for Virtue (200c–201c)

LACHES BEGINS THE FINAL movement of the drama by letting go of his quarrel with Nicias and turning back to Lysimachus and Melesias to advise them once again to "not let go" of Socrates for their sons' education. Nicias for his part agrees: if Socrates is willing to care (*epimeleia*) for them they should seek no one else.[1] Yet each time Nicias has spoken to Socrates about turning his son Niceratus over to him, Socrates mentions others and is unwilling himself.[2] Would Socrates be more heedful of Lysimachus? (200c2–d4)

Lysimachus again says that it is just (*dikaion*) that Socrates obey, because he would be willing to do many things for Socrates that he would not do for others (compare 180d6–e4, 181a4–6, c1–5). So he asks directly (200d5–8), will Socrates heed his request and join their zeal or spirited concern over how the youths might become the best? (Note that Lysimachus says nothing of their souls, as Socrates had at 185e–186a.)

Socrates answers that it would be strange (*deinon*) to be unwilling to join in someone's zeal to become as good as possible.[3] If in their "dialogues" (*tois dialogois*) he had been shown to know and the two generals not to know, it would be right to insist that he teach them. The implication is that justice consists not in the exchange of favors between friends, but in doing the work that one is by virtue of one's knowledge fit to do (see 184e; also *Republic* 369e–370c; *Lysis* 209a–210d; *Crito* 47a–48b). But since they all have fallen into the same perplexity (*aporia*), why should any one of them be chosen over the others? (200e1–a1) Having concluded his apology for not being willing to become the boys' teacher, Socrates exhorts them all to examine what he now will advise them to do. In his most gentle ironic manner, addressing them as real men (*andres*) and mysteriously confiding to them a secret speech, "not to be divulged," Socrates says that we must seek in common most of all as good a teacher as possible *for ourselves*—since we are in need—and then for the youths, sparing neither money or anything else; but to let ourselves stay as we are now, he does not advise. As for the ridicule that we might suffer for going as older men to teachers, Socrates cites Homer, who said that "shame is not a virtue in a needy man" (*Odyssey* 17.347).[4] So let us bid farewell to those who would laugh and take care for ourselves and the boys (201a1–b5).

Lysimachus heartily approves of Socrates' suggestion and is willing, though he be the oldest, to study zealously with the youths. The others remain silent. Lysimachus brings the discussion to an end by asking Socrates to come to his house on the morrow, in order to deliberate on these same things. For now their conversational community may be dissolved. Socrates has the final word, promising indeed to come tomorrow, "if the God is willing" (201b6–c5).[5]

With this last scene, the *Laches* seems to end on a comically peaceful, if somewhat uncertain, note. The promise of a new deliberative community composed of learners who all recognize their need, to replace the contentious community that we watched fall into what was almost a physical quarrel, is hopeful. Perhaps the war between Nicias and Laches can come to an end, and they all together with Socrates can create a new world not torn by conflict (see the interpretation of the *Laches* as a comedy in section 2.8). Certainly it is pertinent to this reading that Nicias and Laches go on to become the foremost leaders for peace over the next several years in Athens history. Has Socrates perhaps taught them something after all? Has he made them see the need for peace and the premier good that it allows, the good of inquiry? But this is too much to suppose; the drama may not fit so neatly into its historical context.

Moreover, the thematic mime that we have begun to identify in the dialogue tells a different story from that of a final harmony (see sections 2.6, 2.7, "Transition to the Inquiry," sections 5.4, 5.5). The basic structural-mimetic action of the *Laches* is the coming together of Laches and Socrates as a team in order to refute Nicias—of the ancient republican city and the philosopher in order to defeat the sophistic wisdom. When we view the dialogue in this light, its characters and their actions rise to another level of meaning: Laches' initial contempt of mere learning, followed by his anger engendered by the realization that the wisdom of enlightenment denies to him the virtue of courage, together with his inability to defeat wisdom in speech but his capacity to frighten it into submission in deed, brings about the downward turn of Laches' *philonikia*. This love of victory proves ultimately to be far more concerned with the spirited defense of what he believes is rightfully his own than with the inward turn to which Socrates would lead him, a turn to the examination of his own principles, his courage, his honor and freedom, his obstinate, unmusical ignorance, his traditional human naturalness. By contrast, there is Nicias' identification of virtue with knowledge, his admiration for all science or wisdom together with his daring disdain of conventional, merely human thoughts and practices, his Promethean claim to an all-embracing mastery of life, his opposition of rationality to unselfcritical tradition, his shallowness and ignorance of *erōs* and the soul (the word *psychē* is never mentioned after Nicias joins the inquiry), his feminine preference for prudence over courage and for what is private and peaceful and good over what is public and agonal and noble, his hidden fear of freedom and of death. But in the midst of this fundamental political conflict there is also the philosopher, who joins together with the city in order to deflate the sophistic wisdom threatening to so enrage the city by its unconventional views that the city will strike out blindly against *all* learning. Like Aristophanes' Strepsiades, who becomes aware of the threat posed by sophistry to the family, Laches has become aware of the threat that sophistry is to the city and its principles; but unlike Aristophanes' Socrates, Plato's Socrates is not self-forgetful of the community upon which he depends, and he realizes that philosophy does not attain her proper form unless she recognizes the complex threat that she poses to the human city. Together with Laches, the philosopher can perhaps establish the rightful if uneasy place of the life of the mind within the human community. This will be accomplished by revealing publicly to Laches and to everyone else that the sophistic wisdom is a fraud and by teaching them that there is a fundamental difference between the sophistic wisdom that rejects and the philosophical wisdom that affirms the common ground of law, a difference between the sophistic wisdom that claims to stand like a human god above the city and the philosophical wisdom that denies it is anything more than simple inquiry and love. Even if the downward turn of Citizen Laches, back to his contentious striving for pride, is indeed the typical human thing—even if the love of worldly honor and wealth and superiority in the city's contests does in the end drown out the quiet voice that still seeks to know—can not even Laches accept this gentle, if sometimes vexing, love in his community? Can he not be brought to see that so long as the Nician-Promethean quest for mastery is human, he needs philosophy as his ally, or there will just be endless war? Can't he?

And yet, despite appearances, the dialogue does not end on a very optimistic note. Granted, there is not the ominousness that marks the end of the *Charmides,* and there is some hope of future learning. But none of the public men make any promises to come on the morrow to learn, not even Melesias, who will become a member of the Four Hundred after Nicias' failure and death in Syracuse. Whatever the immediate effect of the conversation is on their minds and characters, the failures of prudence and courage that they, and through them Athens will suffer, compose the larger historical horizon in which the *Laches* is set (see section 2.8 on the tragic aspect of the dialogue). In regard to the young masters Aristides and Thucydides, we learn from other dialogues that Socrates does indeed take them on as students, but it does not work out well. Aristides bears up under the Socratic testing for a while, and so long as he is "together with" Socrates, he believes himself to be making great progress and is able to appear inferior to none in arguments, but in the end Aristides leaves Socrates and all comes to naught (see *Theages* 130a–e; *Theaetetus* 150e–151a).[6] Of Thucydides we read only that he quarrels with Socrates and lacks the self-knowledge to see what a slave he was before he began his study (*Theages* 130b).[7] The wonderful mime that brings them all together in a new world of learning gives way to the somber reality of history. Philosophy, shameless as it is in its self-knowing neediness, is a rare and ever-endangered species. Proud men would rather fight for the justice they know than become as little children and seek the man who will teach them virtue.

Notes
Bibliography
Index

Notes

Preface

1. Cited in W. K. C. Guthrie, *A History of Greek Philosophy*, vol. 4 (Cambridge: Cambridge University Press, 1975), 124.

2. See the discussion in Dennis Walton, *Courage: A Philosophical Investigation* (Berkeley: University of California Press, 1986), who notes that "ethics in recent times has become virtually obsessed with the strict notions of fairness and equality, and increasingly, it seems, less and less room is left for the moral value of virtues like courage and gallantry," 18.

3. See Thomas Pangle, ed., *The Roots of Political Philosophy* (Ithaca, N.Y.: Cornell University Press, 1987), 240–68; on the necessity for a literal translation, 17.

1. The Historical Background

1. This dating for the action of the dialogue derives from Laches' remarks at 181b, which suggest that the dialogue is occurring after the battle at Delium in 424 B.C. If the dialogue were later than 423, it would be natural for Laches also to mention the more serious Athenian defeat at Amphipolis in 422, in which campaign Socrates also served, but Laches does not; and it would be amazing even for Lysimachus not to have heard of Socrates, whose name Aristophanes that year made a household word in Athens. Furthermore, if the dialogue were taking place after Amphipolis when Nicias and his allies were looking forward to peace with Sparta, Nicias would not speak of the "contest which lies before us" (182a). Now Nicias was head of the government in 423, after the defeat at Delium, before the defeat at Amphipolis, and in that year he arranged a short-lived truce. It is to the period just prior to his arranging that truce, before the production of the *Clouds,* that all the evidence for the dating of the *Laches* points. Compare the discussion in Robert Hoerber, "Plato's *Laches,*" *Classical Philology* 63 (1968): 95–105.

2. For the antithesis of Athenian and Spartan, see Thucydides, *The Peloponnesian War,* trans. Richard Crawley, rev. T. E. Wick (New York: Random House, 1982) 1.70; compare 1.80–85 with 2.35–46. This antithesis, to a certain extent, develops out of and extends the antithesis of Greek and Trojan in Homer, and Greek and Persian, Athenian and Spartan in Herodotus.

3. On the noble Aristides, see "Aristides," in Plutarch, *Plutarch's Lives*, vol. 2, trans. B. Perrin (Cambridge, Mass.: Harvard University Press, 1916), 209–99, 384–407. On Thucydides, see "Pericles" 11–14 in Plutarch, *Lives*, vol. 3, trans. B. Perrin (Cambridge, Mass.: Harvard University Press, 1916), 33–51 and Aristotle, *Athenian Constitution* 27; also the modern historian H. T. Wade-Gery, "Thucydides the Son of Melesias," *Journal of Hellenic Studies* 52 (1932): 205–27. Both Aristides and Thucydides are often identified as leaders of the aristocratic or oligarchic party in Athens, but this description is misleading. In fact, there is good reason to think that Aristides was in favor of a more open form of government in Athens and was by no means an oligarch. Reading between the lines, Thucydides is described in uncomplimentary terms at *Meno* 94c–e.

4. Lysimachus, according to Plutarch, received a state pension on behalf of his father's contributions. Melesias is reported by the historian Thucydides as having served as an envoy to Sparta, and as having taken part in the government of the Four Hundred (*Peloponnesian War* 8.86).

5. Apparently *hoplomachia* consisted primarily in training in the usage of heavy arms—spear, sword and shield—though instructors may also have given lessons on tactics and strategy. See Plato, *Plato's Laches*, ed. M. T. Tatham (New York: St. Martin's, 1966), 43. Whether it was a worthwhile study for young men is debated by Nicias and Laches at 181d–184c, with Laches, who criticizes the "art," seeming to get the better of the argument. Even Nicias admits that it was only really useful in individual combat, after the lines were broken and there was room for maneuver, rather than in the brutal, coordinate fighting that actually decided the battle (182a). Of course, had *hoplomachia* made its students into dominating warriors, it would have been of great value to the city, since the hoplite phalanx ruled the ancient battlefield. Lightly armored soldiers called "peltasts"—from *peltē,* the light shield they carried—and the various special-skills soldiers, such as slingers and archers, were generally used only as auxiliaries, and even the cavalry played a subordinate role. (One should note, however, that even in land battles there were important exceptions, including the Athenian victory at Sphacteria, which was achieved by light-armed troops, and the role the absence of Athenian cavalry played in the disaster in Sicily; see Thucydides' *Peloponnesian War* 4.32–36 and the Spartan comment at 4.40, 6.64, 70, 7.6, 11, 77, 81. In general, however, sea warfare seemed to allow much more for the application of *gnōmē,* intelligence, to the fighting; see *Peloponnesian War* 1.141–42, 2.84, 89, 7.21, 67.) For discussions of ancient warfare, see F. E. Adcock, *The Greek and Macedonian Art of War* (Berkeley: University of California Press, 1957); Hans Delbrück, *History of the Art of War*, vol. 1, trans. Walter J. Renfroe, Jr. (Westport, Conn.: Greenwood Press, 1975); and W. Kendrick Pritchett, *The Greek State at War*, vols. 1–4 (Berkeley: University of California Press, 1971–85).

6. For Nicias, see "Nicias," in Plutarch, *Lives,* 2: 207–311; Lowell Edmunds, *Chance and Intelligence in Thucydides* (Cambridge, Mass.: Harvard University Press, 1975), 109–42; and H. D. Westlake, "Nicias in Thucydides," *Classical Quarterly* 35 (1941): 58–65.

7. It is impossible to square this judgment with that of Aristotle—if the author is Aristotle—at *Athenian Constitution* 28.5, but it is Plutarch's judgment that conforms best to Thucydides' account.

8. See Douglas MacDowell's note to line 947 in his edition of Aristophanes' *Wasps* (Oxford: Oxford University Press, 1971), 255.

9. All quotations of Thucydides, unless otherwise noted, will be from the Crawley and Wick translation of Thucydides' *Peloponnesian War* cited in n. 2, this chapter. On the point made here, however, see also Edmunds, *Chance and Intelligence,* 85–86.

10. This translation is controversial, but seems to convey most precisely the words Thucydides chose to describe Nicias' virtue.

11. For the severe moral appraisal of Nicias by modern historians, see Donald Kagan, *The Peace of Nicias and the Sicilian Expedition* (Ithaca, N.Y.: Cornell University Press), 320.

12. The account given here owes much to Edmunds, *Chance and Intelligence,* 109–42 (see n. 6, this chapter).

13. This fundamental premise of Nicias' life and indeed of the self-regarding traditionalism that he represents is, as it were, tested and found wanting in Thucydides' *Peloponnesian War,* which instead teaches through Pericles and Alcibiades that a man or nation committed to the path of greatness and empire cannot preserve its good fortune without risk and effort, that is, without a constantly aggressive policy. This is not to say that the latter path is not itself questionable, nor is it to say that the daring form of such a policy as represented by Alcibiades is better than the restrained form represented by Pericles. But there seems to be no doubt that the premise of a Nicias— or a Chamberlain—cannot but lead to defeat.

14. To blame Alcibiades for the failure at Syracuse is unfair; Thucydides gives us no reason to think he would not have succeeded where Nicias failed (see *Peloponnesian War* 2.65, 6.15; also 6.48, 8.82, 86). (He also gives us no reason to think that Alcibiades would have rested with the conquest of Sicily.)

15. Nicias' seemingly brave comments at his surrender recorded at 7.85 are undermined by Thucydides' account of his motivations in 7.86.

16. St. Augustine, The *City of God,* trans. Henry Bettenson, ed. David Knowles (New York: Penguin, 1972), 425, 604. There is a closer analogy to Christian piety in the traditional Spartan attitude of patience and an even closer analogy in the form of patience recommended by Socrates at *Gorgias* 512e. The relation between courage and piety will be discussed in sections 5.1 and 5.6.

17. In addition to Thucydides' *Peloponnesian War* 5.74–75, see Kagan, *Peace of Nicias,* 133–34 (see n. 11, this chapter).

18. Literally, "they were still the same in *gnōmē,*" namely in resolve or spirit. For this Spartan notion of *gnōmē* as opposed to the Athenian notion, see Edwards, *Chance and Intelligence,* 39, 98.

19. Who himself battles with two "word warriors" in the *Euthydemus,* experts in fighting with their bodies (*hoplomachia*), fighting in the law courts (rhetoric), and fighting in arguments (eristics), according to Socrates (271c–272b). See also *Laches* 196b.

20. Dicaeopolis appears to speak for Aristophanes (and good sense) when—in a scene that could have been played by Groucho Marx—he says to this man who boasts of his absurd desire "always" to make war on "all" the Peloponnesians: "Your crests make me want to vomit!" (586–87). As for Lamachus as a commander, he was clearly

superior in aggressiveness to Nicias, but while direct assaults based on surprise are often successful and formed a key element in Athens' military success, an assault made without knowledge of the enemy positions can be a disaster (see *Peloponnesian War* 7.42–44). All in all, Alcibiades' plan, which combined finesse with force, would seem to have been the most likely to succeed, particularly if he had been in charge (see nn. 13, 14, this chapter). (This judgment is disputed by Kagan, *Peace of Nicias*, 360–61.)

21. Although the reference to Nicias at 198e2–199a3 has been noted in the scholarly literature, the reference to the battle of Mantinea at 193a3–9 for some reason apparently has not been.

22. It was this discipline that saved the Spartans in the initial allied assault, which came as a complete surprise (*Peloponnesian War* 5.66) and was again expressed in the immediate moments before engagement (5.69). It should be noted, however, that two of the Spartan commanders apparently refused to withdraw from the battle line, as they had been ordered to do by King Agis, who devised a tricky tactic at the last moment (Agis was no Gylippus; see 5.65). The theme of courage and obedience will be discussed in section 4.7.

23. The soft or weakly image of Socrates is incompatible with what we know from Alcibiades regarding his physical hardiness (*Symposium* 219e–220d). See the discussion of Socrates' appearance in Jacob Klein, *A Commentary on Plato's Meno* (Chapel Hill: University of North Carolina Press, 1965), 50; but see also W. K. C. Guthrie, *A History of Greek Philosophy*, vol. 3 (Cambridge: Cambridge University Press, 1969), 386–88.

24. "Actions speak louder than words." See *Apology* 32a.

25. Compare Edmunds, *Chance and Intelligence*, 7–36, 70–75.

26. See Edmunds, *Chance and Intelligence*, 26–27; see also references cited in n. 27.

27. See the discussions by William Arrowsmith, "Aristophanes' *Birds:* The Fantasy Politics of *Erōs*," *Arion* 1 (1973): 119–67; Michael O'Brien, *The Socratic Paradoxes and the Greek Mind* (Chapel Hill: University of North Carolina Press, 1967), 56–82; Bernard Knox, *Oedipus at Thebes* (New Haven, Conn.: Yale University Press, 1957), 107–58; Victor Ehrenberg, *Sophocles and Pericles* (Oxford: Basil Blackwell, 1954), 91–98, 149–54; Edmunds, *Chance and Intelligence*, 7–36, 76–88.

28. See O'Brien, *The Socratic Paradoxes*, 61–63.

29. See the discussion by Herington in Aeschylus, *Prometheus Bound*, trans. J. Scully and C. J. Herington (New York: Oxford, 1975), 6–18.

30. Protagorean political foresight or wisdom is the analogue in the realm of politics to technical foresight or wisdom. As *logos* is to *mythos* in the one part of Protagoras' tale, so it is in the other: it *replaces* the religious way of thinking for the enlightened. See G. B. Kerferd, "Protagoras' Doctrine of Justice and Virtue," *Journal of Hellenic Studies* 73 (1953): 42–45.

31. Pericles never speaks of the gods in his funeral oration. See the discussion in Edmunds, *Chance and Intelligence*, 76–88. On the close relationship between Pericles and the sophistic movement, see now, in addition to the references in n. 27, G. B. Kerferd, *The Sophistic Movement* (Cambridge: Cambridge University Press, 1981), 15–23.

32. See, for example, Laszlo Versenyi, *Socratic Humanism* (New Haven, Conn.: Yale University Press, 1963), pp. 73–75, 105–110; and more recently, his *Holiness*

and Justice (Washington, D.C.: University Press of America, 1982), 129–32. Versenyi calls Socrates "the greatest Sophist . . . of them all" in *Socratic Humanism*, 69.

33. On Prodicus, see the discussions in Guthrie, *Greek Philosophy*, vol. 3, 223–25, 274–80. He was spoken of as a pupil of Protagoras in the doxographic tradition (DK84A1), a point suggested by the allusion to Protagoras as the "father of all the sophists" at *Protagoras* 317a.

2. The Literary Form

1. On Socrates' criticisms of poetry in the *Republic*, see the commentary in Allan Bloom, *The Republic of Plato* (New York: Basic Books, 1968), 351–61; Hans-Georg Gadamer, *Dialogue and Dialectic*, trans. Christopher Smith (New Haven, Conn.: Yale University Press, 1980), 39–72; and Iris Murdoch, *The Fire and the Sun* (Oxford: Oxford University Press, 1977), 5–18, 40–47.

2. See Gadamer, *Dialogue*, 63–65; Murdoch, *Fire and Sun*, 41–45, 65–67, 76–79.

3. The account given here owes much to Jacob Klein, *A Commentary on Plato's Meno* (Chapel Hill: University of North Carolina Press, 1965), 3–31.

4. The dissolution of tolerance into license and then anarchy in democracy is portrayed comically in *Republic* 557d–558b. This passage is generally treated as an absurdity by contemporary critics, who fail to see how applicable it may be as a description of some aspects of our society, for instance, the treatment of criminals.

5. The world of the Platonic dialogues is far more restrained morally than that of either the comic or tragic stage, to say nothing of the world itself. The most violent scenes—themselves playful—occur at the beginning of the *Republic* (327b–e, 336b–d) and the ends of the *Charmides* (176b–d) and *Lysis* (223a–b). Socrates' own behavior generally is exemplary, though the self-restraint he shows at *Charmides* 155c–156d is very different from what we are told of by Alcibiades at *Symposium* 217b–219d. Clearly he was a human being, susceptible to human feelings (and perhaps even moral or religious error; see *Phaedrus* 242b–243e).

6. Socrates himself admits that many would call him impious for his disbelief in the tales of the gods fighting with one another, *Euthyphro* 6a–c, but as was noted in section 1.5, Socrates' stance in the *Apology* conforms both to the legal requirements and to the traditional ideal of piety as service to the god. In the *Cratylus*, Socrates attributes his wisdom concerning the gods to Euthyphro (*Cratylus* 396d–e; but one should also note 400d). Whether the official requirement of *nomizein tous theous* involved "believing in the [state] gods" or merely "honoring the gods" by participation in civic rituals is a controversial point, but there seems little doubt that someone who was well known not to believe in the gods' existence was regarded as impious, for example, a Protagoras or Anaxagoras. There is no doubt that Socrates honored the gods and adhered to the law, and if we follow Xenophon on this point, there is also no need to doubt that he believed in the gods, albeit not gods who were exactly like the Olympians.

7. For an "analytic" as opposed to a "constructive" account of the arguments in the so-called early dialogues, see Gerasimos Santas, *Socrates* (London: Routledge and Kegan Paul, 1979). For the distinction, see the discussion in Laszlo Versenyi, *Holiness and Justice* (Washington, D.C.: University Press of America, 1982), 11–23; also the other references cited in n. 11, this chapter. The problem, from the point of view

represented in this study, is that a strictly analytic approach to the arguments, without attention to the framing drama, the argument's purpose and place in a larger whole, and the hints suggested in the text, results in a fundamental distortion of meaning.

8. The structural importance of the dyad is basic to Platonic thought. See Jacob Klein, *Greek Mathematical Thought and the Origin of Algebra,* trans. Eva Brann (Cambridge, Mass.: MIT Press, 1968), 69–99 and Rosemary Desjardins, "The Horns of a Dilemma," *Ancient Philosophy* 1 (1981): 109–26. On the dyad in the *Laches,* see Robert Hoerber, "Plato's *Laches,*" *Classical Philology* 63 (1968): 95–105. Triads are most evident in dialogues concerned with the nature of the soul, for example, the *Charmides, Phaedrus,* and *Timaeus.*

9. See *Laches* 179a; 179d; 182e; 183a–d; 185d–e; 186c, e; 189e–190c.

10. At *Protagoras* 340a Socrates calls upon Prodicus to assist him against Protagoras, likening himself to the river Scamander, which called upon Simois to aid him against Achilles (*Iliad* 21.308). The idea of two together is a commonplace in Homer. See also 13.236–37 and especially 17.101–5, where Menelaus says that together with Ajax he could even face fighting the gods. Odysseus, of course, is paired with Diomedes in the night raid in 10.245–46. Socrates is not linked as closely to Menelaus in the dialogues as he is to Odysseus, but consider *Odyssey* 4.351–570 in relation to *Euthydemus* 288b–c, *Euthyphro* 15d. On the comparison of Socrates and Odysseus, see Robert Eisner, "Socrates as Hero," *Philosophy and Literature* 6 (1982): 106–18 and compare *Iliad* 3.221–24 and the account of the ever-testing, all-resourceful, all-enduring beggar-king of the *Odyssey* with Socrates, as described by Alcibiades at *Symposium* 215a–222b (compare also *Symposium* 203b–204a). Laches, on the other hand, is a kind of Ajax—strong, stubborn, traditional, shame-bound. In the *Iliad* it is Ajax who saves Odysseus, 11.485–88.

11. On this theme in the Platonic dialogues, see Robert S. Brumbaugh, "Plato's *Meno* as Form and as Content," *Teaching Philosophy* 1 (1975): 107–15; Gadamer, *Dialogue,* 1–20; Klein, *A Commentary,* 17–31; and Versenyi, *Holiness and Justice,* 11–23.

12. Klein, *A Commentary,* 4.

13. A notable exception to this general rule was the older Chicago School headed by Richard McKeon and Ronald S. Crane.

14. This includes the work of men such as Allan Bloom, Thomas Pangle, and others. One must also acknowledge the important revival of interest in Socrates and the so-called early dialogues among analytic scholars and critics of Plato, a revival owing primarily to Gregory Vlastos and his students.

15. Compare Klein, *A Commentary,* 17–20.

16. Compare the analysis in Hoerber, "Plato's *Laches,*" 98–99. The account given here differs in some respects and aims at more completeness.

17. Compare the discussion in Mark Blitz, "An Introduction to the Reading of Plato's *Laches,*" *Interpretation* 5 (1975): 185–225, 198. Blitz does not discuss the three-part division of the dialogue, but it is a natural variation on the interpretation that he offers.

18. See Hermann Bonitz, "Zur Erklärung platonischer Dialoge," *Hermes* 5 (1871): 413–42; also his *Platonische Studien* (Berlin, 1886), 210–26.

19. Bonitz, *Platonische Studien,* 216, "Zur Erklärung," 435.

20. See the discussions in Michael O'Brien, "The Unity of the *Laches,*" in *Essays*

in Ancient Greek Philosophy, vol. 1, ed. John Anton and George Kustas (Albany: State University of New York Press, 1971), 303–15; Gerasimos Santas, "Socrates at Work on Virtue and Knowledge in Plato's *Laches,*" in *The Philosophy of Socrates,* ed. Gregory Vlastos (Garden City, N.J.: Doubleday, 1971), 177–208; Daniel Devereux, "Courage and Wisdom in Plato's *Laches,*" *Journal of the History of Philosophy* 15 (1977): 129–41.

21. See Devereux, "Courage and Wisdom," 135.

22. Devereux, "Courage and Wisdom," 136. Devereux does not seem to realize that Laches is conspicuously lacking in boldness and also in the kind of endurance perhaps most relevant to true courage. All in all, while we do not fall into the error of those who fail to appreciate Laches (or even Lamachus), we are less willing than Devereux or other adherents of the Bonitz thesis to pair him unreservedly with Socrates.

23. Devereux, "Courage and Wisdom," 136.

24. The original work along these lines is attributed by Hoerber to Erazim Kohak, "The Road to Wisdom," *Classical Journal* 56 (1960): 123–32. For development of the idea, see also the essays by Hoerber, "Plato's *Laches,*" 103; O'Brien, "The Unity of the *Laches*"; Devereux, "Courage and Wisdom." For discussion of the Line, see Klein, *A Commentary,* 112–25.

25. Hoerber, "Plato's *Laches,*" 104.

26. Compare the discussion of Nicias in Devereux, "Courage and Wisdom," 135–36. (Devereux does not actually relate the Line to his interpretation of the dialogue.)

27. On comedy in Plato see William Greene, "The Spirit of Comedy in Plato," in *Harvard Studies in Classical Philology,* vol. 31 (Cambridge, Mass.: Harvard University Press, 1920), 63–123, on the *Laches,* 109–15.

28. On the formal structure of Aristophanic comedy, see the introduction to Aristophanes, *Acharnians,* trans. and ed. Alan Sommerstein (Warminster, England: Aris and Phillips, 1980), 9–11.

29. On the functional structure, see again Sommerstein's comments in his edition of the *Acharnians,* 11–13.

30. The comparison of the *Laches* to the formal and functional structure of the Aristophanic comedies, especially the *Clouds,* coupled with the dramatic dating of the dialogue, make it seem to have been, among other things, a kind of Platonic response to that play and its accusations against Socrates. Another Platonic dialogue that may be seen to have a similar purpose is the *Theages.*

31. See too section 3.4 for the relevance of *Philebus* 47d–50e to the *Laches.*

32. On tragedy in the Platonic dialogues, see Helmut Kuhn, "The True Tragedy," in *Harvard Studies in Classical Philology,* vol. 42 (Cambridge, Mass.: Harvard University Press, 1941), 1–41 and its continuation in *Harvard Studies in Classical Philology,* vol. 43 (Cambridge, Mass.: Harvard University Press, 1942), 37–88; Kenneth Seeskin, *Dialogue and Discovery* (Albany: State University of New York Press, 1987), 13–16; Versenyi, *Holiness and Justice,* 18–20. On tragedy in general, see Susanne K. Langer, *Feeling and Form* (New York: Scribners, 1953), 351–66.

33. The closest thing to a definition of irony in the Socratic dialogues is suggested at *Lovers* 133d, where it is defined as speaking in a "double fashion," saying one thing, meaning another. But this is only one aspect of irony in the dialogues. Compare the discussion of irony in Klein, *A Commentary,* 5–6, 18–19; Laszlo Versenyi, *Socratic Humanism* (New Haven, Conn.: Yale University Press, 1963), 120–21. On the various

forms of irony, one may consult D. C. Muecke, *Irony* (London: Methuen and Co., 1970), especially 56–57, 77–81 and, of course, Søren Kierkegaard's *Concept of Irony*, trans. Lee M. Capel (New York: Harper and Row, 1966), especially 72–78.

3. The Origins of the Inquiry

1. Compare *Gorgias* 447a; *Hippias Minor* 363a; *Protagoras* 314e–315d. The *logos* that is the *Laches* can be understood as a reflection upon the mimetic *ergon* of the fighters in armor (themselves an imitation of real warriors).

2. The theme of *epimeleia* and the "care of the soul" is fundamental in the Platonic dialogues. See *Euthyphro* 2d; *Apology* 29d–30b; *Crito* 47d; *Charmides* 156e; *Alcibiades I* 132c; *Gorgias* 501b; *Protagoras* 313a–d; *Phaedo* 82d, 107c.

3. On the contrast, see Werner Jaeger, *Paideia*, vol. 1, trans. Gilbert Highet (Oxford: Oxford University Press, 1939), xiii–xvi. Compare *Protagoras* 312a–c.

4. On the role of exemplary models, see Jaeger, *Paideia*, vol. 1, 32–34. Compare *Lysis* 205b–d; *Charmides* 157d–158b; *Alcibiades I* 103a–104c, 120e. The desire to compare favorably with one's father, in particular, is an important motive in Thucydides. See *Peloponnesian War* 2.36, 6.18.

5. Teachers of all ages have quoted the Homeric motto to their students, though it has been abandoned by modern educational levelers. See the discussion in Jaeger, *Paideia*, 1: 1–8, and compare the astute observations by Allan Bloom, *The Closing of the American Mind* (New York: Simon and Schuster, 1987), especially 47–67, 313–82.

6. We do not know if Lysimachus and Melesias and their sons ate Spartan food, which was a test of endurance (and, one might add, a training in tastelessness). The most famous Spartan dish was a broth made from blood and vinegar. Contrast the Athenian style of "beauty without effeminacy" celebrated by Thucydides' Pericles, *Peloponnesian War* 2.40.

7. Precisely what they call on their sons to do—care for themselves—they have never done, otherwise how could they still hold daddy responsible for who they are today? Contrast the attitude Nicias claims to hold at 188a–b, and Alcibiades' exemplary willingness to take responsibility for his own failures, *Alcibiades I* 118a–b, 127d.

8. See Jaeger, *Paideia*, 1: 3–14, and Alasdair MacIntyre, *After Virtue* (Notre Dame, Ind.: University of Notre Dame Press, 1981), 114–22.

9. In its complete form, this quest to be the best is the heroic ambition to be honored like a god (see *Iliad* 9.538–41). For the Socratic explanation of this phenomenon, see *Symposium* 206c–209e; *Cratylus* 398c–d.

10. On Tyrtaeus and Theognis, see "Elegiac Poems," in J. D Edmonds, *Elegy and Iambus*, vol. 1 (Cambridge, Mass.: Harvard University Press, 1931), 51–79 and 227–401, respectively. Tyrtaeus speaks of military *aretē* as the highest prize for a young man to achieve (compare *Republic* 468c–d). (Theognis absurdly changes this to "wise man.") For discussion of the Periclean ideal as presented in the funeral oration, see Lowell Edmunds, *Chance and Intelligence in Thucydides* (Cambridge, Mass.: Harvard University Press, 1975), 44–70.

11. Compare the discussions in Jaeger, *Paideia*, 1: 99–114; Hannah Arendt, *The Human Condition* (Chicago: University of Chicago Press, 1958) 175–99; Edmunds, *Chance and Intelligence*, 82–88 and notes.

12. See the definitions of virtue given at *Meno* 71e; *Gorgias* 491a–b; *Protagoras* 318e–319a. Compare the discussion in A. W. H. Adkins, *Merit and Responsibility* (Oxford: Clarendon Press, 1960), 6–7, 31–36, 232–35, and the Athenian ideal of the manly, active life, as represented in Plato by Callicles at *Gorgias* 484c–486c and in Thucydides' *Peloponnesian War* by Alcibiades. On the agonal element in Greek life, see especially Friedrich Nietzsche, "Homer's Contest," in *The Portable Nietzsche*, trans. and ed. Walter Kaufmann (New York: Viking, 1968), 32–39.

13. Niceratus is among the auditors in the *Republic*. In the *Laches*, conspicuous for the absence of music, he is not present.

14. On this point, see Mark Blitz, "Introduction to the Reading of Plato's *Laches*," *Interpretation* 5 (1975): 185–225, 191.

15. As a result, we are defended by an army increasingly mercenary in character. The ancient wisdom teaches that we should expect neither self-sacrifice nor loyalty to the republic from such a body. See the discussion of this issue in George Walton's brave book, *The Tarnished Shield* (New York: Dodd, 1973), and in Richard Gabriel and Paul Savage, *Crisis in Command* (New York: Farrar, Straus and Giroux, 1978), especially 3–28.

16. The ideal of war as the most manly of all sports could still be found among German soldiers in World War I. See Desmond Young, *Rommel: The Desert Fox* (New York: Harper and Row, 1951), 21.

17. "To rule or be ruled." Freedom in the full sense, then, includes maximum self-sufficiency or the absence of dependence on others' goodwill. For one who wishes to live the good life, this implies wealth and power over others; for a state it means preeminence in the international struggle (compare *Peloponnesian War* 5.105; similarly, Callicles' account of the good life in the *Gorgias* and the definitions of manly virtue referred to in n. 12, this chapter). Part of Socrates' argument for the superiority of the life of the mind over the life of action is that, despite appearances, the would-be ruler is far more dependent on others than is the philosopher. (It is also part of Plato's teaching, however, that we recognize the dependence of the philosopher on the city. Without freedom he cannot perform his quintessentially human function; but without prowess in the struggle for power, his family or friends and city will not afford him the freedom and culture, *paideia*, that he needs.)

18. Compare *Republic* 411c–d. The whole passage reminds one of Laches.

19. Compare the Aristotelian concept of "second nature," according to which man's original nature is political, shaped by law, convention, no less than by nature herself. Even so, nature still universally and individually limits what nurture and law can attain. See *Politics* 1.1. Compare also the rather different account in James Wallace, *The Virtues and Vices* (Ithaca, N.Y.: Cornell University Press, 1978), 32–38.

20. See Nichols' note on *echthros* in Thomas Pangle ed., *The Roots of Political Philosophy* (Ithaca, N.Y.: Cornell University Press, 1987), 245.

21. As Socrates himself says, quoting Homer, *Laches* 201b. The same passage is cited at *Charmides* 160e. Compare also Aristotle, *Nicomachean Ethics* 2.7.

22. One could hardly find more opposite views than those of Cleinias at *Euthydemus* 290b–e and Nicias at *Laches* 182c about the nobility of generalship. Compare the Stranger's discussion of generalship at *Sophist* 227b and *Statesman* 304e–305a.

23. Of course the Spartan reluctance to admit sophists of *hoplomachia* does not imply they did not themselves employ training methods that were similar in many

respects. Indeed, training in basic sword, spear, and armor movements was an important element in the incomparable success of the Roman army. See the remarks on military science in pt. 1, chap. 5 of Thomas Hobbes, *Leviathan*, ed. Michael Oakeshott (New York: Collier Books, 1962), p. 46, and the discussion of technical courage in Walter T. Schmid, "The Socratic Conception of Courage," *History of Philosophy Quarterly* 2 (1985): 113–29. On confidence in others that is based on ignorance of their true nature, see Hobbes, *Leviathan*, pt. 1, chap. 11, p. 83.

24. See especially *Peloponnesian War* 6.72, 7.36, 55, 67. On the reversal of the Athenian and Spartan characters (which he plays down somewhat too much), see Edmunds, *Chance and Intelligence*, 142.

25. See the discussions of public life and identity in the ancient city in the works cited in n. 11, this chapter. Socrates seems to adopt this point of view at *Apology* 28d, when he says that a man who has taken his stand is bound to take no account of death or anything else before dishonor. Of course, one might think that Stesilaus was better off than those who died in the battle, albeit with reputations intact. See, for instance, Archilochus, "Elegiac Poems," number 6, in Edmunds, *Elegy*, 1: 101, or Hobbes, *Leviathan*, pt. 1, chap. 11, p. 80. Or one might argue that shame was better than ignorance of oneself, that it was worthwhile to have one's real self, however cowardly, exposed, so as to gain in self-knowledge. We may also compare the Christian account, according to which faith explodes the whole ancient mythopsychology of pride, and honor and glory are found not in the eyes of men but in the eyes of God and the Christian community. See 1 Cor. 1.26–31; St. Augustine, *City of God*, trans. Henry Bettenson, ed. David Knowles (New York: Penguin, 1972), 843–94.

26. Compare the discussion of shame in William Schneider, *Shame, Exposure, and Privacy* (Boston: Beacon, 1977), 18–28.

27. See the discussions in Walter T. Schmid, "Socrates' Practice of Elenchus in the *Charmides*," *Ancient Philosophy* 1 (1981): 141–47, and Walter T. Schmid, "Socratic Moderation and Self-Knowledge," *Journal of the History of Philosophy* 21 (1983): 349–58.

28. Laches is bound to courage in a manner somewhat different from that of Alcibiades (see *Alcibiades I* 115d) or Callicles (*Gorgias* 483b). On traditional civic courage and self-respect, see Herodotus, *The Persian Wars*, trans. George Rawlinson (New York: Random House, 1942), 6.102–4; Thucydides, *Peloponnesian War* 1.84; Aristotle, *Nicomachean Ethics* 3.8; also Robert Graves, *Difficult Questions, Easy Answers* (Garden City, N.Y.: Doubleday, 1973), 157–58; Richard Holmes, *Acts of War* (New York: Macmillan, 1985), 300–304; Gerald Linderman, *Embattled Courage* (New York: Macmillan, 1987), 11–16. Compare too Ajax's exhortation to the Argives at *Iliad* 15.561–64.

29. The translation has been slightly corrected. Compare the discussion in Edmunds, *Chance and Intelligence*, 94–97.

30. Of course, Laches does not think of this as praiseworthy. His half-distortion, picturing Athens as being as devoted to music as Sparta is to war, shows just how "Spartan" is Laches.

31. The claim that Socrates holds that this is a universal condition is, however, controversial. See the discussion in David Bolotin, *Plato's Dialogue on Friendship* (Ithaca, N.Y.: Cornell University Press, 1982), 201–25.

32. This is a thoroughgoing world of appearances, because he does not contrast

mere opinion to belief based on empirical knowledge. On the political sense of *idiōtēs* and the reasoning behind this implicit judgment, see again Jaeger, *Paideia,* 1: 111– 13; Arendt, *Human Condition,* 175–88. We should realize, however, that both of these judgments are more influenced by the Athenian, activist notion of the good life than the Spartan, quietist notion. See Victor Ehrenberg, *"Polypragmosynē:* A Study in Greek Politics," *Journal of the Hellenic Society* 67 (1947): 46–67; Edmunds, *Chance and Intelligence,* 115–18, where he contrasts the barbarian Otanes' judgment "neither to rule nor to be ruled" (Herodotus, *Persian Wars* 3.83) to the Greek view, "to rule is most pleasurable" (see Aristotle, *Rhetoric* 1.11).

33. The principle that objective knowledge of this kind is unavailable is fundamental to modern ethical-political thought. See Descartes, *Discourse on Method,* in *The Philosophical Works of Descartes,* vol. 1, trans. Elizabeth S. Haldane and G. R. T. Ross (Cambridge: Cambridge University Press, 1972), 81; Hobbes, *Leviathan,* pt. 1, chap. 8, p. 61 and pt. 1, chap. 13, p. 98, on the equal distribution of prudence among men. Socrates presents Protagoras' own, sophisticated view of this matter at *Theaetetus* 166c–167d. The wise or prudent man can recognize unsound practices and beliefs and substitute, that is to say, persuade the many to adopt, other practices and beliefs that "are and appear sound" (167c). The position is analogous to those of modern thinkers such as Mill or Dewey, who seek to combine a doctrine of progress through science with an ultimately relativistic metaphysics. We reject this sophistic tradition root and branch.

34. Compare the discussion in Blitz, "An Introduction," 200. The topic of course is central to the discussion in the *Republic.* It plays no role in the discussion of the *Charmides,* where the operative principle is that every sickness of the body stems from the soul (156e–157a), though the events of the dialogue call that doctrine into question. See 162d, 169c and Schmid, "Elenchus," 144–45.

35. On Zalmoxis, see Herodotus, *Persian Wars* 4.94–96 and the discussion in Seth Benardete, *Herodotean Inquiries* (The Hague: Martinus Nijhoff, 1969), 109–10.

36. Compare the discussion by John Burnet, "The Socratic Doctrine of the Soul" in *Essays and Addresses* (Freeport, N.Y.: Books for Libraries Press, 1968), 235–59.

37. Note the use of "wonder" at 186c6 *(thaumasaimi)* and 186d5 *(ethaumasa).* The Socratic philosophical inquiry begins with this wonder at the fundamental conflicts of the authoritative opinions. This does not imply that wonder at nature and the contrast of nature and convention, knowledge and opinion, did not precede it. See *Phaedo* 96a– 99a; *Gorgias* 454c–e, 482e–483a.

38. Like some other dialogues, including the *Charmides, Lysis,* and *Euthydemus,* the conversation in the *Laches* occurs at a palaestra or wrestling school, and the agonal nature of the conversation is highlighted. There is also a link to Theseus, mythical liberator of Athens and legendary inventor of the art of wrestling (196d–e)—an art that demonstrates the superiority of art to nature, even in Homer (see *Iliad* 24.700–728). Melesias was well trained in wrestling by his father Thucydides, but this did not make him virtuous (see section 1.2; *Meno* 94a–e). Thucydides' father, Melesias' grandfather, was the greatest wrestling master of his generation in Greece, and he is celebrated in three odes by Pindar.

39. See Socrates' discussion with the young Hippocrates at *Protagoras* 310b–314c, especially 312a; also *Meno* 91c; *Gorgias* 520a; and, of course, *Apology* 18a–20c.

40. Socrates distinguishes between ordinary persuasion, which aims simply at con-

viction, and educational persuasion, which aims at learning or understanding (see *Gorgias* 454d–e), as well as between the art of legislation, to which he contrasts sophistry as an empirical knack of flattery, and the art of justice, to which he contrasts rhetoric (464b–465e). In the *Laches,* however, as in the other aporetic, inconclusive dialogues, his manner of inquiry seems largely confined to the medical or elenctic form of educational persuasion. This is not to say that positive doctrine and distinctively Socratic philosophical ideas and principles are absent. But they are not developed through the agreements of the interlocutors as they are in, for example, the *Gorgias* and the *Republic.* In the *Charmides,* the beautiful speeches comprising the charms that engender moderation in the soul would not appear to be speeches *about* the soul, virtue and truth, or the like, but the very speeches that elenctically cure the soul of its immoderate, inflaming opinions (see 157a–c); and in the *Theaetetus* (150b–151d), Socrates denies that he has *anything* positive to offer in terms of wisdom, an account of his way that seems to be at odds with what we see in many dialogues but is not at odds with his own account in the *Apology* 21a–23b. None the less, as was noted earlier (section 1.5), Socrates makes it clear in the *Apology* and elsewhere that he not only refutes, he also exhorts, and the principles he recommends for the guidance of life are sharply opposed to the principles recommended and acted on by most of his contemporaries (29d–30b).

41. Nicias' use of the phrase "not let go" marks the third or fourth time it has been used in the dialogue to this point. Laches told Lysimachus twice not to let Socrates go; Socrates told Lysimachus not to let Nicias and Laches depart; and now Nicias says that Socrates will not let his interlocutor go. (At 197e Socrates will not let Laches go from his share in the inquiry, although there it has a somewhat different meaning.) The interpretive metaphor would seem to be given in the *Euthydemus,* where Socrates refers to the eristic brothers as being like the "Egyptian sophist" Proteus, who kept changing shapes but when held fast by Menelaus, finally gave up his secret (288b–c). Compare *Euthyphro* 11b–d, 15b–d, and especially *Theaetetus* 169a–b, where Socrates admits his love of "this kind of gymnastic." The interlocutor's words or professed opinion keeps changing, because it is intrinsically fluid, not "tied down" by binding arguments (see *Meno* 97e; *Gorgias* 508c–509a).

42. The translation of the Greek *ton epeita bion* is difficult. Blitz, "An Introduction," 203, offers "the life afterward" and suggests that this could mean his life after death. This interpretive translation plays an important role in his reading of the dialogue, see especially 219–20. W. R. M. Lamb, in the Loeb Classical Library edition, renders it simply as "the rest of your life," which eliminates any possible allusion to an afterlife. Nichols' translates it as "his life afterward" in Pangle, *Roots of Political Philosophy,* 251. This retains the possible ambiguity, but Nichols ignores the afterlife reading in his interpretive comments, 269–80. Variations on the Greek phrase are found in several other places in the dialogues, including *Euthyphro* 16a; *Protagoras* 361d; *Gorgias* 512e; *Gorgias* 527c; *Euthydemus* 293a; and *Phaedo* 90e, where *ton epeita bion* clearly lends itself to the reading, "the afterlife."

43. On the comparison, see Schmid, "Moderation," 342–45.

44. On the distinction, see the note by Christopher Bruell on *Lovers* 133c in Pangle, *Roots of Political Philosophy,* 82.

45. See Cicero, *Tusculan Disputations* 3.32.77.

46. The philosophical depth of the *Protagoras* is to no small degree due to the

presence of Alcibiades, who intervenes decisively at 337b–d, 347b, and 348b to keep the *logos* alive. Of the men devoted to the life of action, Alcibiades is by far the most Zeus-like, *naturally* virtuous of Socrates' interlocutors, the only one Socrates speaks of as his beloved (*Alcibiades 1* 131d–e; *Gorgias* 481d; *Symposium* 213c–d). On Alcibiades' unwillingness to abandon the life of action for philosophy, see Ilham Dilman, *Morality and the Inner Life* (London: Macmillan, 1979), 41–45; Schmid, "Moderation," 347; Kenneth Seeskin, *Dialogue and Discovery* (Albany: State University of New York Press, 1987), 147–48. Seeskin rightly condemns the effeminate waffling that chooses not the philosophical but the poetic or tragic view of life.

47. On this passage, compare the comments by Blitz, "An Introduction," 204.

48. Compare Paul's second letter to Timothy, especially 2 *Tim.* 2.14–17, 3.6–7; but also 2.23.

49. See also *Hippias Minor* 369e–371e. Socrates in effect concedes Hippias' claim regarding Achilles, but then he goes on to reiterate the argument that voluntary liars are better than the involuntary, an argument that Hippias points out is contrary to justice and the law (372a), later calling it "terrible" (*deinon*, 375d3). Socrates replies that if one tends to identify knowledge, wisdom, art, and justice, as does Hippias, this conclusion is unavoidable (375d–376b).

50. See Schmid, "Elenchus," 143–45. Compare the accounts in Richard Robinson, *Plato's Earlier Dialectic* (Oxford: Clarendon Press, 1953), 15–17; Seeskin, *Dialogue and Discovery*, 1–4, 100–103, 139–42; and Gregory Vlastos, "The Socratic Elenchus," in *Oxford Studies in Ancient Philosophy*, vol. 1, ed. Julia Annas (Oxford: Oxford University Press, 1983), 29–53.

51. One may consult, on this and related matters, Montaigne, "Of the inconsistency" (2.1) in *The Complete Essays of Montaigne*, trans. Donald Frame (Stanford, Calif.: Stanford University Press, 1958), 239–44. See also 1.42, "Of the inequality that is between us" and Frame's commentary: "the *vulgaire* are in such a state of flux that they can hardly be said to exist at all," in Donald Frame, *Montaigne's Discovery of Man* (New York: Columbia University Press, 1955), 47.

52. Robinson, *Dialectic*, 16. Compare the discussion in Schmid, "Elenchus," 143.

53. Compare the discussion of the errors of the vulgar intellect by Algazali in the selection from *Incoherence of the Philosophers*, trans. W. M. Watt, in Arthur Hyman and James Walsh, eds., *Philosophy in the Middle Ages* (Indianapolis: Hackett, 1973), 273–75.

54. This self-testing aspect is brought out especially in the definition of moderation presented by Socrates in the *Charmides* 167a. See the discussion in Schmid, "Moderation," 342–45.

55. Compare the discussion in Hannah Arendt, *The Life of the Mind: Thinking* (New York: Harcourt Brace Jovanovich, 1971), 179–93.

4. The Inquiry with Laches

1. It is an inquiry that challenges modern conceptions of courage, which tend to denigrate the central importance of this virtue for moral-political thought. See the discussion in Dennis Walton, *Courage: A Philosophical Investigation* (Berkeley: University of California, 1986), 18 (cited in note 2 to the preface).

2. See especially the discussions in Gregory Vlastos, *Platonic Studies,* 2d ed. (Princeton, N.J.: Princeton University Press, 1981), 266–69; Daniel Devereux, "Courage and Wisdom in Plato's *Laches,*" *Journal of the History of Philosophy* 15 (1977): 129–41. Conflicting views are found in Terence Irwin, *Plato's Moral Theory* (Oxford: Clarendon Press, 1977), especially 302, n. 62, and Terry Penner, "The Unity of Virtue," *Philosophical Review* 82 (1973), 35–68. To speak of an "orthodox" view may overstate the status of the Vlastos position among analytic scholars, but his view does seem to be the most commonly accepted one.

3. The necessity of conventional, patriotic courage is implicitly acknowledged in the *Republic* 372d–373e, 412c–415d, 430b, 465d. Compare the account of the human condition in Carl Schmitt, *The Concept of the Political,* trans. George Schwab (New Brunswick, N.J.: Rutgers University Press, 1988), 25–37. So long as men are political and serious in the sense of being willing to kill and die for justice or glory, and so long as men are divided into a plurality of states and a plurality of views as to the nature of justice, or so long as there is a scarcity of goods necessary for developed society, it would seem that there must be the possibility of war, which only fools will not prepare for. Compare also n. 4 following, chap. 4, n. 47, chap. 5, n. 52.

4. For a contemporary account of the traditional wisdom on this matter, as developed by St. Augustine, see G. E. M. Anscombe, "War and Murder," in *Morality and the Military Profession,* ed. Malham Wakin (Boulder, Colo.: Westview Press, 1981), 285–99. (Compare also in this regard Machiavelli, *Discourses* 2.2.)

5. For the alternative interpretation, see *Theages* 129e–130e; *Theaetetus* 150d–151a. But compare *Symposium* 175c-d.

6. On the other hand, one might rather describe the eye as an organ of the mind, in which case it must be thought of as oriented not only to the sensory but also beyond it. See *Timaeus* 47b.

7. See Aristotle, *Nicomachean Ethics* 2.3, 3.9; *Rhetoric* 1.7.

8. On Prodicus, see section 1.7. On the elenchus, see the accounts in Richard Robinson, *Plato's Earlier Dialectic* (Oxford: Clarendon Press, 1953), 49–53; Kenneth Seeskin, *Dialogue and Discovery* (Albany: State University of New York Press, 1987), 26–35; Vlastos, *Platonic Studies,* 410–17.

9. The oaths are by Lysimachus at 181a4 (Hera); by Laches at 190e4, 190e5, 193d10, 195a6 (Zeus); and by Socrates at 194d3 (Zeus, or God); and again by Laches at 197a1 (the Gods).

10. Aristotle denies that this is true courage, though it is "most like it." See *Nicomachean Ethics* 3.8.

11. Compare G. W. F. Hegel, *Phenomenology of Mind,* trans. J. B. Baillie (London: MacMillan, 1910; New York: Harper and Row, 1967), 228–40. Compare also Thucydides, *Peloponnesian War* 5.89, 105 and chap. 3, n. 12.

12. It is indicative of the largely ahistorical manner of reading the Platonic dialogues that dominates contemporary scholarship that none of the most prominent discussions (e.g., Irwin, Devereux, Santas) identity or discuss the representative aspect of Laches' definition, nor even do such fine outsiders as Nichols and Blitz.

13. J. D. Edmonds, *Elegy and Iambus,* vol. 1 (Cambridge, Mass.: Harvard University Press, 1931), 75.

14. Edmonds, *Elegy,* 1: 347.

15. Compare the account in Robert Graves, *Difficult Questions, Easy Answers*

(Garden City, N.J.: Doubleday, 1973), 156–61, and the other references cited in chap. 3, n. 28.

16. Sprague, however, notes regarding 191c that "Plato's description of the battle is not consistent with the one in Herodotus 9.61–63," Plato, *Laches and Charmides,* trans. Rosamund Kent Sprague (Indianapolis: Bobbs-Merrill, 1973), 32, n. 40.

17. Compare Montaigne, *Complete Essays of Montaigne,* trans. Donald Frame (Stanford, Calif.: Stanford University Press, 1958), 30–31. Montaigne misses the complexity of the third example, however.

18. See *Iliad* 5.251–544; 8.139–56; and compare chap. 2, n. 10 above.

19. Note too that Aeneas' knowledge results in the specific virtue of prowess in war: to be fear-inspiring to the enemy and cause their flight. Compare *Symposium* 221b.

20. This was not good policy on his part, though it is a part of ancient military wisdom to create such necessity. See Homer, *Iliad* 4.297–300, Herodotus, *Persian Wars* 8.80, and Machiavelli, *The Art of War,* trans. Ellis Farneworth (New York: Bobbs-Merrill, 1965), 178 (compare *Discourses* 1.45). Incidentally, one can even see an implicit critique of Spartan piety in the Herodotean story. Contrast the Athenian attitude exemplified by the brilliant Themistocles in Herodotus, *Persian Wars* 7.143, and Plutarch, *Lives,* "Themistocles" 10–11; also the discussion in section 5.6. (Compare also Machiavelli, *The Art,* 175–76.) For a different interpretation of Pausanias' actions at Plataea, see F. E. Adcock, *The Greek and Macedonian Art of War* (Berkeley: University of California Press, 1957), 12.

21. One notes that both in Thucydides and in Herodotus, "Spartan" qualities seem more like virtues in the troops than in their commanders.

22. See the discussion by the editor in *Protagoras,* trans. Martin Ostwald, ed. Gregory Vlastos (Indianapolis: Bobbs-Merrill, 1975), l–li.

23. Thus Gerasimos Santas, "Socrates at Work on Virtue and Knowledge in Plato's *Laches,*" *The Philosophy of Socrates,* ed. Gregory Vlastos (Garden City, N.J.: Doubleday, 1971), 187.

24. *Andreia* is restricted to the guardian nature in the *Republic,* 429a–430d, also 374a–e. While at first it seems that men and women will be represented more or less equally in the army of the just society, a close examination of the text reveals that women may have at best a marginal role. See Arlene Saxenhouse, "The Philosopher and the Female," *Political Theory* 4 (1976): 195–212. (This article is also insightful on the general topic it addresses.)

25. See the account of *tlēmosynē* in Hermann Fränkel, *From Poetry to Philosophy,* trans. Moses Hadas (New York: Harcourt Brace Jovanovich, 1975), 87–88, 134–44, 420–21 and the discussion in Walter T. Schmid, "The Socratic Conception of Courage," *History of Philosophy Quarterly* 2 (1985): 113. The latter discussion does not reflect the fact that traditional civic courage is also founded in endurance of the spirit, nor does it consider the problem of what it is that frees the existentially courageous man from the motivation of political honor and shame for another kind of courage.

26. Of course traditional Greek civic courage provides the model for the definition given at *Republic* 430a. Compare also *Republic* 412d–414b.

27. Santas would appear to be mistaken in his account of the traditional Greek conception of courage in "Socrates in Plato's *Laches*"; Vlastos, *Socrates,* 186–87. Courage had for several centuries been understood both in terms of battlefield bravery

and endurance when confronted with adversity, and as is discussed in section 4.5, classical civic courage was itself conceived of as founded in resolve or psychic endurance or strength of will. We note that Socrates does not include in his list any of the kinds of courageous actions that would be associated with women in particular, such as the courage to conceive and bear children deliberately.

28. See Goethe, *Aus meinem Leben: Dichtung und Wahrheit* (Munich: Goldmanns, 1962), 15: "The common fate of mankind, which we must all endure . . . that in the end, one is thrown back upon himself, and even the Deity relates to man in such a way as not to be able to respond to his faith, hope, and love—at least not in the moment of greatest crisis." Cited in David Bolotin, *Plato's Dialogue on Friendship* (Ithaca, N.Y.: Cornell University Press, 1982), 68.

29. While the actual battles did not usually last very long in phalanx warfare, being decided generally by a vicious, face-to-face killing match of the respective spearmen lines, the exertion of marching, then running in attack, carrying the heavy shields and wielding the spears was extremely wearying, and campaigns were often exhausting, draining both energy and morale. See Alcibiades' description of Socrates' legendary hardiness in the the the Potidaea campaign, *Symposium* 219e–220b. The role of physical endurance has become an even more serious matter in modern warfare, where the physical conditions are often extreme (jungle, desert, freezing cold), and prolonged periods of sleeplessness and virtually constant fighting are common. We have also come reluctantly to recognize the effect of prolonged warfare on the moral constitution of the soldier, which while not caused by a physical condition appears to have it as a basis. See Robert Graves, *Good-Bye to All That,* 2d ed. (Garden City, N.Y.: Doubleday, 1957), 171–72.

30. Compare St. Thomas Aquinas' distinction between courage as an aspect of every virtue and courage as a virtue proper, *Summa Theologiae* 1–2.61.3–4 and 2–2.123.2.

31. For an analysis of the argument in the *Charmides,* see Gerasimos Santas, "Socrates at Work on Virtue and Knowledge in Plato's *Charmides,*" in *Exegesis and Argument: Essays in Honor of Gregory Vlastos,* ed. Edward Lee, Alexander Mourelatos, and Richard Rorty (Assen, Holland: Van Gorcum, 1973), 105–32, 113–17; Walter T. Schmid, "Socrates' Practice of Elenchus in Plato's *Charmides,*" *Ancient Philosophy* 1 (1981): 144.

32. Compare the discussion in Mark Blitz, "An Introduction to the Reading of Plato's *Laches,*" *Interpretation* 5 (1975): 212–13.

33. Nicolai Hartmann, *Ethics,* vol. 2, trans. Stanton Coit (London: Allen and Unwin, 1932), 253–57. We find this account particularly attractive, insofar as it is the most complete in relation to the phenomena, lending itself to both a simpler and a more complex interpretation.

34. Mules are obstinate and sluggish, unlike trained thoroughbreds, which are responsive and fast. In the *Phaedrus,* the dark horse is obstinate until tamed by force (254b–255a). In the *Lysis* 208a–c, Socrates speaks of horse driving and of mule driving, and it is in regard to the latter that Socrates first speaks of "rule," as if to suggest that rule is more difficult and requires more violence than it may seem. See Bolotin, *Friendship,* 87. Ajax is compared to a donkey at *Iliad* 10.558 ("stubborn and hard to move"); compare also 7.191–98, 17.281–83.

35. Odysseus is the Greek hero most closely associated with Socrates; see e.g.,

Laches 201c; *Charmides* 161a; *Republic* 620c; and chap. 2, n. 10. Ajax is the hero associated with Laches.

36. See also *Republic* 440c–d and the ambiguity noted by Allan Bloom in his notes to *Republic of Plato*, 457. The first example is discussed by Bruno Snell, *The Discovery of the Mind*, trans. T. G. Rosenmeyer (Harper and Row, 1960), 159. The second is cited for praise at *Republic* 390d.

37. The goddess stands to Achilles in his act of self-control at *Iliad* 1.188–218, as Odysseus' mind stands in relation to his spirit. On the archaic religion and the capacity for self-control, see Gerhard Krüger, *Einsicht und Leidenschaft* (Frankfurt: Klostermann, 1939), 3–29; see also the discussion in section 5.1.

38. Compare the discussions of freedom of the will by Harry Frankfurt (81–95) and Gary Watson (96–110) in *Free Will*, ed. Gary Watson (Oxford: Oxford University Press, 1982); Mary Midgley, *Beast and Man* (Ithaca, N.Y.: Cornell University Press, 1978), 253–72.

39. The phrase is characteristic. Laches uses it seven times, at 180b1, 186a2, 190b2, 191c6, 192d9, 193b4, and the superlative at 193e5 (affirming Socrates' attribution to him of courage in deed, if not in speech).

40. Compare the discussion of the translation of Greek words in the preface. Frequently, *sophia* and *phronēsis* are not sharply differentiated in Plato, though the conceptual difference would seem to be important, as suggested here and in the contrast between the use of the words in the *Phaedo* and the *Republic*. Thus *phronēsis* is best translated as "wisdom" throughout the *Phaedo*, which largely abstracts from political life, and where the notion of political rule seems largely irrelevant (but see 88e–91c). In the *Republic*, on the other hand, although the rulers are initially called "prudent" (412c), the city in book 4 is called "wise" because of the presence in it of "good counsel" (428a), and we learn in book 7, after the discussion of philosophy and the philosopher-ruler's education, that the philosopher-ruler's art of rule is informed by the synoptic vision of Being and the Good that accompanies dialectic (537c). Even in the *Republic*, however, it seems clear that the knowing that is directed upward toward the perfect Ideas involves the ruler in a state of mind other than the knowing that is directed downward toward the ordering of actual society (see 517c–d, 540a–b). See also the account of the Cave, which contrasts the false wisdom of dwellers within the Cave to the genuine wisdom of the one who apperceives the Sun and its analogies with the rest of being (516c), and then concludes with the judgment that the one who possesses that knowledge of the Idea of the Good would act prudently only after he had reaccustomed himself to the dim, artificial light of the Cave (517b–518b). "Prudence" is clearly tied to political action in a way that "wisdom" need not be.

41. Compare the discussions in Philippa Foot, *Virtues and Vices and Other Essays in Moral Philosophy* (Berkeley: University of California Press, 1978), 16; Peter Geach, *The Virtues* (Cambridge: Cambridge University Press, 1977), 150–60; Alasdair MacIntyre, *After Virtue* (Notre Dame, Ind.: Notre Dame University Press, 1981), 167–68; James Wallace, *The Virtues and Vices* (Ithaca, N.Y.: Cornell University Press, 1978), 77; and Walton, *Courage*, 52–53, 94–95. It is especially noteworthy that the idea prominent in classical political philosophy—that there might be a natural courage in the form of spirited or self-assertive individuality rebelling against social morality— is largely absent in contemporary philosophical discussions of courage (something analogous is found in Freud's *Civilization and Its Discontents*, however). This view is

presented in Plato's dialogues not only by Callicles and Thrasymachus, but also by Socrates himself at *Republic* 560c and 574a. Such courage, or manly self-assertion, might itself be a motive. But see Wallace, *Virtues and Vices*, 77.

42. For the would-be prince's need to be both a fox and a lion, see Machiavelli, *The Prince*, trans. Harvey Mansfield (Chicago: University of Chicago Press, 1985), 61–82.

43. It is a truism of the ancient and medieval wisdom that the love of money saps the power to be brave; see *Republic* 555a, 556a–e. Since the avaricious believe wealth to be self-sufficiency and happiness, they are not directed toward the objects that courage preserves, the city or the divine law; see St. Thomas Aquinas, *Summa Theologiae* 2–2.118.7.

44. Lysimachus had said, "Why, what else can one do, Socrates?" (184d7), and Socrates turned immediately from him to Melesias to begin the deliberation on new grounds (see section 3.5). Here Laches also begins to realize his self-contradiction and *aporia*, which will lead Socrates to turn to Nicias.

45. Compare again, Graves, *Easy Answers*, 157–58, Richard Holmes, *Acts of War* (New York: Macmillan, 1985), 300–304. It is, of course, the extremely rare man in our society who has such a strong sense of honor, but as recently as the first few years of the Civil War this kind of sense of honor was fairly common. See Gerald Linderman, *Embattled Courage* (New York: Macmillan, 1987), 11–16. Contrast his account of the realism that took hold at the end, 134–50 and the remarks on Grant, 210–11.

46. Compare Aristotle *Nicomachean Ethics* 3.6, Thomas Hobbes, *Leviathan*, ed. Michael Oakeshott (New York: Collier Books, 1962), pt. 1, chap. 11, p. 80. For Hobbes, in the absence of a highest good, it is the recognition of the greatest evil that allows for the ordering of goods and the rational conduct of life. Socrates, of course, explicitly denies this principle, which is one reason for his view of things diametrically opposite to those of most men (*Apology* 29a–30b; *Crito* 48d, 49d).

47. This appears to be the attitude of Schmitt, *Concept of the Political*, 35. Compare the discussion by Sigmund Freud, "Why War?" in *Character and Culture*, ed. Philip Rieff (New York: Macmillan, 1963), 134–47, who fails to see that the willingness to die for justice or the fatherland is a distinctively human expression of *erōs*. However much one would like to agree with Freud's final conclusion that "whatever fosters the growth of culture works at the same time against war," it seems dubious in the light of subsequent European history and is inconsistent with his own views as expressed in his *Civilization and Its Discontents*, trans. James Strachey (New York: Norton, 1962).

48. A man of stubborn, comically stupid courage; see especially Herodotus, *Persian Wars* 9.55. His "straight man" and commander, Pausanias, lacked the art of speech (like Laches), and could only call him a "madman" when he refused to obey the order to retreat.

49. See F. M. Richardson, *Fighting Spirit* (London: Bayliss and Son, 1978), 6–13; Holmes, *Acts of War*, 23, 305; and Linderman, *Embattled Courage*, 8, 65. It is the soldier's appearance to his comrades in the fighting unit that matters most, rather than to anyone else. See also J. Glenn Gray, *The Warriors* (New York: Harper and Row, 1959), 89–91.

50. Threat of punishment by the commander is not enough; the ideal of manly courage is incompatible with confining even the common soldier to a merely passive role. See the fighting spirit of the sturdy democratic revolutionary in *Republic* 556c–e,

and contrast Xenophon's Athenian manner of leadership with that of Clearchus in the *Anabasis,* as this is discussed in G. B. Nussbaum's *The Ten Thousand* (Leiden, Holland: Brill, 1967), 30–32. Compare also Thucydides' Pericles on Spartan and Athenian courage, *Peloponnesian War* 2.39–40. There is in the human spirit a natural revulsion from tyranny and a deep will to self-government; see *Republic* 354d.

51. The problem is evident in Walton's *Courage* (see nn. 1, 41, this chap.). It is revealing that when Walton turns from courage in relation to individual actions to courage as a trait of character, his model of the courageous person is the "principled" man of integrity and moral courage (199–202), and he concedes that if we do not think of a man's moral position as a "well thought-out and reasonable one, based on his own sincerely held and justified moral principles," we cannot perceive him as courageous (205–7). But where then should we place the unreflective lifelong soldier or policeman, who on Walton's account might have performed many courageous actions but whose moral position we might not at all be willing to describe as "well thought-out"? Walton edges around the classical problem of the relation between philosophy and autonomy, and their relation to virtue, but he does not face it squarely. Nor even does Alasdair MacIntyre, whose "provisional conclusion" in *After Virtue,* that the good life for man is "the life spent seeking for the good life for man" (204), would, however, seem to take us back to Socrates. One contemporary thinker who does address this issue directly is Charles Taylor, "Responsibility for Self," in Watson, *Free Will,* 111–26.

52. "It is necessary to sail the seas; it is not necessary to live!" Motto of the Hanseatic League, quoted by Freud, "Reflections upon War and Death," in *Character and Culture,* 123.

53. See Walter T. Schmid, "Socratic Moderation and Self-Knowledge," *Journal of the History of Philosophy* 21 (1983): 344–45.

54. Compare Friedrich Nietzsche, "On the Apostates," in *Thus Spoke Zarathustra,* trans. R. J. Hollingdale (London: Penguin, 1961), 198–202; the discussion in Lawrence Lampert, *Nietzsche's Teaching* (New Haven, Conn.: Yale University Press, 1986), 186–87. Also Martin Heidegger, *Being and Time,* trans. John Macquarrie and Edward Robinson (New York: Harper and Row, 1962), 256–73, 349–58 (H 212–30, 301–10).

55. This is only true of course for those who are confronted with the choice of a philosophical life. See Alcibiades' admission at *Symposium* 216b. Compare St. Thomas Aquinas, *Summa Theologiae* 1.1.1, 2–2.2.3.

5. *The Inquiry with Nicias*

1. Compare *Euthydemus* 291a, and Nichols' comment on the passage in Thomas Pangle, ed., *The Roots of Political Philosophy* (Ithaca, N.Y.: Cornell University Press, 1987), 259.

2. On the contrast, see Lowell Edmunds, *Chance and Intelligence In Thucydides* (Cambridge, Mass.: Harvard University Press, 1975), 100–102.

3. See the account of the gods and natural disturbances in Democritus (Diels 68A75, and compare Cicero, *De Natura Deorum* 2.5.14). Democritus may be regarded as the originator of a tradition regarding the gods that extends into modern times and includes among its leading advocates Hobbes, Spinoza, Hume, Marx, and, most recently, Sigmund Freud in *The Future of an Illusion.*

4. In Gregory Vlastos' *Plato's Universe* (Seattle: University of Washington Press, 1975), 3–22, the author plays down the religious aspect of the pre-Socratic thinking, for which compare Werner Jaeger, *The Theology of the Early Greek Philosophers*, trans. Edward Robinson (Oxford: Oxford University Press, 1939), 1–37, and Walter Burkert, *Greek Religion*, trans. John Raffan (Cambridge, Mass.: Harvard University Press, 1985), 305–11. Note too Cicero, *De Natura Deorum* 2.5.15.

5. The hard distinction between science and philosophy did not emerge until the nineteenth century. For ancient man, as for medieval man, the distinction is not so much between knowledge and ignorance in the sense of the absence or lack of factual information as it is between knowledge of reality rather than delusion.

6. This kind of manly attitude is found not only in classical Athens, but both earlier, as in the *Iliad* 12.230–50, and later, as in Machiavelli, *The Prince*, trans. Harvey Mansfield (Chicago: University of Chicago Press, 1985), 98–101. The "courageous" attitude toward nature is to see her as being indifferent or hostile to our well-being, but still capable of being mastered or tamed.

7. The Greek verb *lusitelein* first meant "to pay what is due" and then "to pay," that is, to be profitable or in one's self-interest. Mark Blitz reads Plato as playing on the original meaning to imply that we must at death pay a debt owed. See his "An Introduction to the Reading of Plato's *Laches*," *Interpretation* 5 (1976): 216, 219.

8. This comment, together with the entire discussion, is strongly ironic, given what Nicias' actions will be in Syracuse. I owe this point to Robert S. Brumbaugh.

9. See Thomas Hobbes, *Leviathan*, ed. Michael Oakeshott (New York: Collier Books, 1962), pt. 1, chap. 14, p. 105. Hobbes acknowledges that magnanimous or aristocratic men of manly virtue disdain fear, even the fear of violent death. But this attitude on their part he eventually concludes is vainglorious and irrational, and therefore courage is not a true virtue. See *Leviathan*, pt. 1, chap. 6, p. 50 (courage is listed as a passion), and pt. 1, chap. 15, p. 124 (courage is not listed among the moral virtues). This position is also found in his *De Homine*. As a result of these considerations, Hobbes came to see mortal danger that did not result in actual death as uniquely valuable for rationality and self-knowledge: through it alone arises the true measurement, relative to one's own life, of good and evil, a true appreciation of one's own essential equality with other human beings, and the true willingness to be just. Socrates, we know, explicitly rejects the view that death is the greatest evil, see *Apology* 29a–b, 40c–42a; *Crito* 47d–48a; also *Crito* 54b; *Gorgias* 522d–527a.

10. See particularly the discussions in Gerasimos Santas, "Socrates at Work on Virtue and Knowledge in Plato's *Laches*," in *The Philosophy of Socrates*, ed. Gregory Vlastos (Garden City, N.J.: Doubleday, 1971), 177–208, and Walter T. Schmid, "The Socratic Conception of Courage," *History of Philosophy Quarterly* 2 (1985): 113–29.

11. Compare section 1.3. For battlefields, see Thucydides, *Peloponnesian War* 4.42; Plutarch, *Lives*, "Nicias" 6.7, 6.63, 7.8; offices: *Peloponnesian War* 4.27–28; *Lives*, "Nicias" 7, "Nicias and Crassus" 3.1–4; political contests: see *Lives*, "Nicias" 11; military action: *Peloponnesian War* 7.48; chap. 1, n. 11.

12. Thus conceived, the fool or coward is not oriented by principles but by goals or states of affairs in the world that he seeks to attain or keep from suffering. Compare the discussions by James Wallace, *The Virtues and Vices* (Ithaca, N.Y.: Cornell University Press, 1978), 63–76, Lester Hunt, "Courage and Principle," *Canadian Journal of Philosophy* 10 (1980): 281–93. This conception does not, however, preclude

the possibility that the courageous man will combine his principles with the calculation of risks. See the account in Robert Graves, *Good-Bye to All That,* 2d ed. (Garden City, N.Y.: Doubleday, 1957), 132–33.

13. The "true he-man" (*ton hōs alēthōs andra,* 512e1), Socrates says, lives entirely by his principles and is not at all anxious about consequences. For an example see the career of that supreme man of courage, Winston Churchill, as summarized in William Manchester, *The Last Lion: Winston Spencer Churchill,* vol. 2 (Boston: Little, Brown, 1988), 415–16. This does not, of course, prevent the prudent pilot from doing everything in his power to rule the sailors well and bring the ship safely to port. On the metaphor of life and death involved, see *Euthydemus* 285a–b; also *Crito* 47d–48a; *Phaedo* 64a–69e.

14. See section 1.7, especially n. 33. On the relationship between courage and the Protagorean philosophy, see Roger Duncan, "Courage in Plato's *Protagoras,*" *Phronesis* 23 (1978): 216–28 and Hans-Georg Gadamer, *Platos dialektische Ethik* (Hamburg: Felix Meiner, 1931), 48–50.

15. The translation is by W. R. M. Lamb in the Loeb Classical Library edition of Plato, *Laches, Protagoras, Meno, Euthydemus* (Cambridge, Mass.: Harvard University Press, 1924), 69. Nichols translates *thrasea* as "bold," *tolmēs* as "daring" in Pangle, *Roots of Political Philosophy,* 263. While this has the advantage of treating *thrasea* as a neutral term, it has the disadvantage of covering up the contrast that is important to Nicias between things prudent and courageous, on the one hand, and things merely bold and therefore rash on the other—the latter being on his account what the many foolishly call courageous.

16. On Socrates' role as the new savior in the mythological mime of the *Phaedo,* see Jacob Klein, *A Commentary on Plato's Meno* (Chapel Hill: University of North Carolina Press, 1965), 125–50.

17. On the character traits of the beasts, see Aristotle, *Historia Animalium* 1.1. Nicias appears to be naturally deerlike or timid, whereas Laches is clearly more leonine or wild boarlike. The discussion at 196e–97b raises the important issue of the relationship between ethology and ethics, particularly in relation to the aggressive instincts in man. Compare the discussions in Mary Midgley, *Beast and Man* (Ithaca, N.Y.: Cornell University Press, 1978), 51–82, Anthony Storr, *Human Aggression* (New York: Atheneum, 1968), 59–71. On the question of whether males are by nature more violent and dominance-oriented, females by nature more nurturing and maternal, see also Arlene Saxenhouse, "The Philosopher and the Female in the Political Thought of Plato," *Political Theory* 4 (1976): 195–212; Allan Bloom, *The Closing of the American Mind* (New York: Simon and Schuster, 1987), 105, 129–31. Plato evidently sides with the view that aggression is not simply a function of frustration, at least in some human beings, *Republic* 372c–376c.

18. We recall Nicias' first word in the dialogue was *egō,* and that unlike Laches he seemed more concerned with his private affairs than with his stewardship of public office. In his love of peace at any price he reminds us of Neville Chamberlain. See chap. 1, n. 13 and section 3.3.

19. The first reference is to Menelaus, cited earlier at chap. 2, n. 10. Socrates is associated with Menelaus in the *Euthyphro* by way of the metaphor of wrestling with Proteus (15d). The lion fights "turning." On the second kind of fighting, see also *Nicomachean Ethics* 3.8 and *Iliad* 11.558. The Homer reference is to Idomenus, who

is being attacked by Ajax (who is himself compared to a wild boar at *Iliad* 17.281–83).

20. The sophists can make this distinction, however, as well as a second one, between the merely conventional education "natural" to the customs of each family and city and the artful kind of education that they provide, one guided by wisdom. Protagoras' teaching in the *Protagoras* 320a–328c is better understood if read in conjunction with the teaching at *Theaetetus* 166c–167d. Compare also chap. 3, n. 33.

21. Laches appreciates the passionate aspect of courage, as expressed in action, but he ignores the rational aspect. He is like the Spartans, whose courage, according to Thucydides' Pericles, is unfree (*Peloponnesian War* 2.39, 42 and discussion in Edmunds, *Chance and Intelligence*, 67–68.) Nicias does not understand the relation between human passion and prudence. He is somewhat like Euthyphro in his willingness to look down on mere humans.

22. Ultimately, the sophistic error must lie in its failure to attain self-knowledge in relation to Eros, if indeed it is this that comprises wisdom (see *Symposium* 177e, and more especially the speech of the "most wise" Diotima, 201c–212d).

23. The sophistic pseudowisdom fails to appreciate the religious place of man in the middle of the cosmos, between the gods and the beasts, because it usurps for the wise man the position of the gods. The Socratic human wisdom is distinguished by contrast precisely in this, that it preserves the good sense or prudence that does not arrogate divine knowledge to the human (*Apology* 21a–23b). Together with this, it shows the good sense or prudence not to insist upon the privilege of natural virtue over convention, but conforms to justice and law (29b).

24. Thus "Lachean" civic courage is empowered not simply by desire for some good or fear of some evil, but by fearless, *indignant* anger at the sense of a wrong and slight that has or is about to be committed against one's own communal property or safety or honor. Compare *Republic* 440c-d, Aristotle, *Rhetoric* 2.2, and *Politics* 7.6. On the relevance of this notion to manliness today, see the discussion of macho and feminist ethics in Bloom, *Closing of the American Mind*, 129–31.

25. Certainly this is a fundamental political truth of the ancient world, and quite possibly of the modern world as well. See the references cited above in chap. 4, nn. 3 and 47, and in n. 52, this chapter.

26. Compare the discussion of Nicias' first speech, where he does not clearly distinguish boldness and courage, section 3.3. Because the Athenian view conceives courage as the knowing mastery of fortune, it does not include as an essential element the enduring of misfortune, the virtue of patience. This point will be discussed further in section 5.6.

27. "The law" had a dignity and solemnity in the ancient city that "science" or "wisdom" did not possess. We might say that unfortunately the situation is reversed in modern society. Compare chap. 1, n. 16, and chap. 4, n. 20, on the rational attitude toward prophecy.

28. Justice, therefore, provides the common thread that runs through the virtues, or we might say that the prudence or wisdom of the legislator as embodied in the law provides that common thread. In this regard it is interesting to note the willingness of some of Socrates' interlocutors to identify virtue with justice (e.g., *Republic* 335c; *Meno* 73d; especially *Protagoras* 324d–325b, 326c–e). But the great question remains, Is virtue law or is it wisdom?

29. We do not mean to say that the *Laches* even hints that wisdom does not conform to justice, only that the issue is not squarely joined in this dialogue. The problem, of course, runs deep, both in terms of the actual relationship between the philosopher and the democratic city, and between the philosopher and the just city. Socrates acknowledges that there is a tension between the life of human wisdom or examination (philosophy) as he conceives it and involvement in the affairs of politics and justice (see *Apology* 31c–32a). The question of whether he would violate the law is more complex, as was suggested in section 1.5. At the very least, there could be circumstances in which, even in Athens, he would break the law, if he thought the law demanded that he do injustice or abandon philosophy and he could not persuade his fellow citizens otherwise (*Apology* 29b–d; *Crito* 51e). On the relationship between the life of philosophy and justice as dedication to the city, see Allan Bloom, *The Republic of Plato* (New York: Basic Books, 1968), especially 407–11. It would appear that for Socrates, even the love of justice must be moderated and interpenetrated by the love of wisdom and the moderation that accedes through philosophy. The modern political rationalist, aiming self-forgetfully at pure justice, suppresses this truth in the interests of the historical struggle—thereby missing beauty, truth, and justice. For more on the distinction of wisdom and prudence, see chap. 4, n. 40, chap. 5, n. 40.

30. Compare the description in Martin Heidegger, *Being and Time,* trans. John Macquarrie and Edward Robinson (New York: Harper and Row, 1962), 179–82 (H 140–42); also Aristotle, *Rhetoric* 2.5.

31. However, the "being" of even the most regular laws of natural processes should not, according to Socrates, be confused with the "being" that is the object of knowledge in the strict sense. See *Republic* 530a–b (or with the self-relational kind of "being" characteristic of souls, as suggested at *Charmides* 169a).

32. Compare Heidegger, *Being and Time,* 182–88 (H 143–48), on the concept of existential possibility and its relation to practical self-knowledge.

33. "The fear of freedom." Lacking sufficient knowledge of the good, to choose would seem inevitably to mean to take a risk, trusting in one's power to keep under control or endure the evil that goes along with the good one has chosen. On the intrinsic relation between courage and action, see Hannah Arendt, *The Human Condition* (Chicago: University of Chicago Press, 1958), 36, 186. On Nicias and his desire for refuge from the "dangerous uncertainties" of life, compare the discussion by Nichols in Pangle, *Roots of Political Philosophy,* 277.

34. The main opposing analytic discussions of virtue and its parts are found in the essays by Terry Penner, "The Unity of the Virtue," *Philosophical Review* 82 (1973): 35–68 and Gregory Vlastos, "The Unity of the Virtues in the *Protagoras,*" in *Platonic Studies,* 2d ed. (Princeton, N.Y.: Princeton University Press, 1981), 221–69. For analysis of the argument in the *Laches,* see the articles by Daniel Devereux, "Courage and Wisdom in Plato's *Laches,*" *Journal of the History of Philosophy* 15 (1977): 129–41; Gerasimos Santas, "Socrates in Plato's *Laches,*" 195–208, and Vlastos, *Platonic Studies,* 266–69; also Terence Irwin, *Plato's Moral Theory* (Oxford: Clarendon Press, 1977), 88–89; Penner, "The Unity of the Virtues," 61–63.

35. See Penner, "The Unity of the Virtues," especially 61–63 and Irwin, *Plato's Moral Theory,* especially 88–89, 302, nn. 61–62. The methodological chasm that separates the approach shared by both Penner and Irwin and the approach applied in the present study is evident when we compare their discussion of Nicias' definition as

Socratic with the discussion in sections 5.3, 5.4, and 5.5 of this work. Thus Irwin argues that it is "implausible" that Socrates rejects Nicias' definition, since it is "admitted to be Socratic, and is endorsed at *Protagoras* 360d4–5" (*Plato's Moral Theory*, 302, n. 62). On the approach applied here, however, Socrates may well refute in one dialogic context a definition that he himself might make use of in another, because the meaning supposed in the first context was incorrect or confused, and he may make use of definitions without thereby endorsing them. Thus Socrates' employment of Nicias' definition of courage in the argument at *Protagoras* 359a–360d does not commit him, once and for all, to that definition; it is rather Protagoras who endorses it (with his own meaning) and whose understanding is refuted. Compare Duncan's discussion of Socrates' apparent endorsement of hedonism, "Courage in Plato's *Protagoras*," especially 224–25 and 227, n. 3; Gadamer, *Platos dialektische Ethik*, 48–50.

36. Vlastos, *Platonic Studies*, 221–69. Vlastos' discussion of the final argument in the *Laches* is on 266–69.

37. See Penner, "The Unity of the Virtues"; Irwin, *Plato's Moral Theory*, especially 86–90; also Laszlo Versenyi, *Socratic Humanism* (New Haven, Conn.: Yale University Press, 1963), 83–110.

38. For some reason this clue seems not to have been discussed in the scholarly literature on the *Laches*.

39. This should not be misunderstood. The Athenian notion of courage based on skill and experience is well founded. The Israeli Defense Force motto is, "Knowledge prevents fear." Compare also *Republic* 374c–d; chap. 1, n. 5, above. But courage is needed to acquire mastery in skills that work in risky situations, which also helps explain the ordinary confusion between virtue and virtuosity. The point is rather that Nicias' knowledge of this would-be invincible, superhuman virtue is not based on experience, it simply is based on what he hopes for.

40. Compare the discussion by Blitz "An Introduction," 220–21, and by Nichols in Pangle, *Roots of Political Philosophy*, 277.

41. See *Phaedo* 63e–69c; also Walter T. Schmid, "Courage," 120; editor's comments on *Laws* 804b, in Thomas Pangle, *The Laws of Plato* (New York: Basic Books, 1980), 485. The argument at *Phaedo* 68b–c concerning philosophical versus vulgar bravery assumes the brave are fearless or completely detached from concern for their bodies. Such courage is founded in "pure" prudence or philosophical wisdom (knowledge of the Ideas), not in the political prudence issuing in laws intended to govern in the interests of the common good. On the distinction between prudence and wisdom, compare also chap. 4, n. 40; chap. 5, n. 29.

42. The relation of fear to courage is an important theme in contemporary discussions of the virtue, e.g., in Philippa Foot, *Virtues and Vices and Other Essays in Moral Philosophy* (Berkeley: University of California Press, 1978), 12; Wallace, *Virtues and Vices*, 76–81; Dennis Walton, *Courage: A Philosophical Investigation* (Berkeley: University of California Press, 1986), 80–85; Georg Henrik von Wright, *The Varieties of Goodness* (London: Routledge and Kegan Paul, 1963), 147. Walton denies that the emotion of fear is an essential characteristic of the courageous act (82). His account, however, sidesteps hard questions about the development of the trait of fortitude in dangerous situations, about the conceptual relation between fear and the perception of danger, and about the conceptual relation between perceptions of danger and human nature. Note that in his discussion of this point, Walton relies on examples of what we

have called "technical courage." The "Socratic-Lachean" view would appear to hold, like Aristotle, that some terrors are fearful to all human beings in their senses, but that the brave man can nevertheless master these fears (compare *Nicomachean Ethics* 3.6).

43. It was precisely such military prudence that Thucydides tells us Nicias most conspicuously lacked in Sicily (see especially 6.63). On the necessity of risk and action, compare in Thucydides' *Peloponnesian War* the words of Alcibiades and the deeds of Gylippus, especially 6.18 and 7.21, and such modern authorities as Carl von Clausewitz, *On War*, trans. J. J. Graham (London: Penguin, 1968), 143; Erwin Rommel, "The Rules of Desert Warfare," in Desmond Young, *Rommel: The Desert Fox* (New York: Harper, 1951), 230. The successful commander does not wait to react but himself defines the situation to which his opponent must react—a reaction that will generally come too late to be effective. See also, however, chap. 1, nn. 13, 14, 20.

44. Each of these actions is prudent in the narrow or vulgar sense of the term, hence where Nicias asks Laches at 195c11–12 whether it is not better for many to never arise from their bed of sickness, he is not asking about men sick or corrupt in soul but about men so sick in body that they can never again enjoy life, someone with a painful terminal illness (see *Crito* 47d–e; *Gorgias* 512a; *Republic* 409e–410a). Of course, the man with Nician courage may well, when it is too late and he has made his choice of death, realize his folly.

45. See the discussion in section 5.4, chap. 5, n. 29, and chap. 4, n. 20. The delay almost cost the Greeks the battle, and more endurance was needed than might otherwise have been. Nicias' delay at Syracuse seems not simply to have been out of piety, but also to have been influenced by a realistic fear of private harm if he had returned, defeated, to Athens. See section 1.3, and the perhaps unduly harsh judgment of him cited in chap. 1, n. 11 (compare *Republic* 366c–d).

46. On this view, then, piety ought not to be regarded as a virtue separate from justice, but as an aspect of it. Compare *Republic* 427e, where piety does not appear in the list of the civic virtues.

47. See also the manly wisdom of the Athenians in Thucydides' *Peloponnesian War* 5.103, 105 and n. 6, this chapter. We should also mention that the Platonic teaching presents a still higher vision of art and nature, thereby securing philosophy against disgrace and harm. See Plutarch, *Lives*, "Nicias" 23.

48. From the standpoint of prudence and the city, it is unmanly and foolish merely to endure and accept what fate brings us without trying to conquer fortune and our enemies. But it is unmanly in the highest degree not to distinguish between the things of honor or virtue (action; matters of principle), which are subject to the will, as against the things of fortune (events; consequences), which are not. Compare the doctrine of Epictetus, *Discourses* 2.1.

49. On Nicias' concern with life and death, see also chap. 3, n. 42, and this chapter, n. 44. On the primal fear that Nicias, unlike Laches, is still open to, see *Phaedo* 77e; also *Laws* 790e–791c; discussion by Pangle, *Laws of Plato*, 479; also Schmid, "Courage," 123–24.

50. This is not the self-deceiving artificial light of the imagination, which pictures the life that the "I" will enjoy after death. It is the unselfdespairing light of philosophical love, which walks on the waters of uncertainty, but walks firmly, firmly toward the sun. Note that Socrates does not regard the reality of that order as a settled thing, even on the day of his own death (*Phaedo* 107b; also 85c–d).

51. It would appear to be a Platonic doctrine that contentiousness is the most common cause preventing the ascent to the apperception of truth. See *Phaedrus* 248a–b.

52. This is a rivalry in which the good that is sought can be shared without loss, unlike money or honor or rule. See Socrates' comments at *Charmides* 166d; *Gorgias* 505e; Aristotle's discussion of true friendship, *Nicomachean Ethics* 9.9. It is in the shared relation to the common good of truth that real peace is possible. The modern enlightenment hope—that mankind would find peace through rational fear and the love of "commodious living"—shattered in the death camps and total war of the twentieth century, though we appear to be moving again into a period of exaggerated optimism concerning international relations and human nature. Whether this attitude will continue into the twenty-first century remains to be seen, though no one of good sense can ignore the potential for conflict inherent in the growing scarcity of natural resources and danger of global ecological crisis, on the one hand, and the worldwide capitalist release of the appetites and corresponding spread of democratic consciousness, on the other. The proliferation of nuclear, chemical, and biological weapons may foreshadow yet another century of mass destruction.

53. The whole discussion there, however, should be supplemented with commentary on the treatment of the philosophical nature in *Republic* 5. The elenchus may serve to moderate the unphilosophical man, but its highest virtue must lie in assisting in the genesis and ever-preservation of the life of philosophy, which is so far from being moderate and pious and just as to be called by Socrates a form of madness (*Phaedrus* 249c–e). On these grounds one might argue that the only clear-cut real candidate for the elenchus in the dialogues other than Socrates himself is Theaetetus; a case might be made for the young Alcibiades, but in the end he lacked the courage to let go of his old life and turn to a new one. See the discussion of Alcibiades in Ilham Dilman, *Morality and the Inner Life* (London: Macmillan, 1979), 41–45; Schmid, "Moderation," 347.

54. This is the two-sided crux of Socrates' case against the sophists: they not only fail to make their students aware of their ignorance and baseness, but they steepen them in it with the veneer of science or wisdom. Compare especially, *Gorgias* 458e–461c, 462b–465d; *Protagoras* 313a–314c; discussion in sections 2.1, 2.2.

55. Compare Klein's discussion of Meno in *A Commentary*, 184–202.

6. The Conclusion of the Dialogue

1. On the Socratic care, see chap. 3, n. 2.

2. For discussion of this phrase and the question of Socrates' consent at the end of the dialogue, compare the discussion in Mark Blitz, "An Introduction to the Reading of Plato's *Laches*," *Interpretation* 5 (1975): 224.

3. For the reasons that Socrates believes this is in his self-interest, see *Apology* 25e–26a.

4. This quotation, also used by Socrates at *Charmides* 161a to refute Charmides' definition of moderation as "the sense of shame," stems from what is said by Telemachus about his father, who is disguised as a beggar. On the phrase and Socrates' association with the hero Odysseus, compare chap. 3, n. 2 and chap. 4, n. 35 above; also the

discussion of shame in section 3.4 and its relation to Socrates' refutation of Laches, sections 4.7, 4.8. As Socrates' last word on the matter, the phrase makes especially apparent the ambiguous nature of his so-called community with Laches.

5. Compare the endings of *Crito* 54e, *Alcibiades I* 135d, and contrast the ominous ending of the *Charmides*. Compare, too, *Theaetetus* 210d, where it is Socrates who is eager to continue.

6. On the notion of being "together with," see section 4.2 and also n.5 (section 4.2). For discussion of the account of Aristides in the *Theages*, see Thomas Pangle's commentary on the dialogue in his *The Roots of Political Philosophy* (Ithaca, N.Y.: Cornell University Press, 1987), 170. Pangle also discusses with insight the apparent real meaning of Socrates' inner voice, 167–71, a treatment of the *daimonion* that follows Seth Benardete, "The *Daimonion* of Socrates" (Master's Thesis, University of Chicago, 1953), 29–41.

7. For the sense in which the young Thucydides was (and apparently remained) a slave, see *Republic* 514a–516e.

Bibliography

Adcock, F. E. *The Greek and Macedonian Art of War*. Berkeley: University of California Press, 1957.

Adkins, A. W. H. *Merit and Responsibility*. Oxford: Clarendon Press, 1960.

Aeschylus. *Prometheus Bound*. Translated by J. Scully and C. J. Herington. Oxford: Oxford University Press, 1975.

Anderson, Robert J. "The Theory of Perception in Plato's *Theaetetus*." In *Plato, Time and Education: Essays in Honor of Robert S. Brumbaugh*, edited by Brian Hendley, 61–81. Albany: State University of New York Press, 1987.

Anscombe, G. E. M. "War and Murder." In *War, Morality and the Military Profession*, edited by Malham Wakin, 285–99. Boulder, Colo.: Westview Press, 1981.

Arendt, Hannah. *The Human Condition*. Chicago: University of Chicago Press, 1958.

———. *The Life of the Mind: Thinking*. New York: Harcourt Brace Jovanovich, 1971.

———. *The Life of the Mind: Willing*. New York: Harcourt Brace Jovanovich, 1978.

Aristophanes. *Acharnians*. Translated and edited by Allan Sommerstein. Warminster, England: Aris and Phillips, 1980.

———. *Acharnians, Knights, Clouds, Wasps*. Translated by Benjamin Rogers. Cambridge, Mass.: Harvard University Press, 1924.

———. *Wasps*. Edited by Douglas M. MacDowell. Oxford: Oxford University Press, 1971.

Aristotle. *Athenian Constitution*. Translated by H. Rackham. Cambridge, Mass.: Harvard University Press, 1935.

———. *Historia Animalium*. Translated by A. L. Peck. Oxford: Oxford University Press, 1910.

———. *Nicomachean Ethics*. Translated by H. Rackham. Cambridge, Mass.: Harvard University Press, 1926.

————. *Politics*. Translated by H. Rackham. Cambridge, Mass.: Harvard University Press, 1932.

————. *Rhetoric*. Translated by J. H. Freese. Cambridge, Mass.: Harvard University Press, 1926.

Arrowsmith, William. "Aristophanes' *Birds:* The Fantasy Politics of *Erōs.*" *Arion* 1 (1973): 119–67.

Augustine, Saint. *The City of God*. Translated by Henry Bettenson, and edited by David K. Knowles. New York: Penguin, 1972.

Bacon, Francis. *Selected Writings*. Translated by Hugh G. Dick. New York: Random House, 1955.

Benardete, Seth. "Achilles and Hector." Ph.D. dissertation, University of Chicago, 1955.

————. "The *Daimonion* of Socrates." Masters thesis, University of Chicago, 1953.

————. *Herodotian Inquiries*. The Hague: Martinus Nijhoff, 1969.

Blitz, Mark. "An Introduction to the Reading of Plato's *Laches.*" *Interpretation* 5 (1975): 185–225.

Bloom, Allan. *The Closing of the American Mind*. New York: Simon and Schuster, 1987.

————. *The Republic of Plato*. New York: Basic Books, 1968.

Bolotin, David. *Plato's Dialogue on Friendship*. Ithaca, N.Y.: Cornell University Press, 1982.

Bonitz, Hermann. *Platonische Studien*. Berlin, 1886.

————. "Zur Erklärung platonischer Dialoge." *Hermes* 5 (1871): 413–42.

Brumbaugh, Robert S. *The Philosophers of Greece*. New York: Thomas Y. Crowell, 1964.

————. *Plato's Mathematical Imagination*. New Haven, Conn.: Yale University Press, 1954.

————. "Plato's *Meno* as Form and as Content." *Teaching Philosophy* 1 (Fall, 1975): 107–115.

Buford, Thomas. "Plato on the Educational Consultant: An Interpretation of the *Laches.*" *Idealistic Studies* 7 (1977): 151–71.

Burkert, Walter. *Greek Religion*. Translated by John Raffin. Cambridge, Mass.: Harvard University Press, 1985.

Burnet, John. *Essays and Addresses*. Freeport, N.Y.: Books for Libraries Press, 1968.

Butcher, Samuel. *Aristotle's Theory of Poetry and Fine Art*. New York: Dover, 1951.

Cicero. *De Natura Deorum*. Translated by H. Rackham. Cambridge, Mass.: Harvard University Press, 1933.

————. *Tusculan Disputations*. Translated by J. E. King. New York: G. P. Putnam's Sons, 1927.

Clausewitz, Carl von. *On War*. Translated by J. J. Graham. London: Penguin, 1968.

Cooper, John. "Plato's Theory of Motivation." *History of Philosophy Quarterly* 1 (1984): 3–21.

Dannhauser, Werner. *Nietzsche's View of Socrates*. Ithaca, N.Y.: Cornell University Press, 1974.

Davies, J. K. *Athenian Propertied Families*. Oxford: Clarendon Press, 1971.

Delbrück, Hans. *History of the Art of War*. Vol. 1. Translated by Walter J. Denfroe, Jr. Westport, Conn.: Greenwood, 1975.

Dent, N. J. "The Value of Courage." *Philosophy* 56 (1981): 575–77.

Descartes, René. *The Philosophical Works of Descartes*. Vol. 1. Translated by Elizabeth S. Haldane and G. R. T. Ross. Cambridge: Cambridge University Press, 1972.

Desjardins, Rosemary. "The Horns of a Dilemma." *Ancient Philosophy* 1 (1981): 109–26.

Devereux, Daniel. "Courage and Wisdom in Plato's *Laches*." *Journal of the History of Philosophy* 15 (1977): 129–41.

Dilman, Ilham. *Morality and the Inner Life*. London: Macmillan, 1979.

Dover, Kenneth. *Greek Popular Morality in the Time of Plato and Aristotle*. Los Angeles: University of California Press, 1974.

Duncan, Roger. "Courage in Plato's *Protagoras*." *Phronesis* 23 (1978): 216–28.

Edmonds, J. D. *Elegy and Iambus*. Vols. 1 and 2. Cambridge, Mass.: Harvard University Press, 1931.

Edmunds, Lowell. *Chance and Intelligence in Thucydides*. Cambridge, Mass.: Harvard University Press, 1975.

Ehrenberg, Victor. "*Polypragmosynē:* A Study in Greek Politics." *Journal of Hellenic Studies* 67 (1947): 46–67.

———. *Sophocles and Pericles*. Oxford: Basil Blackwell, 1954.

Eisner, Robert. "Socrates as Hero." *Philosophy and Literature* 6 (1982): 106–18.

Epictetus. *Discourses and Enchiridion*. Translated by T. Higginson. Roslyn, N.Y.: Walter Black, 1944.

Euripides. *Heracles*. Translated by William Arrowsmith. Chicago: University of Chicago Press, 1956.

Falk, W. D. "Prudence and Courage." In *Vice and Virtue in Everyday Life*, edited by Christina Sommers, 209–15. New York: Harcourt Brace Jovanovich, 1985.

Foot, Philippa. *Virtues and Vices and Other Essays in Moral Philosophy*. Berkeley: University of California Press, 1978.

Frame, Donald. *Montaigne's Discovery of Man*. New York: Columbia University Press, 1955.

Fränkel, Hermann. *From Poetry to Philosophy*. Translated by Moses Hadas. New York: Harcourt Brace Jovanovich, 1975.

Frankfurt, Harry. "Freedom of the Will and the Concept of a Person." In *Free Will*, edited by Gary Watson, 81–95. Oxford: Oxford University Press, 1982.

Freud, Sigmund. *Character and Culture*. Edited by Philip Rieff. New York: Macmillan, 1963.

———. *Civilization and Its Discontents*. Translated by James Strachey. New York: Norton, 1962.

———. *The Future of an Illusion*. Translated by James Strachey. New York: Norton, 1961.

Friedländer, Paul. *Plato*. Vol. 2. Translated by Hans Meyerhoff. New York: Bollingen Foundation, 1964.

Gabriel, Richard, and Paul Savage. *Crisis in Command*. New York: Farrar, Straus, and Giroux, 1978.

Gadamer, Hans-Georg. *Dialogue and Dialectic*. Translated by Christopher Smith. New Haven, Conn.: Yale University Press, 1980.

———. *Platos dialektische Ethik*. Hamburg: Felix Meiner, 1931.

Geach, Peter. *The Virtues*. Cambridge: Cambridge University Press, 1977.

Goethe. *Aus meinem Leben: Dichtung und Wahrheit*. Munich: Goldmanns, 1962.

Graves, Robert. *Difficult Questions, Easy Answers*. Garden City, N.Y.: Doubleday, 1973.

———. *Good-Bye to All That*. 2d ed. Garden City, N.Y.: Doubleday, 1957.

Gray, J. Glenn. *The Warriors*. New York: Harper and Row, 1959.

Greene, William. "The Spirit of Comedy in Plato." In *Harvard Studies in Classical Philology*. Vol. 31, 63–123. Cambridge, Mass.: Harvard University Press, 1920.

Guthrie, W. K. C. *A History of Greek Philosophy*. Vols. 3 and 4. Cambridge: Cambridge University Press, 1969, 1975.

Hartmann, Nicolai. *Ethics*. Vol. 2. Translated by Stanton Coit. London: Allen and Unwin, 1932.

Hegel, G. W. F. *The Phenomenology of Mind*. Translated by J. B. Baillie. London: MacMillan, 1910; New York: Harper and Row, 1967.

Heidegger, Martin. *Being and Time*. Translated by John Macquarrie and Edward Robinson. New York: Harper and Row, 1962.

Herodotus. *The Persian Wars*. Translated by George Rawlinson. New York.: Random House, 1942.

Hobbes, Thomas. *Leviathan*. Edited by Michael Oakeshott. New York: Collier Books, 1962.

Hoerber, Robert. "Plato's *Laches*." *Classical Philology* 63 (1968): 95–105.

Holmes, Richard. *Acts of War*. New York: Macmillan, 1985.

Homer, *Iliad*. Translated by Richmond Lattimore. Chicago: University of Chicago Press, 1951.

———. *Odyssey*. Translated by Richmond Lattimore. Chicago: University of Chicago Press, 1965.

Hunt, Lester. "Courage and Principle." *Canadian Journal of Philosophy* 10 (1980): 281–93.

Hyman, Arthur, and James Walsh, eds. *Philosophy in the Middle Ages*. Indianapolis: Hackett, 1973.

Irwin, Terence. *Plato's Moral Theory*. Oxford: Clarendon Press, 1977.

Isenberg, Arnold. "Natural Pride and Natural Shame." *Philosophy and Phenomenological Research* 10 (1949): 1–24.

Jaeger, Werner. *Paideia*. Vol. 1. Translated by Gilbert Highet. Oxford: Oxford University Press, 1939.

———. *The Theology of the Early Greek Philosophers*. Translated by Edward Robinson. Oxford: Clarendon Press, 1947.

Jaffa, Harry. *Statesmanship*. Durham, N.C.: Carolina Academic Press, 1982.

Kagan, Donald. *The Peace of Nicias and the Sicilian Expedition*. Ithaca, N.Y.: Cornell University Press, 1981.

Kerferd, G. B. "Protagoras' Doctrine of Justice and Virtue." *Journal of the Hellenic Society* 73 (1953): 42–45.

———. *The Sophistic Movement*. Cambridge: Cambridge University Press, 1981.

Kierkegaard, Søren. *The Concept of Irony*. Translated by Lee M. Capel. New York: Harper and Row, 1966.

Klein, Jacob. *A Commentary on Plato's Meno*. Chapel Hill: University of North Carolina Press, 1965.

———. *Greek Mathematical Thought and the Origin of Algebra*. Translated by Eva Brann. Cambridge, Mass.: MIT Press, 1968.

Knox, Bernard. *Oedipus at Thebes*. New Haven, Conn.: Yale University Press, 1957.

Kohak, Erazim. "The Road to Wisdom: Lessons on Education from the *Laches*." *Classical Journal* 56 (1960): 123–32.

Krüger, Gerhard. *Einsicht und Leidenschaft*. Frankfurt: Klostermann, 1939.

Kuhn, Helmut. "The True Tragedy." In *Harvard Studies in Classical Philology*. Vol. 42, 1–41. Cambridge, Mass.: Harvard University Press, 1941.

———. "The True Tragedy." In *Harvard Studies in Classical Philology*. Vol. 43, 37–88. Cambridge, Mass.: Harvard University Press, 1942.

Lampert, Lawrence. *Nietzsche's Teaching*. New Haven, Conn: Yale University Press, 1986.

Langer, Susanne K. *Feeling and Form*. New York: Scribners, 1953.

Linderman, Gerald. *Embattled Courage*. New York: Macmillan, 1987.

Lorenz, Konrad. *On Aggression*. Translated by Marjorie Wilson. New York: Harcourt, Brace and World, 1963.

Mabbot, J. D., and H. J. Horsburgh. "Prudence." *Aristotelian Society Proceedings* 36 (1962): 51–76.

Machiavelli, Niccolò. *The Art of War*. Translated by Ellis Farneworth. New York: Bobbs-Merrill, 1965.

——. *The Prince*. Translated by Harvey Mansfield. Chicago: University of Chicago Press, 1985.

MacIntyre, Alasdair. *After Virtue*. Notre Dame, Ind.: University of Notre Dame Press, 1981.

Manchester, William. *The Last Lion: Winston Spencer Churchill*. Vol. 2. Boston: Little, Brown, 1988.

Midgley, Mary. *Beast and Man*. Ithaca, N.Y.: Cornell University Press, 1978.

Mishima, Yukio. *The Way of the Samurai*. Translated by Kathryn Sparling. New York: Basic Books, 1977.

Montaigne, Michel de. *The Complete Essays of Montaigne*. Translated by Donald Frame. Stanford, Calif.: Stanford University Press, 1958.

Muecke, D. C. *Irony*. London: Methuen and Co., 1970.

Murdoch, Iris. *The Fire and the Sun*. Oxford: Oxford University Press, 1977.

Netanyahu, Jonathan. *Self-Portrait of a Hero*. New York: Random House, 1980.

Nietzsche, Friedrich. *The Birth of Tragedy*. Translated by Francis Golffing. Garden City, N.Y.: Doubleday, 1956.

——. *The Portable Nietzsche*. Translated and edited by Walter Kaufmann. New York: Viking, 1968.

——. *Thus Spoke Zarathustra*. Translated by R. J. Hollingdale. London: Penguin, 1961.

Nussbaum, G. B. *The Ten Thousand*. Leiden, Holland: Brill, 1967.

Oakeshott, Michael. *Rationalism in Politics*. New York: Basic Books, 1962.

O'Brien, Michael. *The Socratic Paradoxes and the Greek Mind*. Chapel Hill: University of North Carolina Press, 1967.

——. "The Unity of the *Laches*." In *Essays in Ancient Greek Philosophy*, edited by John Anton and George Kustas. Vol. 1, 303–15. Albany: State University of New York Press, 1971.

Pangle, Thomas. *The Laws of Plato*. New York: Basic Books, 1980.

——, ed. *The Roots of Political Philosophy*. Ithaca, N.Y.: Cornell University Press, 1987.

Penner, Terry. "The Unity of Virtue." *Philosophical Review* 82 (1973): 35–68.

Pieper, Joseph. *The Four Cardinal Virtues*. Notre Dame, Ind.: University of Notre Dame Press, 1966.

Plato. *The Collected Dialogues*. Edited by Edith Hamilton and Huntington Cairns. Princeton, N.J.: Bollingen Foundation, 1961.

——. *Laches and Charmides*. Translated by Rosamund Sprague. Indianapolis: Bobbs-Merrill, 1973.

————. *Laches, Euthydemus, Protagoras and Meno.* Translated by W. R. M. Lamb. Cambridge, Mass.: Harvard University Press, 1924.

————. *Opera.* Edited by John Burnet. Oxford: Oxford University Press, 1903.

————. *Plato's Laches.* Edited by M. T. Tatham. London: Macmillan, 1888. Reprint. New York: St. Martin's, 1966.

————. *Protagoras.* Translated by Martin Ostwald and edited by Gregory Vlastos. Indianapolis: Bobbs-Merrill, 1956.

Plochmann, George Kimball, and Franklin E. Robinson. *A Friendly Companion to Plato's Gorgias.* Carbondale: Southern Illinois University Press, 1988.

Plutarch. *Plutarch's Lives.* Vols. 2 and 3. Translated by B. Perrin. Cambridge, Mass.: Harvard University Press, 1916.

Pritchett, W. Kendrick. *The Greek State at War.* Vols. 1–4. Berkeley: University of California Press, 1971–85.

Rachman, S. J. *Fear and Courage.* San Francisco: W. H. Freeman, 1973.

Richardson, F. M. *Fighting Spirit.* London: Bayliss and Son, 1978.

Robinson, Richard. *Plato's Earlier Dialectic.* Oxford: Clarendon Press, 1953.

Rorty, Amelie. "Two Faces of Courage." *Philosophy* 61 (1986): 151–71.

Rosen, Stanley. *Nihilism.* New Haven, Conn.: Yale University Press, 1965.

————. *Plato's Symposium.* New Haven, Conn.: Yale University Press, 1968.

Santas, Gerasimos. "Socrates at Work on Virtue and Knowledge in Plato's *Charmides.*" In *Exegesis and Argument: Essays in Honor of Gregory Vlastos,* edited by Edward Lee, Alexander Mourelatos, and Richard Rorty, 105–32. Assen, Holland: Van Gorcum, 1973.

————. "Socrates at Work on Virtue and Knowledge in Plato's *Laches.*" *Review of Metaphysics* 22 (1969): 433–60; reprinted in *The Philosophy of Socrates,* edited by Gregory Vlastos, 177–208. Garden City, N.J.: Doubleday, 1971.

Saxenhouse, Arlene. "The Philosopher and the Female in the Political Thought of Plato." *Political Theory* 4 (1976): 195–212.

Schmid, Walter T. "Socrates' Practice of Elenchus in the *Charmides.*" *Ancient Philosophy* 1 (1981): 141–47.

————. "The Socratic Conception of Courage." *History of Philosophy Quarterly* 2 (1985): 113–29.

————. "Socratic Moderation and Self-Knowledge." *Journal of the History of Philosophy* 21 (1983): 349–58.

Schmitt, Carl. *The Concept of the Political.* Translated by George Schwab. New Brunswick, N.J.: Rutgers University Press, 1988.

Schneider, William. *Shame, Exposure, and Privacy.* Boston: Beacon, 1977.

Seeskin, Kenneth. "Courage and Knowledge: A Perspective on the Socratic Paradox." *Southern Journal of Philosophy* 14 (1976): 511–21.

————. *Dialogue and Discovery*. Albany: State University of New York Press, 1987.

Sellars, Wilfred. *Science, Perception and Reality*. London: Routledge and Kegan Paul, 1963.

Snell, Bruno. *The Discovery of the Mind*. Translated by T. G. Rosenmeyer. New York: Harper and Row, 1960.

Solzhenitsyn, Alexander. *Solzhenitsyn at Harvard*. Edited by David Berman. Washington, D.C.: Ethics and Public Policy Center, 1980.

Sophocles. *Oedipus the King, Oedipus at Colonus, Antigone*. Translated by F. Storr. Cambridge, Mass.: Harvard University Press, 1912.

Stendahl, Krister, ed. *Immortality and Resurrection*. New York: MacMillan, 1965.

Storr, Anthony. *Human Aggression*. New York: Atheneum, 1968.

Sun Tzu. *The Art of War*. Translated by Samuel B. Griffin. Oxford: Oxford University Press, 1963.

Taylor, Charles. "Responsibility for Self." In *Free Will*, edited by Gary Watson, 111–26. Oxford: Oxford University, 1982.

Thomas Aquinas, Saint. *Summa Theologiae*. Edited by Thomas Gilby. London: Blackfriars, 1964–75.

Thucydides. *The Peloponnesian War*. Translated by Richard Crawley and revised by T. E. Wick. New York: Random House, 1982.

Umphrey, Stewart. "Plato's *Laches* on Courage." *Apeiron* 10 (1976): 14–22.

Versenyi, Laszlo. *Holiness and Justice*. Washington, D.C.: University Press of America, 1982.

————. *Socratic Humanism*. New Haven, Conn.: Yale University Press, 1963.

Vlastos, Gregory. *Platonic Studies*. 2d ed. Princeton, N.J: Princeton University Press, 1981.

————. *Plato's Universe*. Seattle: University of Washington Press, 1975.

————. "Socrates." In *The Philosophy of Socrates*, edited by Gregory Vlastos, 1–20. Garden City, N.Y.: Doubleday, 1971.

————. "The Socratic Elenchus." In *Oxford Studies in Ancient Greek Philosophy*. Vol. 1, edited by Julia Annas, 23–58. Oxford: Oxford University Press, 1983.

Wade-Gery, H. T. "Thucydides, Son of Melesias." *Journal of Hellenic Studies* 52 (1932): 205–27.

Wallace, James. *The Virtues and Vices*. Ithaca, N.Y.: Cornell University Press, 1978.

Walton, Dennis. *Courage: A Philosophical Investigation*. Berkeley: University of California Press, 1986.

Walton, George. *The Tarnished Shield*. New York: Dodd, 1973.

Watson, Gary. "Free Agency." In *Free Will*, edited by Gary Watson, 96–110. Oxford: Oxford University Press, 1982.

West, Thomas, and Gisela West. *Four Texts on Socrates*. Ithaca, N.Y.: Cornell University Press, 1984.

Westlake, H. D. "Nicias in Thucydides." *Classical Quarterly* 35 (1941): 58–65.

Wright, Georg Henrik von. *The Varieties of Goodness*. London: Routledge and Kegan Paul, 1963.

Xenophon. *Anabasis*. Vols. 1 and 2. Translated by C. L. Brownson. Cambridge: Harvard University Press, 1980.

Young, Desmond. *Rommel: The Desert Fox*. New York: Harper, 1951.

Index

Achilles, 89, 188n.10, 199n.37

Action, life of, activism (*polypragmosynē*), 7, 58–59, 82–83, 125, 144, 191nn.12, 17

Adcock, F. E., 197n.20

Aeneas, and his horses, 102–3, 197n.19

Aeschylus, *Prometheus Bound*, 23

Afterlife, 84, 194n.42, 207n.50

Aggression, 72, 203n.17. *See also* Anger; Human nature

Ajax, 89, 174, 188n.10, 192n.28, 199n.35, 203n.19

Alcibiades, 8–11, 185nn.13–14, 186n.20, 190n.7, 191n.12, 207n.44; and philosophy, 87, 195n.46, 201n.55, 208n.53

Algazali, 195n.53

Alliance (*symbōle*), vs. community (*koinōnia*), 58, 63, 209n.4

Amompharetus, 104, 124

Amphipolis, battle of, 183n.1

Anaxagoras, 16, 21, 136, 175, 187n.6

Ancients, 2, 9, 135, 202n.5, 204nn.25, 27. *See also* Moderns

Anderson, Robert J., xvi

Anger, 115, 146–47, 149–50, 204n.24. *See also* City; Laches

Archidamus, 70–71

Archilochus, 192n.25

Arendt, Hannah, 193n.32, 205n.33

Argument, speech (*logos*), 16–17, 28, 31–32, 86; and deed, 36–38, 86, 88–89, 150; rhetorical vs. philosophical, 39–40, 80–81, 194n.40. *See also* Dialectic; Rhetoric

Aristides, son of Lysimachus, 56, 60, 180, 209n.6

Aristides the Just, 3, 184n.3

Aristocracy, 56, 58–59, 63–64, 202n.9

Aristophanes, 12, 15–16, 49–50, 71–72,

189nn.28–30; *Acharnians*, 13; *Birds*, 7; *Clouds*, 12, 17, 49–50; *Knights*, 8; *Wasps*, 5, 11–13. *See also* Comedy

Aristotle, 112; *Athenian Constitution*, 12, 184n.7; *Historia Animalium*, 203n.17; *Nicomachean Ethics*, 174, 191n.21, 196n.10, 207n.42; *Politics*, 191n.19; *Rhetoric*, 193n.32. *See also* Philosophy

Army, mercenary vs. citizen, 191n.15

Art(s) (*technē*), 20–24, 65, 74, 80–82, 141, 157, 193n.38; art of politics, 141, 186n.30; 199n.40; bowmanship, 75; charioteering, 75, 102–3, 111, 198n.34; eristics, 185n.19, 194n.41; farming, 138, 153; fighting in armor (*hoplomachia*), 4, 55, 64–69, 184n.5, 191n.23; gymnastics, 34, 194n.41; horsemanship, 120; medicine, 75–76, 78–82, 96–97, 121, 138, 153, 194n.40; of music, 28–29, 34, 60, 85–86, 132, 153, 191n.13, 192n.30; piloting, 143, 170, 203n.13; rhetoric, 16–17, 39–41, 72, 81; of war, 20–21, 64–69, 123, 134, 165, 184n.5, 185n.19, 191nn.22–23, 207n.43; writing, 27–33; wrestling, 73, 79, 84, 193n.38, 194n.41. *See also* Knowledge, Virtue

Athens, xv, 1–2, 5–6, 12, 124, 191n.12; and boldness, 126; and Sparta, 2, 21, 190n.6, 197n.20, 201n.50; and the sophists, 20–24, 66, 134. *See also* City; Pericles

Augustine, Saint, 9, 52, 196n4

Autonomy, 125, 197n.25, 201n.51

Beautiful, noble (*kalon*), 56–57, 62, 82, 118–19, 153, 166, 190n.9; gentlemen, 77,

WALTER T. SCHMID is professor of philosophy and religion at the University of North Carolina at Wilmington. In 1969–71 he was in the United States Army, where he served in the military police and adjutant general's corps. In 1971–72 he pursued graduate studies at Heidelberg University, and in 1976 he received his Ph.D. degree in philosophy from Yale University. He has contributed articles to such journals as *Ancient Philosophy, History of Philosophy Quarterly,* and *Journal of the History of Philosophy.* Professor Schmid is married to the former Catherine M. Hooe, and they have three children.